World **Superbike** Winners

Carl **Fogarty**

The Complete Racer by Julian Ryder Second edition

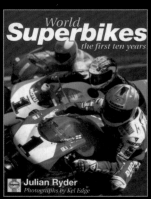

World **Superbikes** *the first ten years*

Julian Ryder
Photographs by Kel Edge

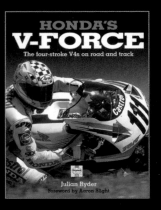

HONDA'S V-FORCE
The four-stroke V4s on road and track

Julian Ryder
Foreword by Aaron Slight

Other titles by Julian Ryder

World
Superbike
Winners

ALL THE MEN, ALL THE RESULTS

Julian Ryder Foreword by Colin Edwards

First published in November 2000

A catalogue record for this book is
available from the British Library

ISBN 1 85960 678 4

Library of Congress catalog card no. 00-131893

Published by Haynes Publishing, Sparkford,
Nr Yeovil, Somerset BA22 7JJ, England

Tel. 01963 442030 Fax 01963 440001
Int. tel. +44 1963 442030 Fax +44 1963 440001
E-mail: sales@haynes-manuals.co.uk
Web site: www.haynes.co.uk

Haynes North America, Inc.,
861 Lawrence Drive, Newbury Park,
California 91320, USA

Printed and bound in England by
J. H. Haynes & Co. Ltd, Sparkford

Contents

Acknowledgements

It would have been impossible to put this book together without the help of many of my colleagues and friends from the press office at both World Superbike and Grand Prix Championships. First, Gordon Ritchie did the work on many of the current generation of top men, specifically Edwards, Haga, Yanagawa, Bayliss, Corser, Gobert, Whitham, Bostrom and Meklau.

Kel Edge, the man who has photographed every World Superbike race since the Championship began in 1988, contributed a good deal of useful advice as well as the pictures. Very special thanks also to Kay Edge whose clear eye and knowledge of the subject contributed greatly to the accuracy of this book. Yoko Togashi, HRC's translator, made sure my ignorance of Japanese didn't scramble what Takuma Aoki had to say and ensured I got my facts straight. Hirofumi Nakamura did the same for Suzuki's Japanese stars. Colin Young and Mark Fattore helped with detail on the fast Aussies who enlivened the Championship in its early years.

This book wouldn't have been possible without their help, or the publishing team at Haynes – Darryl Reach, Mark Hughes and Flora Myer – who refuse to let their standards slip below excellence.

Most importantly I have to thank my wife Wendy. Without her understanding and support you wouldn't be reading this.

Foreword

by Colin Edwards, 2000 World Champion

The World Superbike Championship becomes more competitive year on year and winning the millennium series was always going to be special. At the start I couldn't help looking around me and guessing who would challenge for the title – only for that view to be turned on its head by mid-season. The 2000 chase proved how unpredictable sport can be.

Winning any championship requires focus and that's what I had to maintain, as I'm sure all of the other champions before me had done.

The World Superbike Championship remains a relatively young championship but to have so many race winners as it has seen is a sign of freedom within the championship. Any rider who believes he can win at the highest level can still take his national championship machine along, fill a wild card slot and, as we saw in 2000, win.

If you're going to be the best then you have to be prepared to beat all comers. As I looked at the championship line-up at the start of the year I never expected riders like Hitoyasu Izutsu, Neil Hodgson and even Troy Bayliss to be standing on the top step of the podium.

After two years on the RC45 Honda I knew we had the machine to win the 2000 title when the VTR first appeared. The machine was Honda's first twin-cylinder superbike, it had the biggest piston Honda had ever made and, true to form, Honda did not want to be beaten.

My title win, like many champions and World Superbike race winners before me, was all about a team effort. Naturally, with a new machine, we had our teething troubles as we developed the VTR race by race. Ultimately the VTR had the edge. My season included a mid-season lull and was probably typical of a champion's campaign although I suffered a punishing testing programme through June and July.

To be World Superbike Champion is a great honour and to write this foreword as one of an illustrious group of World Superbike race winners is also satisfying. At a time in motorcycle racing when there are two equal World Championships I am proud to have secured one of those two titles. I can now set about breaking some of the records you can read about in this book!

Introduction

When the rules were laid down for the first World Championship for Superbikes, a word that had meant different things in different countries was finally defined. A superbike would be a racer based on a production bike, keeping the frame, bodywork, major engine casings and fuel-delivery system of its parent road bike.

It was the third attempt to invent a new World Championship class for big four-strokes. Part and parcel of the design was the unspoken consensus between the big four Japanese manufacturers that they would not enter full factory teams but would leave it to local importers whether they took part or not. The Italians had no such compunctions. Bimota carried on where they'd left off in the previous formula (TT F1), while the moribund Ducati broke free from the shackles of protective receivership and built the first of a new generation of motorcycles that would not just resurrect the factory's fortunes but make the marque a worldwide style icon.

Most interest in the fledgeling World Superbike Championship centred on Ducati's new 888, and Marco Lucchinelli duly delivered a fairy-tale win in the first ever World Superbike race, at Donington in April 1988. Both man and machine gave the new series instant credibility – the bike as one of the most desirable you could hope to own and the rider as an ex-Grand Prix World Champion. When all the other manufacturers racked up wins in that first season, the obvious competitiveness of the championship helped too.

Leaving aside the behind-the-scenes financial and political problems, there was no doubt that this new formula was a success. The adoption of the two-races-a-day format was popular with both riders and spectators. If a top man had a first-race disaster the crowd got another chance to see him later in the day and the rider himself got a second chance to score some points. If there was a downside for the spectators it was the variable quality of the support races, although when Supersport arrived first as a non-championship class and finally as a World Championship in 1999 that problem was finally laid to rest.

In the early days, riders had to race on some tracks that Grand Prix men wouldn't have contemplated going near and there was the perennial problem of a disjointed calendar for the teams to cope with.

Superbike's big break came in 1993 with guaranteed television coverage of the whole championship: viewers were treated to the first round of Carl Fogarty's ferocious title fight with Scott Russell. By now, nearly all the Japanese factories had full works teams fighting Ducati, and when Honda joined the fray the world knew that Superbike mattered – really mattered.

The advent of full factory teams altered the character of the championship over the years. It had started, by design, as a series for privateers but Ducati upped the ante first with Lucchinelli, then with Raymond Roche. At first, the riders were ex-GP or experienced four-stroke racers from other classes, but as the championship grew up so it produced its own stars. Names like Haga, Edwards, Russell, Slight and Corser achieved worldwide prominence due solely to their exploits in Superbike, and Carl Fogarty became not just a star in the UK but a genuine household name worldwide. British motorcycling hadn't had such exposure since the days of Barry Sheene.

This book is the story of the men who made the World Superbike Championship what it is today. From the piratical privateers of the early years through the former Grand Prix riders to the Superbike specialists of the new millennium, they represent some extremes of character and attitude but they all share one thing in common. None of them is boring.

Julian Ryder
October 2000
Cheshire

Marco Lucchinelli

Ducati's resurrection man

The adjective 'colourful' could have been coined for Marco 'Lucky' Lucchinelli. His career spanned all branches of motorcycle racing, starting with ultimate success in GPs he then moved to winning as a rider and manager in Superbike. Along the way, a talent many thought had been wasted was allowed a second flowering.

He was a late starter who did not have his first race until the age of 20, but it took him only a year to compete in his first GP at Imola when he was quick enough to finish seventh in the now-obsolete 350cc class. Under the guidance of Roberto Gallina he won nine 500cc GPs and took the 1981 World Championship. With hindsight it is possible to see that he was only truly competitive when riding Gallina's RG500 Suzukis, a fact underlined when, in 1982, he took the number-one plate to Honda and never won another Grand Prix. Marco partied the year away after an early-season crash ruined his chances of retaining his crown.

Such was his sense of style that even the bloodthirsty Italian press was willing to overlook the fact he was not winning races. Japan, however, was not so charitable and in the following years Marco virtually disappeared from sight.

Perhaps 'Lucky' is more than just a nickname, for Marco carved out a second career as a vital part of the resurrection of Ducati. At the start of the 1986 season he rode the Pantah-based F1 racer to victory in the Daytona Battle of the Twins, followed that up with a win in a round of the World F1 Championship and then, at the end of the year, he shared the

prototype four-valve 851 with Virginio Ferrari and Juan Garriga at the Bol d'Or. The bike was retired well into the race while running seventh.

By now the cash and enthusiasm of the Castiglioni brothers' Cagiva company, Ducati's new owners, was starting to make itself felt. The first race win for the new generation of four-valve Ducatis, the bikes that would raise the company's profile to undreamed of heights on and off the track, came at Daytona in 1987. It was a convincing repeat victory in the Battle of the Twins race, and it was Marco Lucchinelli who took the chequered flag. The really impressive thing was not the distance by which Lucky won but the speed of the bike. It was right up there with the Superbikes and light-years ahead of the other twin-cylinder racers – good news as the 851 was always intended for the new World Superbike Championship due to start in 1988. And when the first Superbike field assembled at Donington, there was Lucky and the Ducati 851 on the front row of the grid. And when they held the rostrum ceremony, there he was on the top step with tears in his eyes declaring it was the best day of his life.

So why do so many books show that Davide Tardozzi and Bimota won the first ever World Superbike Championship race? It is true that Tardozzi took the flag at the end of the day's first Superbike race, but as the new regulations concerning two races per day had yet to be ratified, the points were allocated on aggregate over the two races, the first and only time that has happened in the World Superbike Championship. Lucky was second in that first race and led the second, pursued by Tardozzi, and the two would have shared victory if the Bimota man had not crashed leaving Marco to cruise home in splendour. Lucky only managed one more win in 1988 but was only 17.5 points behind the championship leader (Tardozzi) when the circus set off for the season-ending trip to Australia and New Zealand, yet Ducati did not send their team, claiming lack of budget. If they had sent him, there is every chance that Marco Lucchinelli would have been the first World Superbike Champion.

It was Luchinelli's last season racing at the top level. In 1989, he became manager of the official Ducati team with Raymond Roche and Baldassarre Monti as riders. Reliability problems plagued them in 1989 but in 1990 Roche won the title despite the attentions of new team-mate Giancarlo Falappa. This was the year when Marco showed his diplomatic skills in Canada after Roche had carried an officious marshal on his hire-car bonnet along most of the pit lane. Lucky strode out of the pit garage, surveyed the scene magisterially, and pronounced his verdict on the unfortunate official: 'Fuck you', he said with commendable command of the English vernacular, before adding a very Italian afterthought – 'and your sister!' You didn't mess with Ducati's riders or their team manager.

The following year, Lucky's over-enthusiastic partying caught up with him, and he served a jail term for cocaine possession. He returned to Superbike and Ducati in 1999 as manager of the R&D Racing team with his friend Doriano Romboni as rider. When Romboni retired after breaking his leg, the pair pulled off the clever signing of double-125cc GP World Champion Haruchika Aoki.

Circumstances may have prevented Marco Lucchinelli adding the Superbike crown to his 500 GP title as a rider, but he still has a good number of four-stroke firsts to his name. Justice was done when the team he managed gave Ducati their first World Superbike title.

Lucky and the Ducati 888, a partnership that lit up the first year of World Superbike.

Fred Merkel

Born
28 September 1962
Stockton, California, USA

First win
1988 Round 2/Race 1
Hungaroring, Hungary
Honda RC30

2 Championships
1988 Champion
1989 Champion
1990 6th
1991 8th
1992 13th
1993 11th

8 Race wins
1988 Hungary 1
1988 New Zealand 1
1989 Hungary 1 and 2
1989 Canada 1
1990 Great Britain 1
1990 Hungary 1
1990 Germany 1

4 Pole positions
1989 Hungary
1989 Canada
1989 USA
1989 New Zealand

The first Champion

Like Superbike's first winner, Lucchinelli, the first Champion, Flyin' Fred Merkel, carved out a second career in World Superbike after it looked as though his winning days were over. And when his World Superbike winning days were finished, he went back to the States and won a few more races.

In the mid-1980s, the impossibly good-looking Californian was the undisputed number-one of American Superbike racing, winning three consecutive national titles from 1984 to 1986 for Honda. His record of 19 AMA Superbike Championship race wins stood for over 10 years until Miguel DuHamel passed it. In his first National Championship year he won 10 AMA races, a record most authorities now consider will never be broken, and that was against top-quality opposition. Those marks represent a 77 per cent winning rate, also still a record, Wayne Rainey managed 67 per cent in 1987, and Doug Polen 60 per cent in 1993.

UK fans found out what all the fuss was about when Merkel came over for the 1986 Transatlantic Trophy match races and spent Easter duelling mercilessly with Kevin Schwantz. You would never have guessed they were on the same side … one synchronised highside, which both men saved, down a freezing Donington's Craner Curves is seared in the memory of all who were there.

But the golden boy fell from grace after his third US title. There are many theories seeking to explain why American Honda sacked Merkel but none of them can be confirmed. Was it booze-fuelled hotel wrecking sprees? Was it what the Americans coyly refer to as 'substance abuse'? Or was the real reason more prosaic? Was it simply that Fred was surplus to requirements as Honda sought to concentrate their resources behind their new star – Wayne Rainey?

Realising that he would never get as good a ride again in the USA, Fred did what American motocrossers did fairly regularly, but not road racers: he moved to Europe. To be more accurate, he moved to Italy. The country which loves style in all things took Flyin' Fred to its heart. His dirt-track derived style was spectacular in the extreme and his off-track persona matched it. Blond surfer curls, piratical facial hair and bandannas (a decade before David Beckham thought it looked good), the skull & crossbones flag flown from his motorhome, they all marked him out as an archetypal Californian. His willingness to learn Italian didn't, but it all made him an instant favourite. None of which would have mattered were it not for the extravagant sliding riding style which made him unbeatable on tight, twisty tracks like the Hungaroring where he scored his only double. He was not bad on the fast stuff either, as his last career win shows; it came at Hockenheim, the fastest track on the calendar.

Arguably the most important thing Fred gave to the early days of World Superbike was star quality. With the Japanese factories adopting a hands-off approach to the new championship and leaving decisions on whether to enter to individual importers, there were no full factory teams to capture the imagination. Superbike badly needed personality and Flyin' Fred provided plenty. From the warning on the back of his crash helmet – 'If you want blood, you've got it' – to the unrestrained victory celebrations and that oh-so-Californian confidence and quotability when dealing with the media, Fred was God's gift to the series and the prototype for the splendid cast of characters that has characterised World Superbike since.

British and European journalists meeting their American counterparts at new model launches were puzzled to be greeted with, 'Is Merkel being an asshole in Europe too?' As far as the Euros were concerned, he was everything a motorcycle racer should be: fast, dashing, intelligent, eloquent, and able to talk about things other than bike racing. What more could you want?

It would be easy to assume that because he had the new-for-

The unmistakable style of Fred Merkel and the Honda RC30 in full flight.

Superbike Honda RC30 he was a shoe-in for the title in 1988 and '89, but nothing could be further from the truth. The new bike was not reliable to start with and there was very little in the way of help from the factory. Far from being the fastest thing out there, the V4 was blown away on the fast tracks by the Italian machinery from both Ducati and Bimota, and nearly every RC30 in the paddock blew up on Hockenheim's straights in 1988. Fred had to graft to stay in contention, as the fact he only won two of the 17 races in the inaugural season against Tardozzi's four tells you. He led the championship twice, after round two in Hungary and after the final round after putting together rock-solid performances in Australia and New Zealand. In Australia he was only beaten by local men Dowson, Phillis and Doohan, and in the country that would later become his home, he won the first race in the wet. In warm up for Race 2 the long-time championship leader, Davide Tardozzi, crashed and Fred cruised home to become the first World Superbike Champion. As an example of how to stand up to pressure, the way Fred won his first crown would be hard to beat.

Retaining a title is always more difficult than winning it in the first place, so the way Merkel made it two in a row was even more impressive. He became the first man to win three races consecutively and led the championship from Rounds 2 to 7 of 11 and set four pole positions, three of them at consecutive rounds at the start of the year. His fourth pole was at the last round, again in New Zealand, where he had to beat Bimota's Stephane Mertens to retain the title. Fortuitously for Fred, but decidedly not for Stephane, the Belgian crashed out of the first race, apparently because a brake disc disintegrated. Fred's third in the second race was enough for his second championship and, incidentally, Pirelli's first and so-far only road-racing world title.

Merkel might have made it three-in-a-row in 1990 despite the improved reliability of the always speedy Ducati, but a crash at the Suzuka 8 Hours put paid to his challenge. He had led after what would turn out to be that final career win in Germany and was still third in the title chase when he damaged some vertebrae at Suzuka. He certainly looked like the man most likely to stop Roche and Ducati but he never got the chance for another last-round showdown. Fred only rode one more race in the season, opting out of the final three rounds in Malaysia, Australia and New Zealand yet still ending up sixth overall. The following year was the last in which the RC30 was fast enough to finish in the top three – winning was out of the question in the face of Polen and the Fast by Ferracci Ducati, and when Doug did not win, Ducati new-boy Mertens, or Roche did. RC30s got on the rostrum three times: Lopez-Mella at home in Spain, Yves Brisson in the boycotted Canadian race and finally and fittingly Flyin' Fred Merkel in France. Merkel was not even the top Honda rider at the end of the year, that honour going to a young Englishman called Carl Fogarty.

Everyone remembers Fred on a Honda, but his year with Yamaha was blighted by injury.

But Fred's market value was hardly diminished, his next move was to the newly-formed works Yamaha squad run by the Italian importer's racing subsidiary, BYRD. Naturally the other rider was Italian, Fabrizio Pirovano, and no doubt Fred's status as an honorary Italian helped his job application. It was not a happy year, a highside in testing shattered his heel and he did not race until the sixth round of the season. In the circumstances, 13th overall was not a shabby result after what the man himself described as the most painful injury he had ever suffered. The relationship with Yamaha lasted into 1993 but did not see the year out. Merkel left Yamaha and joined a privateer Ducati team. The champ had one more punch left; he got on the rostrum again with second place at a sodden Osterreichring in a race shortened because of the appalling conditions. He had been closing on the leader when the red flag went out.

But another win would have been too much of a fairy tale, and Fred knew it. With his English wife Lorraine and their son Travis, he returned to the US to race for Kawasaki in the AMA Championship. Although he never won another Superbike race, he won a Supersport 750 race for Kawasaki and in 1995 won an amazing seven for Suzuki. That put him joint second in the all-time winners list for that AMA Championship category.

It was just like old times, but it came to an unpleasant end on 23 September at the Firebird Raceway in Chandler, Arizona, three laps into the 750 Supersport final. Fred crashed and hit a trackside wall sustaining serious injuries including broken ribs and a bruised heart, although it was nerve damage to his left arm that gave him no alternative but to announce his retirement from racing the following month.

The Merkel family moved to New Zealand where Fred had bought a farm featuring a trout lake (fishing is a passion) and started a business supplying materials to the construction industry. He also advises a couple of up-and-coming Kiwi Supersport racers on behalf of Suzuki NZ.

Flyin' Fred Merkel remains one of the greats of American and World Superbike racing. It would have been hard to invent a better first champion or ambassador for the sport.

Adrien Morillas

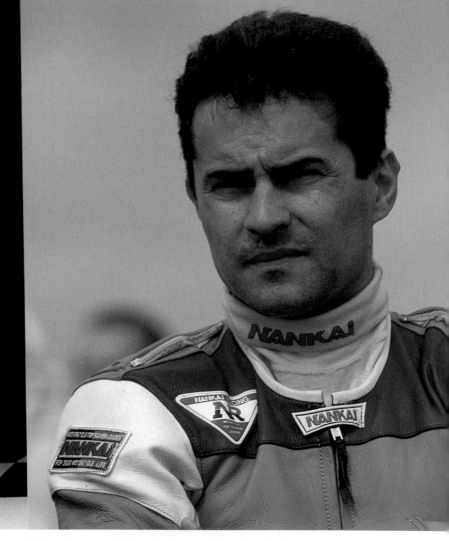

Born
30 May 1958
Clermont Ferrand,
France

First win
1988 Round 2/Race 2
Hungaroring, Hungary
Kawasaki GPX750

Championships
1988 16th
1992 15th
1993 18th
1994 19th
1995 20th

1 Race win
1988 Hungary 2

Green is the colour

There is a certain breed of racer who takes his knocks and victories just the same, the model professional who seems able to race anything anywhere and is silently grateful that he does not have to clock-on at the factory every morning like the rest of his family and friends. Adrien Morillas, the son of a production worker at Michelin's giant Clermont Ferrand plant, is such a man.

He came to road racing late after 10 years as a motocrosser, and immediately won the 1986 French national 500cc Championship, moving up to big production bikes the following year and being signed by Kawasaki France for 1988. When you ride for a French team, your priority is the World Endurance Championship and Adrien immediately showed he had the application for that discipline with a shock third place in the Suzuka 8

Hours on a works F1-spec ZXR750. Just as shockingly, he won a World Superbike race in Hungary on Kawasaki's unfancied, low-tech, steel-framed GPX750, a bike that theoretically should not have been up with the front runners, but the tight nature of the Hungaroring negated any power advantage his rivals may have had. Not only did Morillas beat off first-race winner Merkel and his Honda, but he beat the two factory Bimotas that had filled-out the first-race rostrum. His margin of victory was about half-a-wheel from the notoriously hard-charging Stephane Mertens. Incredibly, the works Bimota team protested on the grounds that the shape of the seat on the Frenchman's Godier-Genoud prepared Kawasaki was illegal. As the legality of Bimota's complete motorcycle was a matter of some debate, the protest was not only petty and mean-minded it was also breathtakingly brass-necked. The jury rightly threw it out and Adrien Morillas became Kawasaki's first World Superbike winner and the only man to win on a GPX.

On the back of these successes, Adrien moved to Grands Prix with the help of his friends the Sarron brothers, who also hailed from Clermont Ferrand. He rode two years in 250cc and, in 1990, showed himself as a more than useful privateer on an Aprilia before moving up to 500s as team-

One of the least expected victories in the whole of World Superbike history: Adrien Morillas and the Kawasaki GPX.

mate to Jean-Philippe Ruggia in the Sonauto Yamaha squad. He scored points in 10 rounds and only finished one place behind his more-fancied young colleague.

Then it was back to French domestic racing, where he won two more titles, and regular works rides in the World Endurance Championship, first for Honda and then back with Kawasaki for whom he won the Le Mans 24 Hours in 1993 and '94. That second victory helped him to the World Championship. In between those commitments he also managed a few World Superbike rounds but never rode a full season.

Adrien Morillas won a World Superbike race at 30 years of age and his Endurance title at 36. It is tempting to wonder what he might have achieved if he had started road racing when he was a little younger than 28.

Davide Tardozzi

Born
30 January 1959
Ravenna, Italy

First win
1988 Round 3/Race 1
Hockenheim, Germany
Bimota YB4EI

Championships
1988 3rd
1989 27th
1990 25th
1991 10th
1992 16th

4 Race wins
1988 Germany 1 and 2
1988 Austria 2
1988 Portugal 1

2 Pole positions
1988 Hungary
1988 New Zealand

From crasher to Ducati's master controller

We should get one fact established right away: Davide Tardozzi did not win the first ever World Superbike race. Sure, he took the flag first in that first race at Donington in 1988 but, uniquely, that round was decided on aggregate positions over the two races, and after Davide bit the dust at the Old Hairpin chasing Lucchinelli's Ducati later in the day he did not even make it to the rostrum. That unforced error summed up Tardozzi and Bimota's first Superbike season. The YB4EI was just about legal by the letter of the regulations but not by their spirit; it was more like a TT Formula 1 bike with its highly modified fuel-injected FZ Yamaha motor in a beautifully crafted aluminium chassis and of course it was right on the minimum weight limit. Because Bimota was and is a tiny concern they only had to make 200 road bikes to homologate it for the series, so their two works bikes were much more like tool-room specials than the road-bike based racers the rules envisaged. They were undoubtedly the fastest things out there and the company's name was then a byword for handling excellence, so in many people's eyes Tardozzi was the pre-season favourite to be the first World Superbike Champion.

True to form, he won more races than anyone else and posted Superbike's first double – predictably at superfast Hockenheim, but as well as winning a lot, he fell off a lot. As well as the Donington crash there were other examples of his rostrum-or-straw-bales approach to the job. It was difficult to reconcile the small, baby-faced Italian with the on-track chancer. Critically, crashes in qualifying for the penultimate round in Australia and a catastrophic get-off on the warm-up lap for the very last race of the year when he had one hand on the title, dumped him to third at close of play.

To all intents and purposes, Davide Tardozzi then disappeared from view after Bimota relegated him to their satellite Speed Shadows team for 1989. When he turned up for the first round with a broken collarbone sustained in a road-bike crash two weeks earlier and then highsided himself at high speed in qualifying, we really did think we had seen the last of him. And when Bimota pulled out of the Championship at the end of the season, we were sure we had seen the last of him. Ducati knew better.

First, Tardozzi went to a dealer-supported Ducati team, and then became the factory's test rider. In 1992, when there were no less than six factory Ducatis on the grid, Tardozzi was the one who tried out new components for his more illustrious team-mates. He did not race every round, but he did get to do a bit of pot-hunting in the Italian and European Championships. Some people might be surprised to learn that Davide Tardozzi won five Italian championships as well as the European Superbike title.

You had to be a serious fan (or a complete anorak) to have known that Davide Tardozzi was still involved with top-flight motorcycle sport, hence the universal surprise outside of Italy when, immediately after he retired from racing, he was made manager of one of the two works teams Ducati fielded in 1993. The Grottini-sponsored team was the only outfit aside from the full-works squad of Fogarty and Falappa to get the latest 926cc motors for their riders, Stephane Mertens and Juan Garriga. Mertens was a proven winner, but Garriga was a massively important signing for Superbike. Garriga was both a top 500cc Grand Prix man as well as a 250cc winner, and

Tardozzi and the super-fast Bimota, pre-season favourites for the first World Superbike title.

Spanish. The World Superbike Championship was desperate for a top-flight rider from that GP-obsessed country and the Catalan was a prime catch. The fact that his enthusiasm for racing did not last the season should not obscure the fact that the Ducati factory thought enough of Tardozzi's management skills to entrust him with such a valuable asset. He was not the manager's first choice for a rider though, as Davide's first 'phone call had been to Carl Fogarty. When Garriga retired mid-season, Tardozzi was given Mauro Lucchiari, one of Ducati's young hopes, to groom for stardom.

After two years running the 'other' Ducati team very much as a reserve squad to the full works operation, an injection of cash from Austrian businessman Alfred Inzinger's Power Horse energy drink company meant that, for 1995, there were two full-works Ducati teams. The newly rechristened Promotor team fielded phenomenally fast young Aussie, Troy Corser, alongside the last rider to win a World Superbike race as a privateer, Andy Meklau, who also happened to be Austrian.

It was now that the wider world started to realise what a clever manager Davide Tardozzi had become. And to add spice to the internal competition within Ducati, it was obvious that Tardozzi and the 'works' team manager, Virginio Ferrari, disliked each other intensely.

Round 1 went to Ferrari when Fogarty cakewalked the 1995 Championship while Corser finished second despite frequent mechanical problems. With Fogarty's departure to Honda, Corser was the bookies' favourite for 1996 and he did not disappoint. Again, not many people outside the Ducati family noticed Tardozzi's contribution but if you asked Troy about him you would get an unqualified statement of admiration. Both men would say it was like a father-and-son relationship, then ask you not to tell the other one what he had just said.

Tardozzi disappeared from view again when Corser and Inzinger went off for an ill-fated year in the GPs only to resurface again for 1998 as manager of the Ducati Performance team (a joint venture between the GiaCoMoto tuning firm and Ducati) which fielded lone riders in Supersport and Superbike, although they were Paolo Casoli and Carl Fogarty … The works team was still under the control of Virginio Ferrari and fielded Frankie Chili and Troy Corser, yet it was the lone Englishman who triumphed and precipitated both Chili and his manager's departure from Ducati. Tardozzi moved to manage the factory Ducati team, taking the Ducati Performance brand name with him, and found himself with two World Champions in his team, both of whom he had already taken to world titles. The differing styles of Corser and Fogarty presented the Italian with his biggest challenge yet, but he stopped them from squabbling and even got them to co-operate on matters such as tyre testing. Fogarty's legions of fans soon realised just what Tardozzi could do. If Carl was having a bad day, Davide seemed to know what to say to him. He knew when to put an arm round his rider's shoulder and commiserate and he knew when 'to kick his arse'. Foggy himself is unequivocal: 'Davide's the best team manager I've ever had.'

Of course, it is vital for a team manger to be able to read his riders but he must also be able to run a large operation. Tardozzi's cleverest trick was to bring together a team with a real feeling of solidarity and togetherness. Nearly all the mechanics, cooks, drivers, IT specialists and other staff are, like their boss, from Ravenna and even socialise together away from the track.

Davide Tardozzi's official job title is Sporting Director of Ducati Corse. As well as the day-to-day running of the World Superbike and World Supersport Championship teams, he is directly responsible for all Ducati's works riders and is required to spot up-and-coming young talent in whom the factory might invest for the future.

Not bad for a rider dismissed 10 years ago because he crashed too much to win titles.

Hard charging on the Bimota (opposite) and first steps with Ducati in 1992. Then comes a change of job.

Gary Goodfellow

Born
19 October 1955
Dunedin, New Zealand

First win
1988 Round 5/Race 1
Sugo, Japan
Suzuki GSX-R750

Championships
1988 8th
1989 35th

1 Race win
1988 Japan 1

First for Suzuki and for New Zealand

Any top-flight motorcycle racing paddock always contains a disproportionate number of New Zealanders; some are riders, many are mechanics or race engineers. How come there are so many Kiwis in racing – it's not like it is the only sport they're interested in? Maybe it is because when you come from a country effectively isolated from the major centres of racing you have to learn how to do things for yourself.

Gary Goodfellow is down in the record books as a Canadian, but in fact he was one of that band of wandering Kiwis. He was a professional motocrosser for six years, including one at World Championship level, before moving to Canada, opening a bike shop and going racing on tarmac to promote it. That did not prevent him from being involved with the greatest of independent bike designers, his good friend and fellow New Zealander John Britten. Goodfellow raced his early creations in the BEARS (British, European & American Racing Series) and in Battle of the Twins racing in the States, and the combination was quick enough to be on lap-record pace at Christchurch's Ruapura circuit. But Goodfellow is best remembered for his exploits on Suzuki Superbikes both in his adopted home and abroad. He was the Open Class Champion of Canada in 1986 and was good enough for the Yoshimura Suzuki factory team. In 1987, he was within six minutes of winning the Suzuka 8 Hours with Katsuro Takayoshi after leading for most of the race when a crash put them out. The team wanted the Japanese rider to take the flag but he crashed into a backmarker exiting the pits after the final rider change.

'Goody' impressed British fans with a fighting second place at the Eurolantic (née Transatlantic) Trophy Challenge at Brands Hatch in 1988 before an injury put him out of the series. Just to prove he was a genuine all-rounder Gary was in on the birth of 600 Supersports racing, winning the Canadian Championship in 1988 and a 600 class race down south at Laguna Seca.

This was a busy year for Gary, for as well as racing at home in Canada, in the States and the UK, there were Japanese events for Suzuki's Don Knit Sugano-sponsored factory squad. The Japanese round of the inaugural World Superbike Championship was part of that team's programme, and so Goodfellow became the first World Superbike winner for Suzuki. Not that it was quite that straightforward. The race started in a downpour but the track dried out dramatically towards the end of the race, so Goodfellow did something unique. Well, uniquely he did it, and still won; he came into the pits to change the rear wheel. Out went the wet-weather rubber, in went a slick. It gave him enough of an advantage to hold off Fred Merkel for the win. To show it was not a fluke he finished third in Race 2, so if they had been deciding the event on aggregate he would have won it that way, too. Late in the season he raced again in Australia and New Zealand, getting on the rostrum in the first race at his (real) home event. His only other appearances in the Championship were in the American and Canadian rounds the following year. He quit racing in 1991 – 'too many kids' – and planned to move back Down Under in 2000.

Strange colour scheme hides a factory Suzuki on its way to the marque's first win.

World Superbike arrived a little late for Gary Goodfellow to really make his mark at world level, so he will have to settle for two firsts: first Kiwi to win a World Superbike race, and first Suzuki-mounted winner.

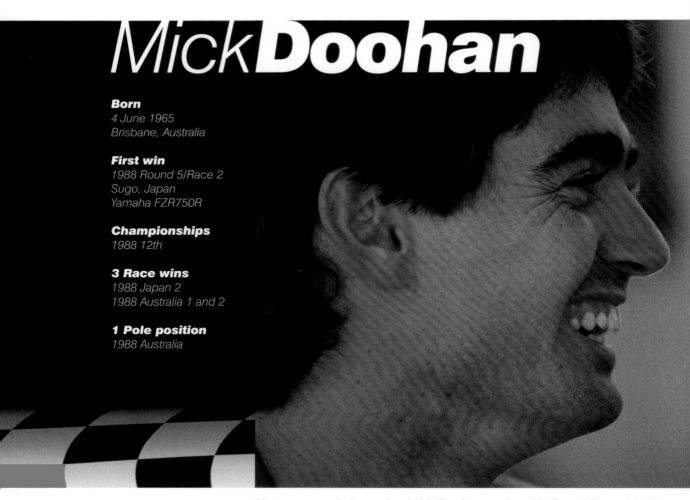

Mick **Doohan**

Born
4 June 1965
Brisbane, Australia

First win
1988 Round 5/Race 2
Sugo, Japan
Yamaha FZR750R

Championships
1988 12th

3 Race wins
1988 Japan 2
1988 Australia 1 and 2

1 Pole position
1988 Australia

Yes, he won in Superbike as well

Not many people know that Mick Doohan used to ride Superbikes, which is not surprising because he did not ride them for very long. In fact, he was only a full-time 750cc four-stroke rider for one season. What is not a surprise is that he was as dominant on an FZR Yamaha as he came to be on an NSR Honda.

Mick Doohan holds a good many records in motorcycle racing besides the five consecutive World 500cc GP titles he won from 1994 to 1998. Away from the Grands Prix, he holds the distinction of being the first Australian to win a World Superbike race and also the first Yamaha-mounted winner. The only man who could have beaten him to that first was Fabrizio Pirovano, but there was plenty of competition to be the first Aussie winner.

Australian racing had just produced its first World 500 Champion in Wayne Gardner and Kevin Magee seemed well on the way to being the second. The domestic scene was ferociously competitive, with tough men like Robbie Phillis, Mal Campbell, Mike Dowson and Peter Goddard battling for wins on well-sponsored importer-run Superbikes. All these Aussies except Campbell would go on to win World Superbike races, but all except Goddard were really at the veteran stages of their careers. He went off on a prolonged excursion to GPs, but would return to the four-stroke fold.

Meanwhile, Mick Doohan was rocketing along what was now a well-established career path: dirt-track, production racing, Superbike, Grand Prix. The production line did not stop with Mick, after him came Daryl Beattie who would also become a good friend, then Mat Mladin, Troy Corser, Anthony Gobert and most recently, Troy Bayliss.

Dirt riding was Mick's first love as a kid but he caught the eye of the big teams when he rode a Suzuki in the 1986 Castrol 6 Hours, the biggest box-stock production race in the world, and followed that up by riding in the 250cc Production class of the Swann Series. He did not win but someone from Yamaha understood what they were seeing and he got an invitation to ride in the Suzuka 8 Hours.

The long-time boss of HRC, Yoichi Oguma, once described the 8 Hours as an exam that any aspiring works rider must pass. Despite a slow bike, Mick did enough to impress the Japanese factories on their home turf and was invited back to ride a Yamaha in an end-of-season meeting. In 1988 he joined Dowson in the mighty Marlboro Dealer Team Yamaha set-up to battle Robbie Phillis and Kawasaki for the Australian title. When Dowson broke his leg, Mick had to fight Phillis single-handedly and although he won more races, he lost the Championship.

Aside from the domestic commitments, Mick had to fit in a good few overseas events and naturally one of them was the Japanese round of the World Superbike Championship. It could have been the end of a promising career. He crashed in qualifying – twice, and he crashed while leading the first race, got back on, got up to third, then crashed again. A few well-chosen words were whispered in the three hours between races and Mick took notice. In Race 2 he did not take risks and kept a big enough cushion between himself and the field to win without any last-lap dramas.

When the World Superbike regulars came to Australia they knew they would be facing the toughest bunch of locals in world racing. What they did not know was that they would be exposed to a stellar new talent. Mick took pole position and won both races, the first time that was done in World Superbike, but it was the manner of the victories that was so impressive. To this day, Mick Doohan rates those two rides as among the best of his career. The only championship regular to get on the rostrum all day was Fred Merkel with third place in Race 2 and he was half-a-minute behind Mick, whose Aussie team-mate Dowson was second both times to underline the strength of MDTY. This was the point at which the Japanese factories started to outbid each other for Mick's services. One year after becoming the number-two rider in an Australian Superbike squad Mick Doohan was a 500cc Grand Prix rider. The rest is history.

Out on his own on a Superbike: a preview of GPs to come.

Fabrizio Pirovano

Born
1 February 1960
Biassano, Italy

First win
1988 Round 6
Le Mans, France
Yamaha FZ750

Championships
1988 2nd
1989 4th
1990 2nd
1991 5th
1992 5th
1993 4th
1994 9th
1995 7th

10 Race wins
1988 France
1989 Great Britain 1
1990 Australia 1
1990 Italy 1 and 2
1990 Malaysia 1 and 2
1992 Italy 1 and 2
1993 Portugal 1

Small is fast

With one exception, every rider who won a race in the first year of World Superbike had some sort of reputation as a racer, be it the 500cc GP ex-World Champion Lucchinelli or the rising star of French racing, Morillas. That exception was Fabrizio Pirovano. The tiny Italian had been a top-notch motocrosser, good enough to be Italian 125cc Champion, before taking to the tarmac for the first time in 1986. In 1987, he won the Italian Superbike Championship and in 1988, just two years after he first raced on slicks, he was challenging for a world road racing title. He never got that elusive world crown but he did win his national title twice more in 1990 and '92.

Pirovano was exactly the type of rider the Championship was originally meant for. A privateer with a modicum of support from his local Yamaha importer plus a host of small trade sponsors (the fairing of his bike looked like a page from *Exchange & Mart)* and he was managed by his sister Cinzia. Nevertheless, he proved that the steel-framed FZ750 was good enough to win races. In fact he only won one race in 1988, the French round (uniquely, there was only one race not two), but that victory put him to the top of the points table and he stayed in the hunt for the title right to the last race of the last round.

Two things became evident in that first year. First, Pirovano was a demon wet-weather rider, and secondly, he was not a man you would pick a fight with. His 'physical' riding style brought complaints from the men

Piro persevered with Yamaha (right) for six years before decamping to Ducati.

usually heard being complained about. Stephane Mertens's team once officially protested about his riding, other riders complained that he 'stopped in corners' after braking later than the rest due to his light weight. Piro nearly came to blows with Giancarlo Falappa at Hockenheim amid unpleasant references to each others' mothers, which is about as abusive as an Italian can get. Time did not mellow him. When Fabri started riding a Supersport Ducati in 1996, a tall young Spaniard called Ruben Xaus put him in the sandtrap at Donington Park. After qualifying the Italian sought him out and told him exactly what would happen if he tried something like that again. Xaus spent the rest of the weekend keeping well out of sight. But the really unnerving thing about Piro was that he did not look or act like a stereotypical Latin nutter. No arm waving, no posing, no shouting

and raving; just a level, cold, detached stare. 'Bloody hell', said a British journalist after encountering him for the first time, 'shouldn't he be in the SAS?'

Perhaps Pirovano's finest achievment in the field of unarmed combat came after he fell at Hockenheim's Sachs Kurve in 1989 and a posse of large German marshalls somewhat officiously tried to prevent him restarting. One was floored with a right cross and another despatched with the boot before the forces of law and order regained control. All of which shenanigans tended to disguise the fact that he really was a rather good rider. Look at the record: twice second in the Championship and never out of the top 10 in an eight-year Superbike career. Pirovano was the first star created entirely by World Superbike.

For 1989 he got one of the new Yamaha OW01s and promptly won the first race of the year but his consistency deserted him and a string of crashes followed, starting with Race 2 at Donington. In 1990, he started the season slowly but put on a late charge winning four races in a row, a first for World Superbike, including a double at a wet Monza. The fact that they were two double wins was also – obviously – a first. It was too late though, Raymond Roche had a big enough lead to win with plenty in hand. Again, Piro's reputation as an ultra-hard competitor was underlined by clashes with Rob McElnea and Raymond Roche. On the positive side, he emerged as the fastest starter in the field, which cannot have been due totally to the fact that he had a significant power-to-weight ratio advantage over the other four-cylinder powered competitors. It was the height of Pirovano's World Superbike career and he never again got near to challenging for the title.

In 1991 he did not win a race and in 1992, armed with the new YZF750 as part of the official Yamaha team, he needed a home circuit and rain to win. So when it rained (as usual) at Monza, Piro reminded everyone of just how good he was with a double at a time when the accepted wisdom was that you had to be on a Ducati to win. Of the four riders who finished in front of him in the Championship, three were on Ducatis and the other one was Rob Phillis. Fabri's last World Superbike win was also Yamaha's last until Noriyuki Haga came along four years later. It came in Portugal after Scott Russell fried his clutch and Carl Fogarty fell, leaving Aaron Slight, Piergiorgio Bontempi and Piro to fight it out. Live on television, Niall Mackenzie was asked who was going to win. 'Pirovano', said the Scot, 'because he's mad', then realised they might have to meet on a race track again … Rumour has it that Fabri took this as a compliment.

Two years on Ducatis followed, the first was on a factory bike, before Piro switched to the new Supersport Open Championship on a 748 Ducati for the Alstare Corona team. He won that series, and then when the championship became the Supersport World Series he and his team were given the task of developing the new Suzuki GSX-R600 for the planned World Championship in 1998. Fabri won one race in 1997 and the following year dominated with five wins. Unfortunately for him, the promised World Championship status did not materialise until 1999 and then, to add insult to injury, his team-mate Stephane Chambon won. None of which changed Pirovano's attitude, having celebrated his 40th birthday he came back for the 2000 season still looking for that world title.

And you still wouldn't argue with him.

The enduring image of Fabrizio Pirovano in Superbike – the little guy on the big Yam.

Stephane Mertens

Born
14 May 1959
Paris, France

First win
1988 Round 7/Race 2
Estoril, Portugal
Bimota YB4EI

Championships
1988 4th
1989 2nd
1990 3rd
1991 4th
1992 7th
1993 7th
1994 14th

11 Race wins
1988 Portugal 2
1988 New Zealand 2
1989 Austria 2
1989 France 1
1989 Italy 1
1989 New Zealand 2
1990 Germany 2
1990 USA 1
1990 Austria 2
1991 Great Britain 2
1991 Austria 1

3 Pole positions
1988 Portugal
1990 Australia
1991 USA

The first to win on three different bikes

Ask any professional motorcycle Grand Prix photographer who earned them the most money in the 1980s and you will get an almost unanimous vote for Stephane Mertens. The lanky Belgian had an unenviable reputation as a crasher. True, he was often trying too hard on uncompetitive machinery, but equally undeniably, he did sling it into the scenery with depressing regularity. Still, the snappers were grateful. Strange then that 10 years later he would excel at a discipline where falling off has even more repercussions, and win the World Endurance Championship.

Mertens started racing late. He was 21 when he took to the track having been a top-class tennis player and athlete as a youngster, but he was fast straight away. In his second year he won the Belgian 500cc Championship and the following year finished runner-up in the European 250cc Championship. The man who beat him was Carlos Cardus of Spain, later to be a GP winner, and behind him were Fausto Ricci and Harald Eckl, later to become manager of the Kawasaki World Superbike team.

Like his fast fellow-countrymen of the late 1980s, the De Radigues brothers, Stephane Mertens came from an upper middle-class background. His father Jean was a powerful man in the Total petroleum company's Belgian operation and used his influence in getting Stephane sponsorship which he then took to the GPs, as his Euro Championship placing entitled him to. From 1984 to 1987, Stephane was a 250cc GP racer, but during that time he only managed nine points-scoring rides and a best end-of-season position of 13th in 1986. That was the year he got his best finishes, a brace of sixth places in Yugoslavia and Sweden. Unfortunately, he had now built up an unshakable reputation as a crasher and there was no way that he was likely to get a works 250.

In the circumstances, a works ride for the new World Superbike Championship was a godsend and Stephane lined up on a factory Bimota alongside Davide Tardozzi. There were, of course, Total stickers on the bikes. Despite never having raced a four-stroke before, Mertens did a good job. He got on the rostrum in Round 2, only being deprived of a win by half-a-wheel, but it took him until Round 7 (of nine) to win. When he won again it was in the strangest of circumstances. He already knew that Bimota had decided to replace him when the grid lined up for the last race of the year with the title still undecided. When Tardozzi crashed on the damp warm-up lap, the Belgian repulsed the team's attempts to reallocate his bike, and then won convincingly when his choice of slick tyres suited the fast-drying track.

Mertens had his most successful Superbike year in 1989 on a Honda RC30.

Although he never really looked like a championship challenger in 1988, in the interests of fairness it should be pointed out that this was largely due to machinery failures not crashing. That old reputation was firmly laid to rest in 1989 but not before one last big crash resurrected all the old jokes. Not that the crash with Joey Dunlop at Brands Hatch's then notorious Paddock Hill Bend was a laughing matter. Both riders were badly hurt, but Dunlop came off far the worse and missed his beloved Isle of Man TT. Mertens' ruptured pelvic ligaments put him out of the first World Superbike round and severely handicapped him for the second at the tight and twisty Hungaroring. Bravely, he raced anyway despite having to be lifted on and off his bike and scored a few valuable points. By the end of the season they looked invaluable.

With one of the three HRC-supplied Honda RC30s in the Championship, looked after by ace tuner Jean d'Hollander, Mertens put together an astonishing run of results. In the next eight rounds he was never lower than eighth in any race and when he was eighth it was usually behind a posse of locals in Japan or Australia. In 16 races he won three times and was on the rostrum another six times. Deservedly, he went to the top of the table with one round left. Stephane Mertens had shown what he could do when he had good machinery, turned round a season that started disastrously and got one hand on the Championship. In a cruel irony, that he did not get both hands on it was down to a crash but most definitely not one of his own making. He was lying sixth on a damp track when a brake disc disintegrated as he entered a high-speed turn. The resulting crash destroyed the bike but Stephane was miraculously unhurt and got on his

Mertens' first Superbike ride was with Bimota in 1988.

Mertens' third and final Superbike mount, a Pirelli-shod Ducati 888.

spare bike to win Race 2. Heroic though it was, it was not enough; Fred Merkel retained the crown.

That was the nearest Mertens got to the Superbike title. Despite keeping the same equipment for 1990 and winning three races, he could not match the consistency of Raymond Roche and the Ducati. A crash in Italy and Pirovano's double in Malaysia even lost him second in the title chase.

Seeing the writing on the wall, Mertens abandoned Honda for Ducati but took the gamble of using Pirelli tyres. In Round 1 of 1991 he crashed in the first race then won Race 2. Along with the rest of the field he then ran into the steamroller that was Doug Polen in his record-breaking first championship year. However, the old brilliance surfaced in Austria when he became the only rider all year to beat Polen in a fair fight with Roche third on an all-Ducati rostrum, at the fastest track on the calendar.

After a couple more years in Superbike, Stephane diversified into Supersport and Endurance, and just to show his crashing days were over he won the Endurance world title in 1995. Nowadays he races cars, in long-distance GT1 events of course.

Of all the characters that inhabited Superbike in its early years, Stephane Mertens was probably the least colourful. Quiet and introverted, he never made the impact on the public consciousness his talent warranted yet he was the first man to win on three different makes of motorcycle and his three pole positions were also spread out between Bimota, Honda and Ducati. It is difficult to see anyone equalling that achievement.

Giancarlo *Falappa*

Born
30 July 1963
Ancona, Italy

First win
1989 Round 1/Race 2
Donington Park, GB
Bimota YB4EI

Championships
1989 6th
1990 11th
1991 9th
1992 4th
1993 5th
1994 15th

16 Race wins
1989 Great Britain 2
1989 Canada 2
1989 France 2
1990 Great Britain 2
1992 Austria 1 and 2
1992 Holland 2
1992 New Zealand 2
1993 Ireland 1 and 2
1993 Germany 1
1993 San Marino 1 and 2
1993 Austria 2
1993 Italy 2
1994 Italy 2

8 Pole positions
1989 Italy
1990 Great Britain
1990 Canada
1992 Spain
1992 Belgium
1992 Malaysia
1992 New Zealand
1993 San Marino

The fans' favourite

If Fabrizio Pirovano was the first star made entirely by World Superbike then Giancarlo Falappa was the first superstar, a favourite not just of his own travelling fan club, but with fans everywhere.

He burst on the scene at the start of the 1989 season with a literally fighting showing at Donington Park. In Race 1, a pack of the usual suspects jostled for the lead with one stranger in their midst; alongside Burnett, Rymer, Pirovano and Merkel there was a muscular white-clad figure on a Bimota who seemed to be riding somewhat unconventionally and certainly never touching the same bit of tarmac twice.

Bimota had arrived with a totally new team: ex-GP man Fabio Biliotti and an unknown newcomer who had won the 1988 Italian 750cc Sport Production Championship called Giancarlo Falappa. No-one outside Italy knew his name, which was not surprising as Falappa had quit motocross in 1983 and had only just got back into racing with Bimota after a five-year break from competition.

To the surprise of all, on and off track, it was the newcomer who was up with the fast men although his style of sitting upright while pushing the bike down into the corner motocross style made him look like an accident waiting to happen. He also seemed unaware that a breather was spraying petrol on his rear tyre, as Roger Burnett observed to his pit crew when he got back to the pitlane: 'Who's that wanker on the Bimota? He doesn't know what's going on!' Falappa actually lost the chance to win his debut World Superbike race when he centre-punched an errant backmarker, but made no mistake in Race 2. A star was born.

His competitors may have preferred to keep their distance, but the fans loved Falappa. His no-prisoners style came directly from motocross with precious few concessions for the track and he had a nice line in standing celebration wheelies, but it was his looks which hit you. Or rather he looked like he would hit you. I've seen less-threatening looking bodyguards surrounding Mike Tyson. In fact the gangster looks disguised a surprisingly quiet, charming guy who was patently devoted to his girlfriend Paola.

When Bimota withdrew from World Superbike after the 1989 season Falappa was snapped up by Marco Lucchinelli to partner Raymond Roche in the factory Ducati team. Unfortunately, it was a season that started with some minor crashes and ended prematurely with a massive crash and serious injury.

First there was a broken wrist in an Italian Superbike round a fortnight

Falappa's finest hour, a damp but dominant double at Brands in 1993.

Giancarlo and the Ducati 888 in 1991.

before the second round of the World Championship at Donington Park, despite which, Giancarlo set pole and then infuriated Roche by mugging him for the win one corner from the chequered flag in Race 2. He then crashed hard in Hungary and Canada, breaking his wrist. After missing the American round, Falappa returned for Austria with a light cast on his injury. Lucchinelli did not want him to ride, and events proved the manager sadly right. The Osterreichring was the circuit on which Stephane Mertens won races three years in a row, and in 1990 he was decisively fastest all through qualifying. This did not stop the Italian from trying to go faster.

It takes a lot to shock a top-level bike racing paddock but Falappa's crash turned Zeltweg into a very quiet place indeed. He had lost the front on the fastest part of the track and smashed through an advertising hoarding, coming to rest with his legs folded up behind him and his helmet twisted on his head. Davide Tardozzi was among the first on the scene and twisted Giancarlo's helmet round to stop the strap from strangling the fallen rider – not recommended procedure perhaps, but strangulation was a serious possibility. The damage was bad enough, a rebroken wrist, shattered shoulder blade and both thighs broken. Frankly, he was lucky to be alive and most men would never have gone near a racing motorcycle again. Most men in Falappa's condition would not have got a ride again, but for 1991 Ducati kept faith with their man and he quietly worked his way back to full fitness for 1992 when he rode alongside the all-conquering Doug Polen in the Police (sunglasses) sponsored works team. Giancarlo was now fully fit and just as fast and aggressive as ever, although most (but not all) observers noted a new weapon in his armoury, tactical awareness. He had certainly not lost any of his courage. At the Osterreichring, the track that so nearly killed him, he scored a magnificent double win, his first.

Things looked even better in 1993 when Giancarlo won the first three races, including a perfect double at a wet Brands Hatch's entertainingly titled Irish round that opened the season. It was that brace of crushing victories that opened the eyes of most spectators to the fact that Falappa could ride with the delicacy of touch you need in the wet as well as swap paint with the hardmen in the sort of last-lap battle that would intimidate the average axe murderer. And if you were lucky enough to get to eat in the Ducati team's camp there would be Giancarlo urging you try some pasta or other treat, and making sure you had the right condiments for maximum enjoyment. Paola was the chef and he was so proud of her.

Other riders still did not know what to make of him, including new team-mate Carl Fogarty who simply described him as unpredictable. Scott Russell, who Falappa torpedoed at Albacete, held with the more popular and less complimentary view. Indeed, despite his awesome start to the year, Giancarlo could not match the consistency of Russell or the sheer speed of Fogarty and faded to the point where he was almost uncompetitive.

With the advent of the Ducati 916 in 1994, Falappa stayed in the factory Ducati squad with Carl Fogarty under new manager Virginio Ferrari. After Foggy broke his wrist in Germany, Falappa was Ducati's main weapon in chasing Scott Russell. When the two traded wins at Misano in Round 3 and Falappa went second in the points table, it looked as if he could at last challenge for the title rather than simply win a few races.

Just another day at the office.

Unfortunately, that hope disappeared in untimed practice for the very next race when Giancarlo highsided in a slow corner and suffered severe head injuries. At first he seemed unhurt but lapsed into a coma and local Spanish doctors warned that the situation was very serious. Just as you would expect, Falappa was a fighter and when, against expectations, his condition stabilised the Castiglionis (owners of Ducati) had him flown home to Italy. He was kept in intensive care for nearly two months before starting his rehabilitation with the objective of racing again firmly in his mind.

Sadly, this was not to be. Giancarlo had been as close to the edge as you can go and still come back. He recovered enough to do most normal things; unfortunately motorcycle racing does not come under that heading. There was also the matter of some minor injuries that had been untreated in the battle to save his life, so Giancarlo had to undergo a series of operations. As a result, the Falappa seen around the paddocks in the following year was a shadow of his former, muscular self. The pale, unsteady figure came as a shock to those who had not realised just how seriously he had been injured. It was now that he decided that it was unfair to Paola to continue their relationship and he moved to Monte Carlo where he has an apartment right on the F1 car circuit. He seemed genuinely surprised to be mobbed when he went into the Redgate Lodge pub at Donington. 'But I'm not a rider any more …'

It took a lot of hard work with the physiotherapist, but Giancarlo got himself well enough to play his part in the Superbike paddock, first running a Ducati team in Supersport and then helping the NCR satellite Superbike squad which took over Ben Bostrom when things got tough in the works team. Like those English fans in the Redgate Lodge, Ducati remembers its heroes.

Raymond Roche

Born
21 February 1957
Ollioules, France

First win
1989 Round 4/Race 1
Brainerd, USA
Ducati 888

1 Championship
1989 3rd
1990 Champion
1991 2nd
1992 2nd

23 Race wins
1989 USA 1 and 2
1989 Germany 1 and 2
1989 Italy 2
1990 Spain 1 and 2
1990 Hungary 2
1990 Canada 1 and 2
1990 Japan 1
1990 France 1 and 2
1991 Malaysia 1 and 2
1991 Germany 2
1991 Italy 2
1992 Spain 2
1992 Great Britain 1
1992 San Marino 1 and 2
1992 Malaysia 1
1992 Austria 2

9 Pole positions
1989 Great Britain
1989 Australia
1989 France
1989 Germany
1990 Spain
1990 Germany
1990 Japan
1992 Australia
1992 San Marino

Ducati's tough guy

The honour of being Ducati's first ever World Superbike Champion went to a man who had already been a World Champion and who, you suspect, would have traded at least one of his titles for a 500cc Grand Prix victory. It is difficult to tell though because Raymond Roche often gave the impression of not really being worried about anything at all. Communication with journalists was never a priority, either. Asked by the author where his bike was faster than the others, he shrugged and pretended not to understand. When the question was repeated in appallingly accented French he winced and replied: 'In the pits'.

For Raymond, Superbike racing was a job. In 1989 when he went to Ducati the options were a factory Superbike or trying to score the odd point as a GP privateer. Roche had spent five years in 500 GPs, first as a well-supported privateer on a Honda triple and then as a works V4 pilot for Honda, Yamaha and finally, none too successfully, Cagiva. Before any of that he had been World Endurance Champion for Kawasaki in 1981 and won the 1983 Bol d'Or as part of Honda's mighty factory squad. But right at the very start of his racing career Raymond was a 250cc hotshot who won the French title in his second year of competition. Like any fast young Frenchman, he got offered good rides in Endurance; he did not like the discipline much but how else was an impoverished privateer supposed to get so much track time and get well paid for it? It was in Endurance that he made his name outside France as a tough guy and he took that reputation into the GPs. In 1983, he was top privateer in the 500cc World Championship and was given his chance on an NSR in 1984. That year he finished second four times and third four times, had eight rostrums without a victory and twice he only lost the lead in last-lap duels. The first was with Mamola at Assen's chicane and then at Anderstorp when he outbraked

A smile from the French racer of an Italian bike with the flag of Europe in Japan.

Eddie Lawson and himself at the end of the back straight. He finished third in the Championship and despite his fearless riding style he did not crash once in a race all season. Here was a man who resented American domination of the 500s and had not just the nerve but also the skill to try to do something about it. But that elusive win never materialised and Raymond slid slowly down the rankings.

After a couple of years on the Cagiva 500, Raymond moved across to another part of the Castiglionis' empire and promptly won more races in the 1989 World Superbike Championship than anyone else. Unfortunately, the bike was not as reliable as Roche and he only finished third in the Championship.

As you would expect from a man with so much experience, Raymond was totally professional if not always enthusiastic. When he could get the bike right, he won. Look at the percentage of double wins in his record – 60 per cent of his 23 victories were racked up in pairs. Again, as you would expect, they were mainly on the fast tracks but there was a double at Albacete and wins at Sugo and the Hungaroring to show just how hard Roche was trying. If he was almost terminally laid-back with some Mediterranean charm breaking through from time to time, that did not stop him from venting his dissatisfaction with some aspects of the machinery and the organisation of Superbike, or from rowing ferociously with his team-mate Falappa. His famed and feared temper also appeared in an encounter with a Canadian marshall as well as the legendary incident in which he drove down the pitlane with a gateman on the bonnet of his hire car. Even if he had rather have been somewhere else, you crossed Raymond Roche at your peril.

In 1991, the 888 Ducati was at the height of its powers and Roche was the bookmakers' favourite to retain his title. They reckoned without Doug Polen and his Dunlop-shod Fast by Ferracci Ducati. Even the reigning champion could not cope, crashing in qualifying for the very first race as he chased Polen's pole time. That resulted in injured fingers and when he did the same again in the States he broke his foot. The second half of the season was a gutsy and professional recovery of lost ground. In 1992 Roche gave Polen a much harder time, leading the Championship for the first three rounds and chasing the Texan right to the last round. That was enough for Roche, he moved up to manage the team in 1993.

On the Donington rostrum in 1992, Raymond famously told Carl Fogarty that one day he would be World Champion, 'but not this year'. Now his first act as a team manager was to sign the Englishman to ride alongside Giancarlo Falappa. Foggy remembers him as a manager who got involved with the detail of bike set-up, although the first incident he talks about has nothing to do with bikes. Roche used to pass a bit of time at the tracks practising his golf swing, on one occasion he tried out his new driver in the pitlane garage using an apple as the target. Carl subsequently went out to race with his helmet, leathers and other riding kit plastered inside and out with atomised fruit.

Raymond Roche may sometimes have given the impression that he did not care, but that was off the motorcycle, the difference in his attitude when he won was always indicative of his real feelings. There is no doubt, however, that he spoke from the heart when he said that his World Superbike title was for Ducati, not for himself.

He may have been a reluctant Champion, but Raymond Roche is in the history books as Ducati's first.

Alex Vieira

Born
14 December 1956
Vila Nova de Ouren,
Portugal

First win
1989 Round 5/Race 1
Osterreichring, Austria
Honda RC30

Championships
1988 6th
1989 15th
1990 30th

1 Race win
1989 Austria 1

1 Pole position
1988 Germany

The unsung hero of Honda's V4 years

Like the other French winners featured here, Adrien Morillas and Raymond Roche, Alex Vieira made his name in the World Endurance Championship, so that makes him a steady rider, right? Wrong! His solus Superbike victory came on the fast and scary Osterreichring after a 10-bike dice that lasted from flag to flag and involved such notable chargers as Roche, Mertens, Monti, Pirovano and Mal Campbell. And it happened in a year when, despite Fred Merkel being the Superbike World Champion, Alex could justifiably claim to be the best four-stroke racer in the world.

The record books show he won just one World Endurance title, in 1991, but if the series had had world title status in 1989 and '90 then Vieira would be a triple World Champion. He will have to make do with the six Bols d'Or on the sideboard alongside five winner's trophies from the Le Mans 24 Hours.

The Portuguese-born Frenchman first came to notice as the third man in Honda's mighty factory endurance team, one of the reserves who only rode in the 24-hour events. Shorter-distance events required only the two lead riders.

Like most of the French Superbike men, Vieira subjugated the Superbike World Championship to his World Endurance and even national championship commitments, therefore he never did a full season, which makes his achievements all the more noteworthy. When most teams were struggling with the new RC30's reliability, it was blindingly obvious that the Honda France team's endurance experience was getting their men to the flag. In 1988, it even put Vieira on pole at the fastest track in the world, the Hockenheimring, and then put him on the rostrum twice.

That win in Austria came as part of a year of domination of the races he contested. In the 1989 World Endurance Championship, Vieira won the 24-hour races at Le Mans, Spa and Circuit Paul Ricard as well as the Suzuka 8 Hours, for a clean sweep of the championship. That equates to 2,500 racing miles (4,000km) hounded by works opposition without a single crash. At the Bol d'Or he had to deal with a frighteningly feisty Fred Merkel in the

In the first year of the Championship, Honda France provided Alex Vieira with one of the best RC30s on the grid.

first hour on the second works Honda. It was a fair fight and Alex dispatched the reigning World Superbike Champion with aplomb. And along the way, there was that breathtaking Superbike win in Austria.

Although he was born in Portugal, Alex always pointed out that he lived in France, travelled on a French passport, raced on a French licence and was married to a Frenchwoman. He was, however, more than happy when the Portuguese media discovered that they had a potential World Champion on their hands and turned him into a celebrity back in the land of his birth.

As the unsung hero of Honda's V4 racing, it is somehow appropriate that Alex was the first man to win a race of any importance on the RC45; a round of the French Superbike Championship.

Doug Polen

Born
2 September 1960
Detroit, Michigan, USA

First win
1989 Round 7/Race 1
Sugo, Japan
Suzuki GSX-R750

2 Championships
1989 20th
1991 Champion
1992 Champion
1994 4th

27 Race wins
1989 Japan 1
1991 Great Britain 1
1991 Spain 1 and 2
1991 USA 1 and 2
1991 Austria 2
1991 San Marino 1 and 2
1991 Sweden 1 and 2
1991 Japan 1 and 2
1991 Germany 1
1991 France 1 and 2
1991 Italy 1
1991 Australia 2
1992 Germany 1 and 2
1992 Belgium 2
1992 Andorra 2
1992 Malaysia 2
1992 Japan 1 and 2
1992 Holland 1
1992 New Zealand 1

The dominator

No-one, not even Carl Fogarty, has ever dominated a World Superbike season like Doug Polen in 1991. And he was not even on one of the full works bikes. Doug Polen, the Fast by Ferracci Ducati of ace Italian-American tuner Eraldo Ferracci, and Dunlop tyres made an unbeatable – nay, unapproachable – combination. Consider the numbers: 17 wins in 26 races including a run of seven consecutive victories, 10 out of 13 pole positions, six lap records and not one single crash. Domination is just too weak a word; totalitarian oppression of any hint of opposition is more like it.

It is true that the 888 Ducati, now right on the minimum weight limit and still benefiting from a 25kg advantage over the fours, was the only bike to have if you wanted to win. The Honda RC30 was now well past its sell-by-date and the Yamaha OW01 was never quite competitive, which left Robbie Phillis and the factory Kawasaki as the only four-cylinder opposition. The factory Ducatis were in the hands of reigning World Champion Raymond Roche and the convalescent Giancarlo Falappa and used Michelin tyres. Stephane Mertens ran his own team with Pirelli rubber. Polen certainly benefited from the seriousness with which Dunlop attacked the series but his ability to assess new equipment was a major asset. Both Roche and Mertens crashed trying to match the Texan, and the only time that another Ducati rider got the better of him in a race, when neither man had problems, was when the Belgian won at his favoured Osterreichring. The only non-Ducati win of the year (apart from the largely boycotted Canadian round) was when Kevin Magee got the benefit of a photo finish in Australia.

Polen was as unlike the earlier American World Superbike Champion Fred Merkel as it is possible to be. Sure, he was talkative, but Doug was very much the devoted husband – he even had his wife Dianne's name on one sleeve of his leathers and had a reputation as a

No-one dominated a Superbike season like Doug Polen and the Fast by Ferracci 888 Ducati.

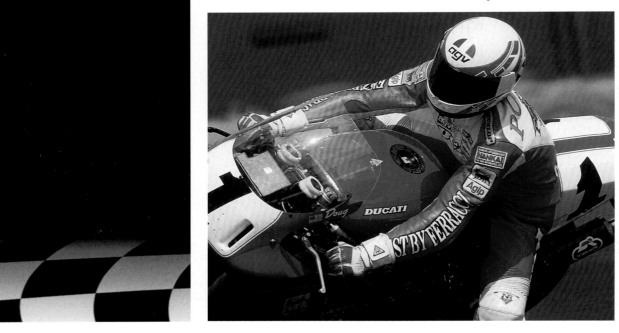

calculating businessman rather than as an emotional glory seeker. That stemmed from his 1986 campaign when he came back to racing having retired after a club-racing injury in Texas. With 750 and 1,100cc Suzuki GSX-Rs, he criss-crossed the States to events – usually club level – paying contingency money. His pot-hunting is reckoned to have earned him nearly $100,000.

When he did deign to enter Superbike races he did well enough to attract the interest of a top privateer team for which he scored two rostrum finishes in 1987 before being signed by the works Yoshimura Suzuki team for 1988. He was only four points behind works Honda man Bubba Shobert at the end of the season.

Along the way Doug monopolised the Supersport classes, winning the 600 class in 1987 and '88 and the new 750cc class in 1988 as well. There was also the small matter of a testing accident that resulted in his bike's chain sawing all the toes off one foot.

The next stop in what cynics always reckoned was Doug's never-ending search for a better payday was Japan. In 1989, he won both the F1 and F3 titles. No foreigner had ever won one Japanese title and no-one had ever won the 750 and 400cc titles in the same year, and all this on long-in-the-tooth GSX-Rs that theoretically should not have been in the same league as the Hondas. That same year he took his debut World Superbike win at Sugo in torrential conditions that negated the opposition's power advantage. HRC would remember all this.

But first there was Doug's Ducati phase during which he set all the marks for wins, poles, etc in a season. That sequence of seven wins has never been threatened, even Fogarty in his pomp could only string four together in 1995, and even Troy Corser cannot approach the record of 10 poles in a year. A repeat of that first championship year would have all

Polen's first win was on a Suzuki in 1989, the year he was also Japanese Champion.

but destroyed the series, but fortunately for everyone, especially spectators, Doug had to work hard in 1992 following a bad start to the season. In fact, the title went down to the last round, and despite arriving in New Zealand with a sizeable points lead, he went out and won Race 1. That shut up the moaners who were always on about Polen only winning because he had the best bike and that he was only in it for the money.

Typically, Doug then returned to the USA to tie up some unfinished business, the American Superbike Championship. He had tried to win it in 1992 alongside the world title but a young man called Scott Russell had put a stop to that plan. So, while Scott battled Foggy around the world, Doug Polen took his – and Ducati's – first AMA crown. That was his last ride on a works Ducati. In 1994, he joined the new Castrol Honda works World Superbike team as the lead rider. The men at Honda head office remembered what he had done to them in 1989, saw that he was the most successful Superbike rider at world level, and signed him on a two-year contract.

Doug's year on the new Honda RC45 in 1994 was not a happy one, compared with his Ducati domination.

The first year of the RC45 was not happy for anyone in the squad, although third and fourth places in the Championship behind Fogarty and Russell does not look too shabby. Unfortunately, the bike did not win a race and Doug was outshone by his new team-mate Aaron Slight. The Kiwi finished 119 points in front of Doug and outscored him in rostrums by 10 to three. Both team and rider had little to say through the winter break, and when the silence was broken, the 1995 season was only a week away. Doug and Castrol Honda went their separate ways and Slight was left to fly the flag on his own. The reason for the strange timing? No-one has said, but it is assumed that some delicate financial negotiations over who paid the bill for buying Polen out of his contract were the cause. Doug did race in World Superbike again, on the German importer's Ducati, but only in a handful of races and to no great effect.

Most people thought that was the last they would see of Doug Polen, especially when he went back to the States and had another average year, but the man had other ideas. He went back to his Suzuki roots, joining Peter Goddard in their World Endurance team and won both the world title and the Bol d'Or. In 1998 he was back on a factory Honda and won the World Endurance title again, this time with Christian Lavieille. Two titles in both Endurance and Superbike is a unique achievement and one that points out just how good Doug Polen was in his heyday. It would be a shame if some of Superbike's more recent converts only remember him for that tricky year on the Castrol Honda. Doug's straight-armed, stiff-backed style may have looked ungainly at times, but at the start of the 1990s he was even more dominant than Carl Fogarty became five years later.

Michael **Dowson**

Born
*10 June 1960
Wonthaggi, Victoria,
Australia*

First win
*1989 Round 7/Race 2
Sugo, Japan
Yamaha OW01*

Championships
*1988 22nd
1989 10th*

2 Race wins
*1989 Japan 2
1989 Australia 2*

1 Pole position
1989 Australia

Aussie elder statesman

Nowadays, when the World Superbike regulars go to Japan they expect to have their collective butt kicked by a posse of fast local men. This is not down to local track knowledge, not at this level, but is an indication of the strength of the All-Japan Championship. All four factories field well-financed full and semi-works teams on the latest development machinery ridden by experienced racers. Back at the start of the World Superbike Championship in the late 1980s, the regulars had to wait for the Australian round to get their come-uppance and the reasons were much the same. Australian domestic racing was populated by a generation of fast, tough experienced racers with full factory bikes at their disposal. Such was the strength of the local scene that of the 18 rostrum positions available in the first three years of the Championship going Down Under, 14 of them went to locals. The first non-Aussie to win an Australian World round was Doug Polen in 1991!

The team to beat was the Marlboro-sponsored Yamaha squad of Michael Dowson, who over the years was teamed with such names as Peter Goddard and Mick Doohan as the Australians gleefully humbled their visitors. Dowson is also credited with being the first established star to give Mick Doohan a helping hand. Unlike his erstwhile team-mates, there was not time left in Dowson's career for him to cash in on Japan's enthusiasm for Australian riders. He had to content himself with national championships and such astonishing feats as winning the Castrol 6 Hours, the most important box-stock production race in the world, on a Yamaha RD500LC. One of the riders on the second-placed Honda was Wayne Gardner.

Unlike his contemporaries in Australian racing, Dowson is from Western Australia, a whole continent away from the tracks such as Surfers' Paradise and Oran Park. This necessitated a move to Brisbane and he was in the right place to become a key part of the mighty Marlboro Yamaha Dealer Team when Warren Willing set it up. He had been at the Grands Prix and seen how Kenny Roberts's Marlboro Yamaha team, aka 'The Evil Empire' dominated the paddock. Back home in Australia the Yamaha Superbikes were painted in exactly the same colour scheme as the GP bikes

Wet or dry, the Aussie on the Yamaha was quick, very quick.

and Willing ran the squad in as professional manner as that team.

The senior rider in the squad was Michael Dowson with a new hot shot called Magee as his team-mate and when the youngster went off to the GPs a kid called Doohan replaced him. As elder statesman, Dowson provided stability and helped the younger riders – not that those two needed much help. Age and injury conspired to keep Michael Dowson off the world stage and today he runs a motorcycle dealership in Bunbury, a small town near Perth, selling Yamahas and KTMs, but the respect in which he is held by fellow Australian racers can be gauged from the turn-out for his 40th birthday bash. Names like Doohan and Beattie were there and some of them even recovered in time to catch the flights they were booked on. That's respect.

Peter Goddard

Born
28 June 1964
Wollongong, New South
Wales, Australia

First win
1989 Round 10/Race 1
Oran Park, Australia
Yamaha OW01

Championships
1989 28th
1990 15th
1998 9th
1999 12th
2000 22nd

2 Race wins
1989 Australia 1
1990 Australia 1

1 Pole position
1990 Australia

Been there, won that

If you're looking for the archetypal Australian racer career path, look no further than Peter Goddard. Like Gardner and Doohan, he started on the dirt-tracks before going on to 250cc production bikes and being headhunted for a major superbike team. Like most of his Australian Superbike colleagues of the late 1980s, he took great pleasure in beating the World Championship regulars when they came to call. Unlike most of his contemporaries, Goddard then spent three years on a 500 before coming back to the big bangers, first at home and then abroad.

On the dirt Peter was good enough to win four Australian titles in various capacity classes and also did a year in the USA racing the Camel Pro Flat Track series – not a championship to be taken lightly. Given this background, it is not surprising to hear that his first foray on tarmac was with a dirt bike fitted with road racing tyres. Goddard was 20 years old then but he did not get serious about road racing for another three years; then everything happened very quickly.

First it was the obligatory Yamaha TZR250 and a win in the production race at Bathurst's big Easter meeting. He was on a Superbike before the end of the year and got the rookies' prize in the Swann Series. That was 1987. This was the time that promising Australian racers spent a lot of time in Japan, so in 1988 he rode a Moriwaki in the All-Japan F1 Championship before returning home to join Mike Dowson for a two-year spell in the

Recent converts to Superbike will recognise Goddard on a Suzuki (right) but maybe not with the Yamaha (overleaf) on which he won two races.

Marlboro Yamaha Dealer Team that saw him win his World Superbike races. There were also plenty of important commitments in Japan. In 1989 he won a round of the F1 Championship and finished third in the Suzuka 8 Hours, and the next year again won a round of the Japanese F1 Championship; just the sort of result to impress the men at head office.

They must have been impressed because Peter got a ride on one of Kenny Roberts's 500 GP bikes as a wild card in the Australian GP. They were even more impressed when he finished eighth. There was talk of Goddard becoming a full-time Team Roberts rider and indeed, he became a full-time 500 rider in 1991, but in the All-Japan Championship. On a thinly disguised works Yamaha, he won the Championship thanks to a finely judged wet-weather win (one of two) in the very last round. This

achievement should not be underestimated, the last domestic 500cc Championship in the world was populated entirely by factory riders on works machinery, but it was not enough to get Peter a works ride. Instead, he rode one of the new 500cc Roc Yamahas and ended the season as the top privateer with four top-10 finishes including a best of fifth at Donington Park.

He really could not have done much more, but no works ride was forthcoming so Peter severed contacts with Yamaha and returned to the All-Japan Championship on a 500cc Lucky Strike Suzuki. He did not repeat the success of previous years, although he again won one round, so it was back to domestic Australian competition on a Superbike in 1994.

Peter spent three years with the Suzuki importer's Ansett Air Freight-sponsored team, managing it for two, finishing fourth, second and finally as Champion in 1996 on the completely new GSX-R750. That was the year when the works team was seriously embarrassed at Phillip Island by Goddard. Next season it was his team-mate, Troy Bayliss, who handed out the lessons, although Goddard would have added to the official riders' discomfort if the new SuperPole regulations had not negated his fastest time in regular qualifying. Goddard competed in the World Endurance series for Suzuki in 1997, starting the year by winning Le Mans and then filling in with four rides for the troubled Grand Prix team. He was the saviour of Suzuki's corporate pride in more than one series that year, and got his just reward when he and Doug Polen won the World Endurance title. He had to wait until 1998 to win a Bol d'Or.

Suzuki's new GSX-R750 Superbike has always had top-end power but was originally afflicted by handling and stability troubles and then by problems in getting that power to the ground. Goddard was now revealed as a development rider of considerable ability. When he joined the World Superbike team for the 1998 season, his team-mate, Jamie Whitham, would marvel at how much time Peter spent going through information from the data loggers or analysing it on a laptop computer. There was talk of Peter moving into managing the team, but when Suzuki moved their team away from Harris Performance to Alstare, Peter was picked up by the new Aprilia team.

In many ways it was a thankless task, a brand new bike run by a privateer team, not a full factory squad, and with no team-mate to help with development work. Things started tolerably well but an outbreak of crashes and precious little sympathy from the bloodthirsty Italian press seemed to sap his morale by the end of the year. The sight of Peter pushing his oft-dislocated shoulder back into joint as he rolled to a halt following a massive highside at Donington Park's Coppice Corner summed up his year, as well as underlining just what a tough character he is, and how hard he was trying.

For 2000, Peter reverted to domestic Superbike competition again, this time in the UK and on a Kawasaki for the first time. Significantly, his manager is Simon Buckmaster who was team co-ordinator for the Harris Suzuki team when Peter rode for them. And that is where many people expect Peter Goddard to go next – team management. Whichever factory employs him they will get a rider of massive experience in all forms of motorcycle racing and one of the deepest thinkers in the paddock on how a racing motorcycle works.

Terry Rymer

Born
28 February 1967
Folkestone, Kent,
Great Britain

First win
1989 Round 11/Race 1
Manfeild Park,
New Zealand
Yamaha OW01

Championships
1988 10th
1989 7th
1990 7th
1991 6th
1992 32nd
1993 8th
1994 10th

2 Race wins
1989 New Zealand 1
1990 New Zealand 1

Britain's first winner

One should not use the word 'if' when talking about any sport, let alone motorcycle racing, but it is so tempting to use it about Terry Rymer. Although he was the first Briton to win a World Superbike race, he never got to challenge for the title as many thought he should. If he had been on more competitive machinery; if he could have done a full season without the distractions of domestic competition; if …

The lanky South Londoner made a habit of bursting on to various scenes. First the British Championship when he beat hot favourite Keith Huewen in the first two rounds, then the World Endurance Championship when he qualified a well-used RC30 in second place at Spa in his first race abroad; and then the World Superbikes. Shy and a little gawky when dealing with the press, he used as few words as possible, or preferably a

'Too Tall Tel' won on a Yamaha (below) but finished his Superbike career on a Kawasaki (right).

serious stare and silence. Accused of being a Brands Hatch specialist, he replied 'Huewen was riding round here when I was at school.' When the European press tried to find out how he had gone so fast in qualifying at Spa they had to deal with, 'Real race track, innit?' in a South London accent. It probably lost something in the translation.

He got that same Honda on the Superbike rostrum in Portugal, beaten only by Tardozzi and Mertens' works Bimotas and in front of both his boyhood hero, Marco Lucchinelli, and champ-to-be Fred Merkel.

Not surprisingly, 'Too Tall Tel' was snapped up by the British Yamaha importer's Loctite-sponsored team for the 1989 season to ride alongside the vastly experienced Rob McElnea. He had a heavy schedule with the British Championship which took precedence as he missed two World

The young Rymer and his Yamaha promised much.

rounds to race at home. It all started so well; third and second in the first round of the year put him in the joint lead of the Championship. Unfortunately, his team's packed schedule allowed no time for testing and development and it was obvious that as the season wore on his bike was not improving at the same rate as other Yamahas. Then there were his Dunlops, which were fine for the shorter duration of British events but seemed unable to last the 40-odd minutes of a World Championship race. He crashed hard in Canada trying to make up in the corners for what he had lost on the straights and did the same in France when his tyres went off. When Dunlop gave him some experimental tyres for the last round of the year, he left the rest for dead to become the first Briton to win a World Superbike race. Just as importantly, it was a major morale boost for the 1990 season when Tel would surely challenge for the title.

That title turned out to be the British Championship, which Terry dominated, while the World series was a replay of 1989 – even down to the win in the last round in New Zealand, although the track was dry this time. Once again his equipment was not quite up to the job and again, he hurt himself too often trying to make up for it. Just one win in the year was not the form of a potential champion. And it did not get any better; 1991 was more of the same, unfortunately without the win.

Things looked even worse in 1992 when the private team Terry joined made the mistake of believing its own publicity and disintegrated, one side-effect of which was to cost Terry a lot of money. It looked like the end of a promising career, but there were not one but two proverbial silver linings to the dark clouds. At home, he rode the screaming, brutal rotary-engined Nortons that were attracting crowds back to British circuits, while abroad, he discovered his true calling: Endurance racing. Along with another hungry young Englishman, Carl Fogarty, Rymer was recruited to the Kawasaki France-managed factory Endurance team as second string to the established French stars. The Englishmen dominated the Championship, winning all three 24-hour races and the two six-hour rounds off pole. Unlike other Superbike winners who have been Endurance Champions, such as Roche and Fogarty, Rymer actually enjoyed the special discipline of the long-distance events so much it became his main career priority. He

also found time to make his 500cc GP debut at Donington on a cobbled together privateer Yamaha. He finished a more than creditable sixth behind top privateer Peter Goddard and in front of Miguel DuHamel on a factory Yamaha.

Terry's last year in Superbike ended early despite a final rostrum finish in Germany.

For 1993, he ran his own privateer team in World Superbike before joining the works Kawasaki team the following year as team-mate to Scott Russell. When he stepped on to the rostrum at Round 2, despite an elbow full of stitches, it looked like he was back to his best, but his motivation was sapped over the year and he ended up being replaced by young Australian Anthony Gobert for the last round. Replacement rides for Lucky Strike Suzuki in 500 GPs and a succession of British Championship rides followed, but if you really want to judge Terry Rymer's worth as a rider check out his record in the World Endurance Championship. That 1992 world title was followed by four more Bols d'Or in 1995, '97, '98 and '99 plus a win at Le Mans in 1994. His 1999 campaign made him World Champion again, this time for Suzuki. On paper that makes him one of the most successful Endurance racers of all time – right up there with Jean-Claude Chemarin, Jacques Cornu and Alex Vieira. Once Vieira had retired he was undoubtedly the best man for the job. His ability to maintain ferocious motivation and consistently high pace over the long distances is unequalled. Terry says that once he has got his crash helmet on he treats it like a war – as the privateers he laps will tell you.

Terry now plans to take that talent to four-wheeled endurance racing and if everything goes to plan he will be the first man to ride the two- and four-wheeled Le Mans 24 Hours races in the same season. Don't bet against him becoming the first man to win both.

Doug Chandler Mo.

Born
27 September 1965
Salinas, California, USA

First win
1990 Round 6/Race 2
Brainerd International
Raceway, USA
Kawasaki ZXR750

Championships
1990 15th
1997 35th
1998 32nd

2 Race wins
1990 USA 2
1990 Japan 2

1 Pole position
1990 USA

America's nearly man

Doug Chandler never wanted to be a road racer, but the quirky way the American Grand National Series used to be organised forced him into it. He was a top-notch dirt-tracker, good enough to be Rookie of the Year in 1983, but both oval and tarmac racing counted towards the title so anyone with aspirations for the championship needed to score points at least in the secondary discipline. Happily, Chandler found that he both liked and was good at road racing.

In the mid-1980s, he raced an F1 Honda sponsored by Freddie Spencer and started on Superbikes when they took over from F1 as the blue-riband class in 1987, scoring his first rostrum finish in the last race of the year at Sears Point. Five more rostrums followed in 1988, after which he was hired by Kawasaki to concentrate exclusively on road racing. He won his first race and then the Championship a year later in 1990, winning four out of eight rounds and completely dominating the season.

There was also the chance to ride World Superbike rounds at home and in Japan, where the 24-year-old Chandler showed the rest of the world just how good he was with third and first places at both venues. With a little luck, the results would have been even better. Off pole at Brainerd, he took the lead on Lap 10 out of 20 and pulled away steadily only to be reeled in when leaking oil got on his rear slick. He did brilliantly to hang on to third place after Mertens and Roche went past. No such problems in Race 2 despite another bad start. Chandler jumped from the pack to get up with the leaders, passed Mertens and Rymer on consecutive laps and won by 2½ seconds. It was only Kawasaki's second victory in the Championship.

As American Championship bikes run to less stringent technical regulations than those in the World Championship, there were dark mutterings from the defeated about all sorts of machine irregularities. No-one put their money where their mouth was for an official protest but the scrutineers stripped the bike anyway and found nothing amiss.

Two races later in Japan, he proved it was not a fluke. Only kept off pole by an epic Roche charge, he finished third in Race 1 when the red flag went out five laps early as the top five were separated by 1½ seconds. In Race 2 he was only headed off the line but got the two men in front of him in Turn 1 before opening up a four-second lead. What the others did not know was that the Muzzy Kawasaki team had run out of brake pads and Chandler planned to conserve his equipment once he had opened up a lead. Goddard and Baldassarre Monti helped him by having a ferocious battle for second, and when the Aussie got clear and started to close up on Chandler, he was able to press again and protect his lead.

Like the rest of the racing world, another ex-dirt tracker – Kenny Roberts Senior – was quite impressed and promptly hired Chandler to ride 500 GPs in what was planned to be his B-team but ended up as a non-branded single-bike satellite operation to the 'evil empire' of the Marlboro Yamaha squad. Incidentally, Chandler's young team-mate was more than capable of keeping the green banner flying and he won the US title in 1992. His name? Scott Russell.

After one year on the 500 Yamaha, Chandler was snapped up by Suzuki as team-mate to Kevin Schwantz. In his first GP as a Suzuki rider, Chandler finished second at a wet Suzuka, beating his team-mate into third. He backed that result up with another second place in Hungary plus two pole positions. When he went to Cagiva he scored two rostrum places for them too. Second place was the best Doug ever did in GPs, but his time on two-strokes was bedevilled by injury and no small amount of bad luck. If you are looking for someone who holds the dubious distinction of being the best rider never to win a 500 GP, then Doug Chandler would definitely be very high on your list, and most probably at the top.

Injuries followed him back to the States in 1995 when he rode for Harley-Davidson, but he reminded racing just how good he was by winning the 1996 and '97 AMA Superbike Championships when reunited with Muzzy Kawasaki. The 1996 title, his second, was a season-long fight with Miguel DuHamel that went down to the wire. The follow-up in 1997 was more a case of playing the rules to perfection as Doug won only one race compared with Honda's DuHamel and Ducati's Mladin with four each.

More than a decade after he first took road racing seriously, Doug still poses a genuine threat to the World Superbike Championship regulars when they go to Laguna Seca. He excelled as a dirt-track, Superbike and GP racer, and one thing everyone in those varied disciplines is agreed on is that Doug Chandler is not just one of the most professional racers to grace the sport, but also one of the nicest guys in the paddock.

Doug Chandler's GP career was sandwiched between American Superbike Championship victories.

Rob Phillis

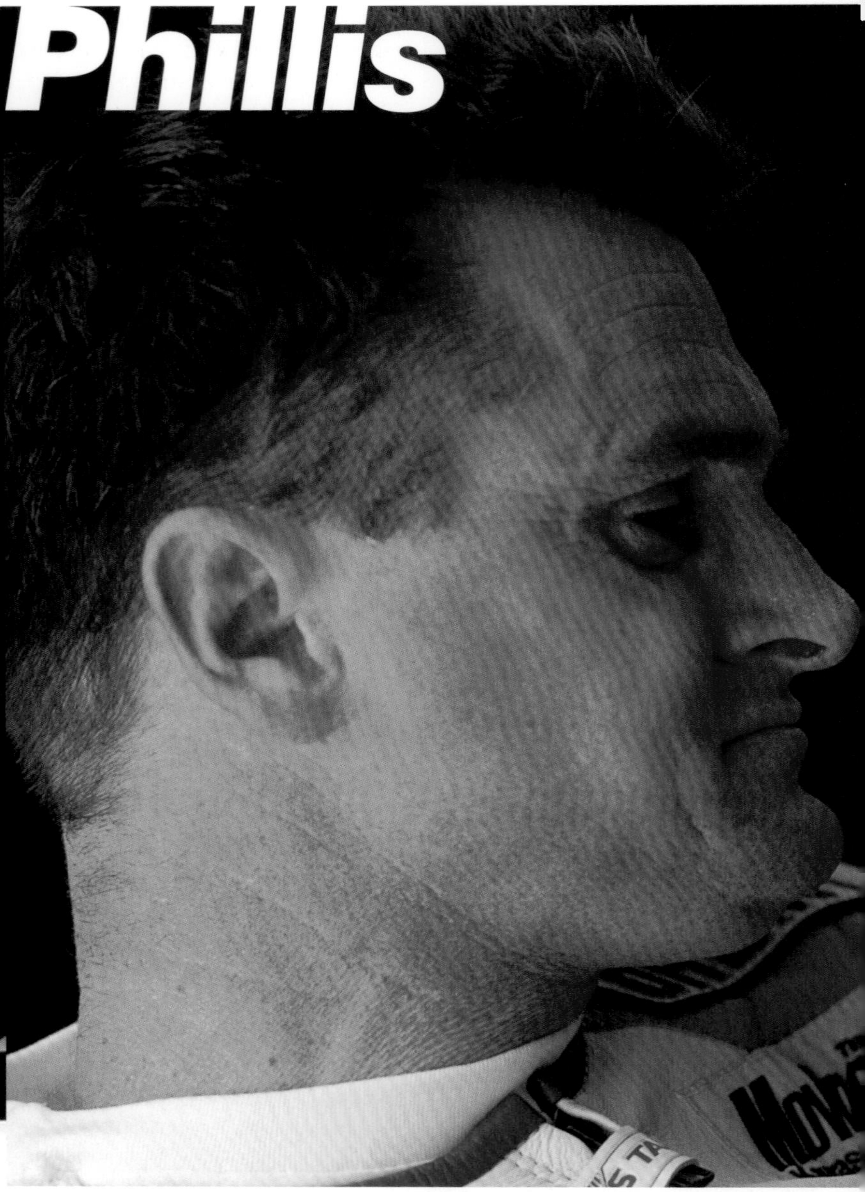

Born
27 February 1956
Wagga Wagga, New
South Wales, Australia

First win
1990 Round 12/Race 2
Phillip Island, Australia
Kawasaki ZXR750

Championships
1988 6th
1989 11th
1990 4th
1991 3rd
1992 3rd
1993 39th
1994 33rd
1996 32nd
1998 32nd

4 Race wins
1990 Australia 2
1990 New Zealand 2
1992 Belgium 1
1992 Andorra 1

3 Pole positions
1990 Malaysia
1990 New Zealand
1991 France

Green meanie

When Ducati dominated and Doug Polen was setting all his records, only one man regularly refused to be outgunned. Already in his 30s and with nine Australian titles under his belt, Robbie Phillis kept Kawasaki's green flag flying as he led the first Japanese works team to compete in a full year of the World Superbike Championship.

That was in 1990, but before then he had served notice on the regulars that he would be a force to contend with. In the first season of the Championship he only raced in four rounds yet finished the year with sixth place in the points table. In 1989 he raced three rounds, never finishing lower than sixth.

But that was not what persuaded Kawasaki to send him to the World Championship full-time. That was the brave move of sinking his life savings, 13,000 Australian dollars, into a trip to the Austrian round of the Championship with fellow Aussie hard man, the Honda-riding Tasmanian Mal Campbell. *Australian Motorcycle News* helped out, and so did the Oran Park track boss Jim Ferguson who travelled with the riders. This was the memorable occasion on which a German journalist asked the duo if they were there to win, and was told that they weren't there to fuck spiders.

When he did get to do a whole Championship, Robbie came up against the 888 Ducati and Doug Polen when that combination was nigh-on unbeatable. In 1990, his first full year at world level, an early-season crash at Hockenheim ruined his chances of challenging Roche and the still-unreliable V-twin. The thing that Robbie regrets most about that crash is not the collection of fractures he suffered but that he brought down Mal Campbell: 'I probably cost him a works ride …'

Polen and the Ducatis dominated, rarely letting a pole position, fastest lap or a win out of their grasp, but when the twins' grip did slip it was invariably Phillis who pounced. His first win came at the end of the season at home in Australia. He won Race 2 after leading Race 1 by an enormous margin until the track dried and Peter Goddard's slicks started working. Rob is more likely to reflect on the loss than tell you about the win.

There is a hint there of the complicated, nay contradictory, character

The only man to challenge Ducati domination regularly was Rob Phillis and his Kawasaki.

that made Robbie one of the most popular men in the paddock. He was always a hard racer – there were very few who could tough it out with Phillis – yet he was never a serial crasher. In fact he won three Australian titles on Suzukis with no crashes. Those bikes were sponsored by Mick Hone from whom Robbie learnt his preferred tactic of waiting and watching the opposition before making the decisive pass as near to the flag as possible. This did not always work at world level and as the man himself admits there was more than one occasion on which he led out of the last corner yet did not get to stand on the rostrum.

In direct contradiction to his tough reputation, he always said the thing he hated most was pain, yet he was at his best on the more dangerous tracks like Spa, the old Osterreichring and back home at Bathurst. Rob's

win in Belgium came after he passed Doug Polen at the ultra-fast left-hander before the bus-stop chicane – on the last lap, of course. He still cannot believe he won there, 'it's so dangerous', and is justifiably proud of holding the lap-record at the Austrian track before it was neutered and turned into the A1-Ring. Another contradiction? Dianne Polen, Doug's wife and a nervous spectator at the best of times, was always least stressed when her hubby was racing with Robbie because he was safe. Rob, in his turn, says that Mal Campbell is the man he felt safest racing elbow to elbow with. Not that they were ever friends, it is a matter of respect.

But the competition for Rob's favourite racer is no contest: Aaron Slight. The Kiwi joined Rob as team-mate for the 1992 season. He stayed at the Phillis's house for three months and from the moment he walked through the door, says Rob, his 2½-year-old daughter loved him. 'Aaron's like my little brother, and he's like a second dad to my kids. I'm his biggest fan …' His brow furrows. 'No, that'd be Carol [his wife]'.

The stories of the Aussie team – effectively the same crew that ran Rob in the Australian Championship – and the Kiwi living in caravans parked out the back of Kawasaki Germany's headquarters are legion. Like the time they borrowed a couple of road bikes and rode up for a spot of practice at Spa, a circuit largely composed of public roads. They got thrown off after about eight laps. Then there were the lengthy faxes back home to *Australian Motorcycle News* complaining about Aaron's treatment in the paper – usually written after a few beers. Tough times? 'Jeez no', says Rob, 'it was fun. There was the forest out the back. It was beautiful.' Rob is a country boy at heart. Was his relationship with the factory strained when Polen was dominating? 'It was easy going, there was never a drama.' He is given to talking himself down entertainingly then suddenly grimacing and wondering what would have happened if he'd done a full championship a year or two earlier.

In fact, Phillis alternates between giving the impression that the world was against him – 'I couldn't hang in the slipstream of one Ducati, I needed two' – and then reminding you that all they were really doing was having fun and subtly giving the impression that motorcycle racing is not that important. He is rightly famed for being the first man into the bar after a race as well as usually being the last one to leave. The intervening period was never suitable for those of a nervous disposition.

Despite having retired, Robbie has been lured back on the track a few times. In 1998 he stood in at short notice for an injured rider and finished third in the Castrol 6 Hours production race. Typically, after he has told you that, he screws his face up and mutters 'Should have been second.' Aussie fans are also enjoying seeing men like Phillis and Campbell in a new Legends series that is attracting crowds back to the tracks and he is also to be seen in the Grand Prix paddock as racing advisor to the Petronas Sprinta team. Phillis did a good deal of racing – and winning – in Malaysia and the bosses at the national oil company thought he'd be the right man to keep their 250cc squad on the straight and narrow.

In the late 1980s, Australia produced a wave of talented Superbike racers, Dowson, Goddard, Campbell and Phillis being the crest of the wave, with Magee and Doohan following in their slipstream. They were all fast, they were all hard-bitten campaigners. But the toughest of the lot was Rob Phillis.

Not the face you wanted to see looking at you when it came down to a last-lap showdown.

Pascal **Picotte**

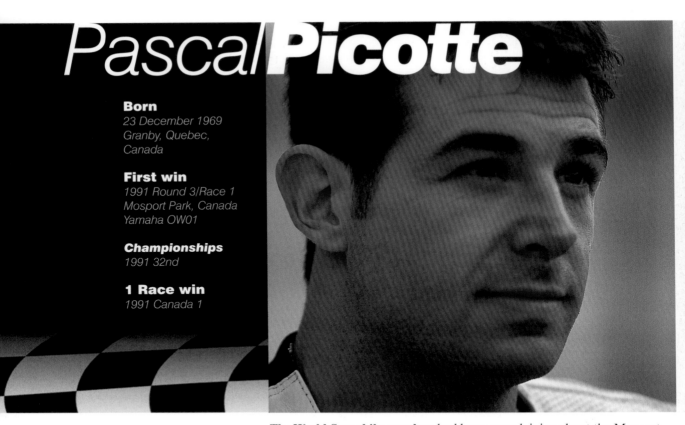

Born
23 December 1969
Granby, Quebec,
Canada

First win
1991 Round 3/Race 1
Mosport Park, Canada
Yamaha OW01

Championships
1991 32nd

1 Race win
1991 Canada 1

Canadian boycott victor

The World Superbike regulars had been complaining about the Mosport Park track's surface since the Championship first went to North America in 1989. The owners made some improvements but in 1991 the riders' representative, Rob McElnea, visited Canada before the start of the season and on his return advised his fellow riders not to race. This was in the days before riders and teams had to enter complete Championships, so in a rare show of solidarity the works riders and the privateers who intended to do the whole season simply did not enter for the Canadian round.

This left the field open to the local men and a few privateers from the USA. Race 1 saw three Canadians on the rostrum, headed by Pascal Picotte. He had been introduced to racing by a friend who took him to a race school in the late 1980s. In 1987 he gave up his streetbike completely and concentrated on racing, turning professional and scoring his first AMA Championship points in the SuperSport 600 class in '89. The following year he raced a Superbike for the first time for Yamaha of Canada as well as his 600. In 1990 he did a full season of Superbike as well as acting as a development rider for Fast by Ferracci Ducati, winning three Pro-Twins races. He became Pro-Twins Champion in '92, the last year it was an AMA Championship class, then rode in the shadow of his team-mate Doug Polen the following year before winning his first AMA Superbike race at Laguna Seca on the Ducati. A year on Muzzy Kawasaki followed by two with Suzuki before he joined Harley-Davidson. A fouled-up pit-stop kept him off the Daytona podium in 1998 but he scored two podium finishes in '99.

As befits a Canadian, when he cannot ride a bike he spends the winter riding snowmobiles.

Tom Kipp

Born
17 November 1968,
Willoughby, Ohio, USA

First win
1991 Round 3/Race 2
Mosport Park, Canada
Yamaha OW01

Championships
1991 31st

1 Race win
1991 Canada 2

1 Pole position
1991 Canada

American boycott winner

Just like Pascal Picotte, Tom Kipp got his name on the World Superbike Championship roll of honour because of the boycott of the 1991 Canadian round. Unlike the Canadian, Kipp had a long history as a motocrosser and had not even ridden a streetbike before he went to a racing school on a borrowed bike. Like Picotte, he started road racing in the SuperSport 600 class but then quickly won two AMA Endurance Championships with the Dutchman Racing team.

The family firm, Wiseco, backed his first Superbike forays and it was on a Wiseco Yamaha he won at Mosport. In 1992 he won his first AMA title, in the SuperSport 600 class on a Honda, and looked set for great things. But a very badly broken leg put him out for most of the 1993 season, and only an act of faith by the boss of Yoshimura Suzuki got him a ride in 1994. He repaid that trust with his second SuperSport title, this time in the 750cc class and retained it in 1995 on a Vance & Hines Yamaha. It was Yamaha's first 750 SuperSport title. It was also a good Superbike year, he finished third in the AMA Championship without winning a race, a feat he repeated in 1996. He stayed with Vance & Hines when the team ran Ducatis in 1998 before going back to Suzuki and winning another 750 SuperSport title in 1999.

Unable to secure a works Superbike at home, Kipp took the chance to get some restorative surgery done on an old wrist injury in 2000. The break from racing also enabled him to look after his cylinder-liner company Advance Sleeve Corp and towards the end of the season to take up an offer to race in the UK as replacement for the injured James Toseland on a Honda SP-1.

Kevin Magee

Born
16 July 1962
Horsham, Victoria,
Australia

First win
1991 Round 13/Race 1
Phillip Island, Australia
Yamaha OW01

Championships
1991 14th
1992 12th

2 Race wins
1991 Australia 1
1992 Australia 1

Healthy again, and fast too

By common consent Kevin Magee, or 'Magoo' as he is more usually known in the paddock, should have been a World Champion. He looked on course to be a GP champ when serious head injuries all but ended his career after just one win. After what, given the nature of his injuries, seemed like a miraculous recovery, he won two World Superbike races at home in Australia, both times beating Doug Polen into second place in the American's championship years.

Magee arrived on the GP scene via the well-trodden path of Aussie proddy racing followed by Superbikes both at home in Australia and in Japan. At the end of 1985, he was, to put it mildly, in demand. He had won the Victorian and Australian equivalents of the Yamaha LC Cup, won the Winton 500km production race with Mike Dowson and got a top-ten finish at the

Suzuka 8 Hours with Robbie Phillis. Having decided that Honda would be the logical choice, he then signed with Yamaha because it felt right. He did not win an Australian Superbike race but he did win production races and got a storming second on a Superbike-spec FZ against the F1 bikes at the Suzuka 8 Hours, again with Dowson. Yamaha promptly invited him to the end of season international race at Sugo where he finished second to Christian Sarron and was then invited to test a GP 500. Australian commitments prevented that so he was given a 500 for the Swann Series in which he was able to judge himself against works Yamaha rider Rob McElnea on similar machinery. The Brit won the series but Kevin convinced a lot of people from Yamaha, including Kenny Roberts, that he was the real deal.

Superbike didn't see enough of Kevin Magee, but when he turned up he won.

Magee was now desperate to race a 500 at the season-opening Suzuka GP and got his wish as part of a season centred on the all-important All-Japan F1 Championship but including the 8 Hours and three GPs. He raced at Suzuka but crashed in both qualifying and the race. A broken leg sustained at the Bathurst 500km looked to have jeopardised his plans, but the rest of the racing world now found out just how good Magoo was. He went to Europe, to Assen no less, and put a bike sourced from team Roberts' parts bin on the front row. He then went back to Japan and won two highly significant races. First he and Martin Wimmer won the 8 Hours, harassing Japanese Suzuki man Takayoshi into a crash in the last minutes. Magee had done two-thirds of the riding as the Yamaha hunted down Takayoshi and Gary Goodfellow and, as Wimmer readily admitted, it was the Aussie who won the race. 'My job', said Wimmer who had no Superbike or F1 experience and was a late replacement for local superhero Tadahiko Taira, 'was not to fuck up'. You can tell he had trained as a lawyer …

Magee then went on to win the Japanese round of the World F1 Championship before returning to Europe for the Portuguese GP, held at the Spanish Jarama circuit near Madrid. He got it on the front row again and this time on the rostrum too. He finished third but only relinquished second to team-mate Mamola on team orders. Beating Wayne Gardner into fourth must have been nice …

It was obvious that Magee would be on a factory bike in 1988; winning the 8 Hours and getting on the rostrum in only his fourth GP is the mark of a very special talent. He did indeed ride a Roberts-run Lucky Strike Yamaha and although the season did not start well he notched his first GP win off pole at Jarama after a duel with Eddie Lawson. Just to underline his status as Yamaha's favoured son he went to the 8 Hours again and won it again, this time with fellow GP newboy and team-mate Wayne Rainey.

The following year, Magee did not get on the rostrum all season, but that paled into insignificance beside the events at Laguna. Frustrated with fourth place, Magee stopped after the flag to wreak revenge on his rear tyre with a burnout. Bubba Shobert, congratulating Eddie Lawson on second, did not see the stationary Yamaha and ran straight into Magee. The Australian suffered a broken ankle but Shobert was helicoptered away with serious head injuries. He never raced again.

Not unnaturally, Magee was not looking forward to returning to California in 1990 and in an incident laden with terrible irony he too ended up being helicoptered away for emergency brain surgery after crashing horribly close to the scene of the previous year's collision. He was lucky that medics on the scene realised what was happening when he lapsed into unconsciousness after the crash, and doubly lucky to be in California near some of the most advanced neurological facilities in the world.

This extended GP chronology is included here to show just how good a racer Kevin Magee was, and this is why his one-off rides in 1991 and '92 are important. This was a time when the Superbike Championship was still unsure of itself and its status. Magee, who made a total recovery from his injuries, was the first of the current generation of GP winners to race against the regulars. Sure, Lucchinelli had won GPs, but came to Superbike well after his GP career was over. Magee was an entirely different matter and although he had had an enforced break from racing at the very top level he was provided with works Yamahas in the colours of the local sponsor, Peter Jackson. How good was Magee? In 1991 the only other non-Ducati winners were Picotte and Kipp at the boycotted Canadian round. The World Champ got his revenge in Race 2, but Kevin had proved both how good he was and how good Doug Polen was. And if Doug Polen was good then so was the whole Championship. There was a replay in 1992 in which Kevin beat Doug in Race 1 only to get beaten by Raymond Roche in Race 2.

Magee now commentates on motorcycle racing for Australian television, something he can do with authority. He's one of a very select band that has won both a 500 GP and a World Superbike race, and when he raced the big four-strokes it took a World Champion to beat him.

Aaron Slight

Born
19 January 1966
Masterton, Wellington,
New Zealand

First win
1992 Round 1/Race 1
Albacete, Spain
Kawasaki ZXR750

Championships
1992 6th
1993 3rd
1994 3rd
1995 3rd
1996 2nd
1997 3rd
1998 2nd
1999 2nd
2000 8th

13 Race wins
1992 Spain 1
1993 Italy 1
1995 Spain 1
1995 Indonesia 2
1996 Germany 1
1997 Australia 2
1997 Great Britain 1
1997 Germany 1
1998 Germany 1
1998 San Marino 1 and 2
1998 Austria 1 and 2

7 Pole positions
1993 Spain
1993 Portugal
1995 San Marino
1995 Indonesia
1997 Australia
1998 Italy
1998 Austria

The best man never to become champion

Only one man has scored championship points in every year of World Superbike from 1988 to 2000, and he is Aaron Slight. Along the way, he has earned the dubious distinction of being the best man never to win the title, endured the presence of more difficult team-mates than anyone should have to suffer, given blood in the cause of developing Honda's RC45, and most recently has gone through a brain operation to cure a congenital problem.

He was aware of a problem with his concentration and fatigue for a large chunk of the 1999 season but the racer's peripatetic lifestyle meant he did not see the same doctor twice. Then, at the start of 2000 he was diagnosed with a condition akin to a burst blood vessel in the brain – unrelated to motorcycle racing – and operated on almost immediately. Medical opinion reckoned that if he was able to race a motorcycle again he would have to wait between six months and a year. The operation was in February; he raced again in May, exactly 12 weeks later aided by the fact that he always has been one of the fittest men, if not the fittest, in the paddock.

His entry into Superbike racing came courtesy of Kawasaki Australia and Rob Phillis. The Aussie veteran took the young Kiwi under his wing and when Kawasaki sent what was effectively their Australian importer's team to contest the World Championship, Slight got his chance of a full world-level campaign in 1992. When he won the first race of the season, beating reigning champion Doug Polen into second place, it was clear he was the genuine article.

One reason the number in the wins column of Aaron's CV does not do him justice is the team-mates he has had to contend with. In 1993, Scott Russell replaced his old mate Phillis and promptly engaged in the first round of his war with Carl Fogarty. Team orders came into play at Donington when Slight was told to move over and hand Russell the win, despite the fact that no such signal had been given the round before in Italy, when Slight won Race 1 from Russell.

When Honda entered their first works team in World Superbike in 1994 with Castrol backing, Slight was signed as team-mate to Doug Polen, the most successful Superbike racer ever. Everyone expected Slight to spend the year in the shadow of the double World Champion but the new RC45 proved less competitive than expected and of the 13 rostrum finishes the Castrol team scored, all but three were Slight's. The team-mates finished third and fourth in the championship but with a massive gap of 119 points between them. When Polen quietly left the team just before the start of the 1995 season, Aaron was left to carry the Castrol Honda flag alone.

It was not an easy job. Honda's flagship was less than happy on anything bumpier than a billiard table and the RC45 had not won a World Superbike race in its first season. Aaron was the first man to win with one, defying the perception that the bike was only suited to fast circuits, by beating Fogarty's Ducati at twisty Albacete. Actually, that first win was as much down to clever tyre conservation as anything and came the round after he got the RC45's first pole position at a circuit much more suited to it, Monza. As legions of HRC engineers laboured to cure the RC45's problems Aaron spent 1995 as the lone works rider and just missed out on second place behind Foggy in a season-long struggle with Troy Corser.

By now, the prevailing opinion was that Aaron was living proof that nice guys do not win. For 1996 he went for a change of image, adopting a series of radical mohican haircuts in a variety of colours teamed with a variety of goatee beards; new race, new hairstyle. It was a conscious decision to change the public's perception of him, but it did not really work because everyone still thought he was a nice guy. He and Carl Fogarty, Castrol Honda team-mates in '96 and not the best of friends in the previous two years, rubbed along okay for their year together, at least managing to stay civil in public and Slight went to the last round with a chance of the title. The next year was not so easy. John Kocinski joined Castrol Honda and in a wonderfully self-centred season, ended the team's tradition of sharing information between the riders. Yet again Aaron suffered in silence for most of the year but pointedly said he would not obey any team orders.

There were other changes too, and not just at the barber's. Up until now, Aaron's championship challenges had been based on consistent points scoring rather than wins. This time he ripped off three wins in the first four rounds, more than he had ever managed in any season before and – uncharacteristically – he also crashed twice. That was taking the change of image a bit too far.

Aaron was much happier about his 1998 team-mate, Colin Edwards, and the RC45 had finally been developed into probably the best package on the track. If one thing still irritated Aaron it was the fact he had never had a double-win and when his new team-mate opened his World Superbike account with a double at Monza their friendship was a little

Aaron's aerodynamic haircut obviously helped this Donington victory (left) on the Honda, which came long after the Kawasaki years (below).

strained. Aaron only had to wait three races before he scored his first double and to make it even more special it was at Misano, the track on which the Castrol Honda team was humiliated three years earlier. Then he had managed only 13th and 16th places but this time he hammered the Ducatis on the nearest track to their factory and a place where they had dominated since the start of the Championship. Having done it once, he did it again in Austria and set up the tightest finish in the history of the Championship when he went to the final round in Japan only half-a-point behind Troy Corser with Fogarty just 5½ points further back. It was Aaron's best chance for the title but somehow, with all their resources, HRC and Michelin managed to give all the Honda riders totally uncompetitive set-ups and he never got within range of the crown.

Aaron rode the four-cylinder bikes when the V-twin Ducatis were doing

all the winning and he always felt the double-whammy of capacity advantage and different minimum weight limits was too much. Ironically, the advent of the big V-twin SP-1 Honda was not really the answer to this Kiwi's prayer. Aaron's style has always suited the multi-cylinder motors better. His idea of riding a bike involves 15,000rpm on the tacho and exiting corners with tons of wheelspin leaving big black lines on the tarmac rather than, for instance, the reliance on carrying speed at the apex of a corner that defines Fogarty's style.

If 1999 was yet another last chance for Aaron it did not start well. Fogarty started like he was going to repeat his runaway 1995 title win and at Round 3 Slight and his team-mate Edwards came together on the exit of Donington Park's Melbourne Loop. Slight fell, got back on, made a disparaging gesture at the American when he lapped him and fell again re-injuring a finger. It took a long while for Slight to recover his composure and start talking to Edwards again but he then complained vociferously about brake problems. It was very unlike Slight and he went through the rest of the season without a win. We now know that midway through the season Aaron was suffering from fatigue and lack of concentration. He consulted lots of different doctors without finding any answers and at the start of 2000, as he was heading for a scan in an Australian hospital, his wife Megan voiced her thoughts: 'I hope they don't find anything.' Aaron replied vehemently that he hoped they did. One brain operation later he was just hoping he would be able to race a bike again. That he managed to get back on a bike so quickly and go so fast is a confirmation of his fitness as well as his will to win. As an English racer once remarked, Aaron Slight

Not many racers can say they've won on a straight-four and a V4 – Aaron Slight can.

is one of those guys who simply looks fast when he's standing still.

His value to Honda is immense: he won the 8 Hours twice for them in the first two years of the RC45, in 1994 with Doug Polen, and the following year with Tady Okada, notching up a unique hat trick – he had won it in 1993 for Kawasaki with Scott Russell. If he carries out his threat to go touring car racing after he retires from two-wheeled racing then expect Honda to be sympathetic.

Carl Fogarty once paid him a massive but unintentional compliment when describing a race he had been leading. Carl had hit the front and tried to make a break by pressing hard but lap after lap his signal board showed the gap was not going up. 'I didn't have to look behind me, I knew who it was,' said Foggy. 'Only Aaron puts pressure on like that.'

Carl Fogarty

Born
1 July 1965
Blackburn, Lancashire,
Great Britain

First win
1992 Round 2/Race 2
Donington Park,
Great Britain
Ducati 888

4 Championships
1991 7th
1992 9th
1993 2nd
1994 Champion
1995 Champion
1996 4th
1997 2nd
1998 Champion
1999 Champion
2000 26th

59 Race wins
1992 Great Britain 2
1993 Spain 1 and 2
1993 Czech Republic 1
1993 Sweden 1 and 2
1993 Malaysia 1 and 2
1993 Japan 1
1993 Holland 1 and 2
1993 Portugal 2
1994 Great Britain 1
1994 Spain 1 and 2
1994 Austria 1 and 2
1994 Indonesia 2
1994 Holland 1 and 2
1994 San Marino 2
1994 Australia 1
1995 Germany 1 and 2
1995 Great Britain 1 and 2
1995 San Marino 1
1995 Spain 2
1995 Austria 1

Carl Fogarty is more than just the most successful Superbike racer in the history of the Championship. Before the word Superbike was even in the vocabulary of most fans he had won TT F1 world titles and Isle of Man TTs, set a Mountain Circuit lap record that lasted seven years, and won the World Endurance Championship. Just as importantly, off-track he rescued British motorcycle racing from the slough of despond into which it had slipped. Foggy's success meant that for the first time since the days of Barry Sheene British riders were taken seriously by the manufacturers' works teams and he brought the crowds back to British tracks, culminating in the astonishing 121,000 attendance at Brands Hatch in 1999. It was the biggest single-day crowd at a sporting event in the UK that year.

Fogarty's career is littered with such landmarks. Ironically, he never wanted to be a four-stroke racer. His initial ambitions lay with the 250cc GP class until a twice-broken leg cost him a season early on in his career. It gave rise to one of the few real moments of doubt that ever afflicted Carl. He had been a hotshot on the 250 but when his leg would not bend enough to fit on one any more his father, George, plonked him on one of Honda's new RC30 Superbikes. With a minimum of planning or preparation Carl promptly won the 1988 World TT F1 Championship and successfully defended his crown in 1989. He did it again in 1990 as well, but the closed-roads-based F1 series could not muster enough rounds to call itself a World Championship so Foggy won an FIM Cup this time.

But TT F1 was being sidelined by the emergent Superbike formula and Carl's first full season was 1991 when he rode the RC30 to seventh overall in the last year it was entered by an importer team. Foggy was top Honda rider in the championship, ahead of of ex-champ Fred Merkel on a better-supported V4. Despite his image as a crash-happy young charger that season did not include one race crash. That season was supported by Honda Britain, largely as a reward for Carl riding the Isle of Man again, but 1992 was crunch time.

The only paying ride he picked up was in the World Endurance Championship for Kawasaki France. Carl was teamed with fellow Brit Terry Rymer as back-up to the more-fancied team of French riders. The idea was that the chore of 24-hour racing would finance the Ducati he would ride as a privateer in World Superbike, but racing is never that simple. Just a few rounds into the season Carl was seriously contemplating concentrating on the endurance ride to pay the bills, and as early as April it became clear that the Donington round of the World Supers was a make-or-break race. It started well, tourned sour, and finally ended in triumph. Carl qualified on pole, crashed while leading the first race, and won the second by a distance. It was a true privateer victory and vindication of Carl's – and his family's – faith in his own abilities. That first Superbike win set up an astonishing year of success in a variety of types of racing: with Rymer he won the World Endurance title, set that TT lap record, and for good measure, ran with the top 500 men as a wild-card entry at the British GP. All that plus domestic championship racing in the UK and Malaysia.

His Donington win propelled Carl into the factory Ducati team under the management of Raymond Roche, who had memorably told Foggy on that rostrum that he would one day be a World Champion. This was when the world outside of UK racing first started noticing Fogarty. They saw a

The greatest

scary young man who more often than not gave the impression that he thought that the world was against him. It was the year when not just Foggy but the World Superbike Championship itself had to prove a point. The Championship lost its top three riders from the previous year but for the first time it got extensive TV coverage, especially in the UK. Both viewers and racers got lucky: we were treated to the opening salvo of what would prove to be a long-running war between Carl Fogarty and Scott Russell. The Briton won 11 races, the American just five but it was Russell who took the title, something that added fuel to Fogarty's conspiracy theories. In 1994, Ducati's new weapon arrived in the shape of the gorgeous 916 and Fogarty took revenge. He did not get both hands on the trophy until a dramatic last-round showdown with Russell in Australia that started with Carl winning Race 1 and ended with Russell, rear tyre destroyed, waving him past in Race 2. A richly symbolic transfer of the crown. The two champions had disliked each other from the first time they met, and for a very good reason; they were very alike in their attitudes to racing. Both men were there to win, for both of them second place simply meant first loser. At first the dislike was genuine – Scott really did not want to acknowledge Carl on the rostrum let alone shake hands and Carl really did mean it when he said he could not believe Russell's luck and made rude gestures on the slow-down lap in Portugal.

Fogarty was now enshrined as the success-starved British bike fans' idol. The man himself was slowly emerging from his shell; shy as a kid, he could still seem tongue-tied and sometimes self-contradictory but he could also be painfully honest. No journalist was ever refused a post-race quote by Carl, no matter how bad a day he had had, and he genuinely felt the expectations of his fans weighing heavily on his shoulders. The fans adored Carl because he was identifiably one of them: a blue-collar hero with a total lack of pretension. It was about this time that Carl and his wife Michaela briefly considered doing what a lot of their contemporaries have done and moving to Monte Carlo or Andorra. They rejected the idea because they wanted their kids to grow up in a normal environment. That meant their home town of Blackburn. Actually it meant a big house in the hills outside Blackburn and private school for their daughters but it underpinned Foggy's image as a man of the people. Of course, the British delight in building a hero up only to shoot them down again – the Aussies call it Tall Poppy Syndrome – so there was the usual collection of moaners who reckoned Foggy had an unfair advantage because the regulations favoured Ducati, or reckoned he was just miserable.

Carl never gave the impression that he cared a jot about what other people thought of him but sniping at Ducati irritated him. Why, he reasoned, should Ducati be penalised for building a good bike? And anyway, Ducati always attracted the best riders so they were bound to win, weren't they.

That was never truer than in 1995 when Foggy defended his title. He stormed through the year aided and abetted by the fact that none of his competitors put together a decent season. Perhaps the most memorable Foggy episode was the 1995 European round at Brands Hatch in front of a then record crowd of over 60,000. He had never won a race at any level at the Kent track before but after qualifying on pole on Saturday he trounced the field in both races in front of his ecstatic public. British bike fans had not had a day like it for decades, and an awful lot of them went to see him retain his title two races later at Assen. In between came Sugo and a massive highside in Race 1. Cue another piece of Foggy mythology; despite cracked bones and horrendous bruising he won Race 2 and declared himself pleased that he hadn't won the title in Japan as he could now win it at the next best thing to a British track – Assen. The Dutch track is the place that suits Carl's style best, it puts a premium on the ability to maintain high corner speeds and string a succession of corners together. He won there in F1 and brought the habit to Superbike, doing doubles in 1993, '94, '95, '96 and '99, and in the two years he didn't win both races he won one.

This is what Superbike means to so many fans: Foggy in full flight on the Ducati 916 on his way to the victor's laurels.

Having won the 1995 title with two rounds (that's four whole races!) to spare, Foggy then astounded the paddock by leaving Ducati for Honda. It was immediately assumed that money was the main factor but that would be a gross oversimplification. It is true that Carl was disappointed with the money Ducati offered him but he was also tired of the unplanned way in which Virginio Ferrari organised such basics as team travel and accommodation. The Castrol Honda team, run by old family friend Neil Tuxworth, looked better organised on all fronts. There was another incentive: the whisperers still saying that Fogarty could only win on a Ducati. Scott Russell, Colin Edwards and others did not so much whisper as shout that opinion.

Honda's RC45 had not had a happy first two years of competition and it was plainly a handful on bumpy corners and Aaron Slight had won just two races on it. Carl's season did not start well with a crunching crash in

qualifying for the first round at Misano and was followed by a miserable Donington round (eighth and seventh) which Carl described as the worst weekend of his career. Things got even worse when Slight won the first race of Round 3 at Hockenheim with Carl 25 seconds adrift in fifth. This was the nadir of Carl's Superbike career. Along with the team, Carl gambled on some radical alterations to chassis set-up. Time for another piece of the Fogarty legend to materialise: he won Race 2 from his team-mate. Carl said he was inspired to win by his older daughter, Danielle, crying after Race 1 because she did not like it when Daddy did not win.

Another Honda-mounted win at Monza set the scene very nicely for Assen. Foggy won Race 1 comfortably but Race 2 was a different story. John Kocinski, on Carl's old Ducati, went with him all the way in a no-holds barred duel. Fogarty led to the final chicane, Kocinski went past on the inside but was in too hot, and as the American struggled to get the Ducati turned Fogarty banged the Honda into bottom gear and drag raced to the line and the most dramatic win in the history of the Championship. It was also the first time an RC45 rider had done the double. Another element of the legend was put in place.

Assen had another surprise in store. Just as it looked as if Carl and the Honda were getting to understand each other, he announced he would be moving back to Ducati for 1997. It seemed like the sensible thing to do but when he got to try the new Ducati he found it almost unrideable. By his own admission he was over-riding the thing, barging through for wins he should never have got. The fact he scored six wins speaks volumes about Foggy's determination; the fact he fell off more than he'd ever done tells you just as much about the bike. Carl had to suffer the sight of John Kocinski winning the Championship on the Honda he had just abandoned. He has never been one to brood on what might have been, but even Carl wonders what might have happened if he had stayed for a second season with the improving Honda.

Ducati put Carl in a one-man team separate from the Virginio Ferrari works team with Davide Tardozzi as manager. It was a marriage made in heaven, but it was not until over halfway through the 1998 season that Carl felt totally happy with the bike again; time for him to do the impossible again. From fourth in the Championship after Round 8, 33 points behind the leader, Foggy arrived at the 12th and final round in Japan third and only six points off a third title. Three men could be champion: Corser, who made a mistake and crashed out in Sunday-morning warm-up; Slight, whose Honda simply never worked all week-end; and Carl Fogarty. Third and fourth places behind fast local men was enough. Fogarty became the first man to win three World Superbike Championships and the first man to regain a title. The parallels with the first triumph were obvious; both went down to the last round, both times he was riding number 2 and both times his reaction was emotional not triumphal. In Japan he stopped and slumped over the tank before returning to the pits.

Continuing the pattern, his third title defence was a mirror image of the 1995 campaign. No-one headed him in the points standings all year and he even got on pole position for the first time since 1995. The highlight was his first Dutch double since 1996 at an Assen that looked more like Brands Hatch thanks to an army of travelling fans. Add in Iain MacPherson's win in World Supersport, Karl Harris's in European Superstock and Webster & James's sidecar victory and you have a British clean sweep. It was British bike fans' best day out since, well, Foggy's Brands double of '95.

The 'R' word – that's retirement – had been bandied about for a couple of years. Carl's third title had brought him more recognition outside the bikesport world than the other two put together and the fourth one elevated him to the status of a genuine household name. He was now the most successful four-stroke racer ever with little left to prove. His wild-card forays into GPs showed that he could ride a 500 too; does the fact he was never offered a works ride there bother him? Carl simply shrugs and says the right ride never came up. But the one thing Fogarty loves above all others is winning. Not taking part, winning; and in '99 he found it as easy as he'd ever done which is why he carried on into 2000.

The omens were not good. A pre-season testing accident knocked him out for the first time in his racing career then he failed to win the first race of the year – something he has done all four times he has been Champion. Worse still, he crashed out of the second race of the year. The worst happened next time out in Australia: a glancing collision with Robert Ulm sent Carl off the track and left him unconscious with the top of his humerus badly broken. It was even worse than it looked. The breaks would take months to heal, although the concussion would bother Foggy more. Glimmers of hope kept Carl going until late September when a test at Mugello showed just how badly he was affected. Would anything ever replace the adrenalin rush of racing? Well, yes. The only other thing he cares about: his family.

Everyone remembers Fogarty's Ducati years (below) but not everyone remembers the Honda RC30 season (left) or the RC45 year (bottom).

Scott **Russell**

Born
28 October 1964
East Point, Georgia, USA

First win
1993 Round 2/Race 2
Hockenheim, Germany
Kawasaki ZXR750

1 Championship
1991 17th
1992 11th
1993 Champion
1994 2nd
1995 18th
1997 6th
1998 10th

14 Race wins
1993 Germany 2
1993 Czech Republic 2
1993 Japan 2
1993 Great Britain 1 and 2
1994 Great Britain 2
1994 Germany 1 and 2
1994 Italy 1
1994 Japan 1 and 2
1994 San Marino 1
1994 Europe 1 and 2

8 Pole positions
1993 Ireland
1993 Germany
1993 Italy
1993 Austria
1994 Great Britain
1994 Germany
1994 Italy
1997 Italy

The only straight-four champ

There are many things that make Scott Russell unique in the Superbike world, chief among which is the distinction he holds of being the only man to win the world title on an across-the-frame four-cylinder motorcycle. This is the economically efficient engine layout which powered most of Japan's street Superbikes from the 1970s right through to the ascent of the affordable V-twin at the end of the century. This distinction is important. Where Honda and Ducati produced homologation specials – racers with lights on – Scott's Kawasaki was based on something much nearer to a roadster.

That is not the only thing that is different about the lanky Georgian. Unlike most of his American compatriots he did not come out of a dirt-track background, instead he gained lots of track time in endurance racing. Unlike most top Superbike riders he made the move to 500 Grands Prix and was a success. And unlike anyone else in the world he has won Daytona five times. That is what makes him a hero in the USA where the 200-miler enjoys the same sort of status as the Isle of Man TT does in the UK. If you read an American account of Scott's career it will mention his Daytona wins before his world title.

But what the rest of the world remembers is the demonic green nemesis that stalked Carl Fogarty through the early 1990s and then went to GPs where he was really the first man to prove that a top-flight Superbike rider can also be a world-class 500 racer. Remember the 1996 Czech GP where Alex Criville beat Mick Doohan by two-thousandths of a second? Well, Scott Russell brought his Suzuki home in third place, just 2.6 seconds behind the two World Champions. And he got another rostrum finish at Suzuka before being let go inexplicably by the team and returning to Superbike, this time on a Yamaha.

His early racing was done in the 750 Supersport class before moving to Yoshimura Suzuki and in 1990 to Muzzy Kawasaki where he was back-up to Doug Chandler. When Chandler went off to GPs Scott took over the number-one spot and in 1991 was the only rider to win more than one AMA Superbike round. He won four races but a puncture in the last round robbed him of the title. Winning every 750 Supersport round made up for some of the pain. He won the Supersport title for the next two years as well, and for good measure took the AMA Superbike title in 1992.

Scott's first full season outside the USA was 1993 when he joined Aaron Slight in the works Kawasaki team, but he had done four rounds the year before at the start of the season scoring two rostrums at Donington and one at Spa. He had shared that second British rostrum with another young charger with whom his career would be entwined for the next few years: Carl Fogarty. The World Superbike Championship got season-long TV coverage for the first time in 1993, and viewers had a treat. For the next two years the slow-talking American and the gimlet-eyed Lancastrian brought an intensity to the fight for the title that has never been equalled. They found plenty of reasons to dislike each other: Scott was convinced the Ducati gave Fogarty an unfair advantage, Carl saw the fact he won many more races, yet was behind on points, as evidence of nothing short of robbery. They really did dislike each other, and the reason was obvious. Their attitude to racing was identical, they raced to win not to come second. Mutual respect did grow, but it took a while to get over the initial antipathy.

The Troy Lee logo and crash helmet design sum up Scott perfectly.

British fans loved to hate Russell but the American saved the most spectacular demonstration of his will to win for the 1993 Donington Park round. Scott led the points table by nine points with three races left. On the Saturday, towards the end of final qualifying, he screamed into the pits to put on a new tyre, all the time yelling at his crew before ripping out of the pits with the engine bouncing off the rev limiter. Going down the 100mph-plus plunge of Craner Curves, the cold rear tyre let go and slammed Russell into the tarmac. After a lengthy session in the medical centre Scott was pushed back to his motorhome in a wheelchair. His crew rebuilt the bike, they padded the seat and lowered a footrest so Scott could sit on it. With a borrowed oversize boot on his swollen foot he went out on Sunday and won both races, beating Foggy in Race 1 and towing him into a mistake

Fans want to remember Scott this way, charging on the Kawasaki.

in Race 2. As a display of pure, bloody-minded will to win it was hard to beat. He actually won his title under bizarre circumstances when the final round in Mexico was cancelled after a pick-up truck crossed the track in front of Scott while he was doing the best part of 190mph down the main straight.

The 1994 season was a continuation of the duel. Russell held the early advantage but two crashes in Spain followed by two testing get-offs took the momentum out of his season and Fogarty took over the lead at the next round. Russell fought back and the fight went down to the wire – the last round in Australia. Fogarty won Race 1 to get one hand on the championship and in Race 2 he shadowed Scott until the American, his rear tyre disintegrating, waved Fogarty through.

Fogarty later said that this was the moment that Scott stopped being a

winner but that is not borne out by what happened in 1995 and '96. At the third race of '95 he turned up with broken bones in his foot; a mountain-bike accident was the story but it was a cover as Scott had actually been in Brno testing the Suzuki Grand Prix 500. He then left Superbike for two seasons.

Russell went to Suzuki mid-season because Kevin Schwantz had finally decided his battered body had had enough and retired. When injury took Daryl Beattie out of the picture, Scott kept the flag flying single-handedly. His rostrum finishes were the only ones Suzuki scored in 1995 and '96 and the Grand Prix press welcomed him as a future star – not exactly the form of a man who has stopped wanting to win. Personality clashes rather than performance problems seem to be the reason why Scott and Suzuki split and Yamaha quickly snapped him up for a return to Superbike.

Unfortunately for Scott and those that remember him in 1993, things did not go well. No Yamaha won a World Championship road race in 1997 until a new star called Noriyuki Haga won at the penultimate round of the Superbike Championship. Russell had a second and a third place plus a storming pole at Monza and ended up sixth in the Championship. Over winter, he persuaded his team to let him use Michelin tyres while his team-mate, Haga, stuck with the Dunlops the Yamahas had always used. Unfortunately for Scott, the French rubber was not the magic ingredient and he was comprehensively out-performed by his new team-mate. More worryingly, there was an outbreak of non-finishes for reasons that were never wholly explained. The second race at Laguna summed it up: a jump start followed by a crash while leading before the black flag could come out, and then a long walk back to the paddock where very few of his team appeared to want to talk to him.

No-one was surprised when Scott returned to AMA racing in 1999 but most people were surprised when he signed to ride Harley-Davidson's underachieving VR1000. If Scott managed to win Daytona on a Harley he would be a national hero. Things went from bad to worse when Scott was attacked in a night club early on the Friday morning before race weekend and sustained facial injuries that were bad enough to keep him out of the race. This, said the detractors, was typical Russell. Too much partying, not enough racing. The Millennium Daytona was no better; Scott was out-qualified by his team-mate Pascal Picotte and then broke down in the race. In fact Picotte was regularly outperforming his team-mate. Scott was now saying that he would forego all the money he had been paid by Harley, for a competitive bike as he was sure he had still got some wins in him with the right equipment.

Racing is not usually that kind to its heroes once they have toppled off their pedestal, but most insiders devoutly hope that it will make an exception for Scott Russell. If it doesn't, then we will have to be content with that unique world title and those Daytona victories in 1992, '94, '95, '97 and '98.

His opponents might not always have liked Scott but the fans certainly wanted to know him.

Andreas Meklau

Born
7 June 1967
Spielberg, Austria

First win
1993 Round 5/Race 1
Osterreichring, Austria
Ducati 888

Championships
1993 15th
1994 6th
1995 13th
1996 18th
1997 18th
1998 18th
1999 11th
2000 13th

1 Race win
1993 Austria 1

The last privateer winner

In some ways, Andreas Meklau's career has mirrored that of the World Superbike Championship. Being too tall for lots of smaller two-stroke machinery, the Ducati 888 'Meki' campaigned suited not just his size but his riding style, which placed a premium on front end grip and a curious mix of precision and hard riding. In fact, the machine suited him well enough to propel him into the elite group of race winners.

Way back in the dim and distant past of 1993, the 26-year-old Meklau did a Fogarty and won his home race even though he was not part of the full championship. Unlike Fogarty, he was not seen as the man to carry the desmo banner forward to world glory, and he spent the next few years as a privateer in both the German Pro-Superbike and World Championships, where he always acquitted himself well.

With a machine capable of winning the German Championship, as Meklau did in 1998, and a team with a Red Bull-enhanced budget in 1999, Meklau has found that his top-spec privateer Dukes are capable of upsetting the lower order works teams in World Superbike once again.

It was not always thus, but in the last few seasons (as one half of the Austrian Gerin WSBK dream team with Robert Ulm) he has found that his machines are fully competitive with virtually everything – often posting fastest top speeds against works Hondas and the like.

But Meklau hasn't converted his competitiveness into a podium since 1994 when he got a brace of second places behind Carl Fogarty – again at home in Austria. It may take the same circumstances which presented themselves to him at the old Zeltweg circuit all those years ago to repeat his only World Superbike win.

Taking what looked like a gamble by going for slick tyres when all others opted for something with treads, Meklau was just demonstrating his superior local knowledge of the awesome but scary Osterreichring. Well, we can assume that that sort of thing must come naturally when your house is less than a kilometre from the circuit gate!

His clever idea was transformed into a win after keeping his cool head down, and was proved to be more than a freak result when he took a fine third in race two, once more finishing ahead of the top factory Ducati,

The Osterreichring in 1993 – Meklau shows the rest how to ride it in the wet.

ridden by Carl Fogarty, no less. He scored the fastest lap in both races, too. His 1993 win made his transition from World Championship part timer to full timer possible and in the 1994 season Meklau finished a career-best sixth in the table, albeit yielding the top privateer mantle to Simon Crafar right at the end of the year. It should be remembered that sixth is a championship position a lot of full works riders have yet to achieve.

Still as fit as he's ever been, Meklau goes about his business in a serious, sometimes dour manner, but in conversation a smile is always present as is a strong Austro-German accent. With maybe his best years behind him, Meklau is still a serious pain to any works rider not earning their keep and is well capable of top-ten championship finishes in the new millennium.

James Whitham

Born
6 September 1966
Huddersfield, Yorkshire,
Great Britain

First win
1994 Round 6/Race 1,
Sentul, Indonesia
Ducati 916

Championships
1993 16th
1994 7th
1995 22nd
1996 17th
1997 8th
1998 8th

1 Race win
1994 Indonesia 1

The people's champion

If you need an example of how typical British racers of a certain age went about the business of building a career, then James Whitham is a good candidate. The former 80cc British Champion's very beginnings may not have been particularly typical, but in every other sense the talented young Whitham was offered the same ladders (and then the usual UK snakes) as any other aspirant racer. That is, production-based racing, proper TT style road racing, little in the way of support for competitive World Championship assaults, and many nibbles of the big cherry without being allowed a proper bite until it was too late.

Born into a better-than averagely well-off family in the Yorkshire dales, Whitham's obsession with all things mechanical had a sound grounding in and around his father's airfield.

In the increasingly impoverished British racing scene, which was a fairly pitiful place in the late-1980s, production (ie cheap) racing was the making of many a local rider, and with his second major success being the 1988 British Unlimited Production title (plus runner-up spot in the TT F1 series) Whitham was on the upslope of what could have been a glittering career before he reached his mid-20s.

This being Britain of course, Whitham was left chasing around in the same circles for season after season, only getting his first big break into the

Jim's ready wit and cheerful demeanour hide an intelligent, thinking racer.

very big time of World Superbike racing for a first full season in 1994.

In the intervening years Whitham had been in hospital with a double leg fracture sustained at the North West 200 road race, had been a factory rider for Honda Britain, a factory rider for Heron Suzuki, British TT Superbike champion, *MCN* Man of the Year, a top-ten 500 GP finisher, double British Superbike champion for Yamaha, a stand-in Yamaha World Superbike rider (scoring a podium at Donington) and a TT racer of some note. It will have been noticed by now that James Whitham has had a very diverse and hectic racing life.

It would take several chapters of any book to do James Whitham's whole career justice, but in terms of his World Superbike life 1994 was the big turnaround. Given a full season on pretty much factory machinery, the

Moto Cinelli British Ducati importer team only had to wait until the first race of round six to be rewarded with a win. It came after Fogarty's Ducati broke down, and Whit's first words were typical of the man's wit: 'That wasn't in the script.'

Three podiums and seventh overall were not seen as enough for Whitham to keep a factory ride in 1995, but with the same Moto Cinelli outfit Whitham took 11 wins in 16 British Superbike races during an epic battle against Steve Hislop. It took Hodgkin's disease (lymphatic cancer) to stop him seeing out the season.

Successfully recovered after intensive chemotherapy, Whitham was back to his best the following season, as he slugged another just-unsuccessful UK Superbike campaign out, this time against his firm friend Niall Mackenzie, only just losing out in the final round.

Once more *MCN* Man of the Year – and no wonder – Whitham was running Carl Fogarty close for the affections of the British racing fraternity in the winter of 1996. His track exploits were well known to the brothers Harris (of the eponymous Harris Performance race team) who had just finished their first factory World Superbike campaign, and James found himself signed for a Suzuki assault on the World Championship in 1997.

Whitham was characteristically enthused to be given a second chance to at least go for race wins. He was never to get his wish, defeated by the fickle nature of the uncompetitive Suzuki. Power was not the problem, the two rostrums he did score came on the fastest tracks in the calendar – Hockenheim and Monza.

By that time though, the Suzuki team had been turned over to Francis Batta's big-money Alstare Squad, and clearly neither James Whitham nor his team mate Mike Hale were deemed worthy of a place in this brave new Suzuki world.

Holding out for a Superbike ride in 1999, Whitham had possibly the most varied and ultimately destructive season of even his tumultuous life. Signed to ride for Suzuki France alongside Terry Rymer in World Endurance, Whitham had an astonishing Le Mans (crashing twice but eventually finishing third), before a one-off ride on a Belgarda Yamaha 600 gave him a win in the Supersport World Championship race at Donington Park.

Offered a full Supersport season there and then, Whitham preferred to keep his Superbike options open, but even he was stunned to be given the chance to ride the unfancied Modenas in 500 GPs, drawing praise from no less a deity than Kenny Roberts Senior, who reckoned Whitham was the only guy to have ever really 'raced' his creation.

A bit too hard as it turned out. Whitham's desire to give his boyhood hero a good result at Brno saw him break his pelvis and put himself out of action for months. Fed up with racing for tenth place and well aware he had to be among the front runners if his career was to continue – Jim has always been bright – he signed for a full season of World Supersport racing for his old buddies at Belgarda in 2000.

Wherever his future may lie, Whitham's past is as inspirational a story of determination and guts as anyone could have dreamed up. If you'd have submitted it as the plot for a novel it would have been rejected as utterly implausible. Life is, for James Whitham at least, one big roller-coaster ride. And he enjoys it.

Three rostrums was scant reward for the Suzuki years. His one chance to stand on top of the rostrum came during his Ducati year.

Anthony Gobert

Born
5 March 1975
Sydney, Australia

First win
1994 Round 11/Race 2
Phillip Island, Australia
Kawasaki ZXR750

Championships
1994 17th
1995 4th
1996 8th
1999 24th
2000 25th

8 Race wins
1994 Australia 2
1995 USA 1
1995 Australia 2
1996 USA 1
1996 Australia 1 and 2
1999 USA 1
2000 Australia 2

2 Pole positions
1994 Australia
1995 Australia

Motorcycle racing's bad boy

In one way at least, Anthony 'Go Show' Gobert has been a true World Champion. An unrivalled genius in fact. Sadly for him (thus far), this ultimate accolade has yet to be earned for exploits on a race circuit. Off track, in the column inches dedicated to scandal, gossip and rumour, Gobert has been the Mick Doohan of his generation.

Ever since his first amazing World Superbike win in 1994, Gobert has been hitting headlines, hitting Gazza-esque personal and professional highs and lows, hitting track barriers and pretty much hitting anything unwise enough to cross his path on the wrong day.

Gobert's fondness for beer and high times has actually been one of his great attractions in these days of PR-stifled riders, but even the young Aussie now admits that it was to the detriment of his career. It has been the spectre of drugs, however, which has been Anthony's biggest problem, even if it manifested itself long after he first burst on to the racing scene way back in 1991, following a successful motocross upbringing. Teamed up with Troy Corser in the Winfield Honda team in Australia in 1993, Gobert went on to win the title the following year, proving his early credentials beyond doubt and earning the RC45 an important title in its first season.

Being famously sucked into the Muzzy Kawasaki squad at the last meeting of 1994 at Phillip Island (dethroning the terminally disgruntled Terry Rymer in the process), Gobert went on to win the second race, guaranteeing himself the full-on Muzzy Kawasaki factory ride the year after. His leap from Honda to Kawasaki before the end of the season also guaranteed he would never ride a factory Honda.

Teamed up with Scott Russell (who would defect to the Lucky Strike Suzuki 500 GP team mid-season) Gobert was an instant sensation – for all the wrong reasons – as the 1995 version of the Muzzy Kawasaki proved to be slow and fickle to set up.

Gobert's impact on Superbike was immediate: he won his second race on the Kawasaki.

Frequently crashing in practice, Gobert struggled and only found success at what are still the only two circuits at which he has (officially) won World Superbike races, Laguna Seca and Phillip Island. He tried though, he tried very hard, and his spectacular sideways style guaranteed him media attention.

Gobert's off-track antics became legendary too, to the point where you could not make them up. Urinating in one of his main rival's crash helmets, scrapping with other riders with depressing regularity, Gobert was massively popular with the fans but equally unpopular with his peers. Naturally talented in a way most of those rivals could only dream of, Gobert was demonstrating a hedonistic streak of self-destruction, and after a second season for Muzzy he started a game of race-team pinball he has

It's never been easy to ignore Anthony Gobert – check out that helmet fin complete with brake light!

never really stopped flipping in and out of ever since.

Signed to ride for Lucky Strike Suzuki in 1997, Gobert's season was over after a drug test by his own team at the Donington Park GP (allegedly) found metabolites of cannabis in his bloodstream. Immediately booted out after the single high point of qualifying on the front row at Imola, Anthony was in limbo land and had now guaranteed he would never ride for another Japanese factory – and all at the age of 21.

Seen as a pariah by the ultra-conservative Japanese factories, Gobert has now had a good go at riding for everyone else in the paddock. His career was saved by his induction into the American Superbike series with the Vance & Hines Ducati Superbike squad in 1998. Here, his turbulent history repeated itself with not one but two more positive drugs tests, a visit to a rehab clinic, and three crushing wins on the weekends when he was on form. Missing key races, Gobert could do no better than finish ninth, although team boss Terry Vance kept faith with his unruly star for a second season when Gobert won five more AMA races plus a dominant Race 1 victory at the Laguna World Superbike round. Gobert was a real contender in 1999 but his almost customary last-minute no-show at the final AMA round at Las Vegas (he said he had hurt his shoulder motocrossing), ensured he burned his bridges with yet another manufacturer. His anger with Ducati in general stemmed from the fact that the ride he claims to have been promised – full time team-mate to Fogarty for the 2000 season – had been given to his V&H team-mate Ben Bostrom.

Appearances on the MuZ GP 500 at the tail end of the year only muddied Gobert's waters still further with fleeting competitiveness only giving him a top-ten finish at the Rio GP – plus his usual, somewhat unconventional approach to timekeeping and attendance meaning team boss Rolf Biland will never allow him near one of his bikes again.

The blind optimism of Virginio Ferrari – founder of the 2000 season's

After his GP excursion, Gobert scored a win on both Ducati (below) and Bimota (right).

bravest new world, the MVR Bimota squad – gave Anthony what many felt was his final real crack at getting back into the World Superbike Championship. A fairy-tale win, once more at home, in the wet at Phillip Island, provided the latest spike in Anthony's racing chart; the demise of the team by mid-season, the latest trough. The spin-off of his latest misadventure is that Gobert has equalled Stephane Mertens's record of winning World Superbike races on three different types of machinery.

Even being given a ride on Kenny Roberts' Mark 3 Modenas KR3 at the Donington GP in 2000 was a fruitless and one-off coupling, leaving Gobert to contemplate once more where his career is headed. And the real tragedy is that even if that place is nowhere, he would still be able to get there faster than most other people, such is his abundant natural talent.

Mauro Lucchiari

Born
31 March 1968
Vescovana, Italy

First win
1995 Round 2/Race 1
Misano, Italy
Ducati 916

Championships
1993 10th
1994 12th
1995 9th
1999 24th

2 Race wins
1995 Italy 1 and 2

Sacked despite a double

When Spanish GP refugee Juan Garriga quit Davide Tardozzi's Grottini Ducati team after the third round of the 1993 World Superbike Championship, the factory turned to a young man who they had had their eye on for a while: Mauro Lucchiari. He did not let them down, getting on the rostrum in second place at his very first race. Fortuitously, that happened to be a home round, the San Marino round at Misano – a track that would play a big part in his career, but the man who beat him was Falappa and the man in third was Pirovano on the factory Yamaha.

Lucchiari was already a factory Ducati rider, campaigning the gorgeous little Supermono in the Italian Singles Championship which he duly won in 1993. He was thought of well enough to do some test riding for the Cagiva 500 Grand Prix team, which made the shock even greater when he signed to ride for Belgarda Yamaha in 1994. Long-time Yamaha man Pirovano had given up the unequal struggle against the Ducatis and joined the red hordes, leaving Belgarda with a big problem just a few weeks before the start of the season. As the team also raced in the Italian championship they needed Italian riders so they coaxed Lucchiari into signing just weeks before the start of the season, pairing him with another young hopeful,

Massimo Meregalli. As the works Ducati team had Fogarty and Falappa in their line-up perhaps Mauro's decision to sign for another team was not as surprising as it first appeared.

However, the relationship only lasted three races. When Giancarlo Falappa had his catastrophic testing accident at Albacete, team manager Virginio Ferrari was quick to recall Lucchiari to the Ducati fold. This was the first year of the 916 and Mauro made good use of the new bike, finishing the year 12th overall. The management was impressed and Mauro got to keep his seat for the 1995 season alongside Foggy in the works team.

If there was ever a time that the V-twin Ducatis had an advantage (fair or otherwise) over the four-cylinder bikes then this was it. Nowhere was this more impressively demonstrated than at the track closest to Ducati's Bologna factory, Misano. This was the year when the Red Bikes filled the top four places in both races with Mauro Lucchiari winning both times and setting the fastest lap on each occasion. The only thing he did not do was set pole – that was Foggy.

Neither win was handed to Mauro, he had to fend off fellow Ducatisti Fogarty and Corser in both races. It was the highpoint of Lucchiari's year – and of his career. His winning double put him second in the Championship after two rounds but he never got on the rostrum again and gradually slid to ninth overall at the end of the year. It was not good enough to keep his Superbike ride, and so he went to the Supersport class that runs as support to the World Superbike Championship, finishing third in 1996 on a Ducati 748 run by the semi-official Endoug team. He stayed in Supersport for two more years before coming back to World Superbike in 1999 on a Gattalone Yamaha, but his best finish was a lowly seventh at a wet A1-Ring.

Getting sacked after doing the double at your home race may seem harsh, but that is what happened to Mauro. His ride was taken by Neil Hodgson who did not have a happy time either. Proof yet again that the second seat in a works team alongside a proven winner is a very, very precarious position.

Mauro Lucchiari was part of Ducati's armada when the factory dominated the Championship in the early 1990s.

Frankie Chili

Born
20 June 1964
Bologna, Italy

First win
1995 Round 4/Race 2
Monza, San Marino
Ducati 916

Championships
1995 8th
1996 6th
1997 7th
1998 4th
1999 6th
2000 4th

14 Race wins
1995 San Marino 2
1996 Italy 2
1996 Europe 1
1997 San Marino 1
1997 Italy 2
1997 Europe 1
1998 Spain 1
1998 Germany 2
1998 South Africa 1 and 2
1998 Holland 1
1999 Austria 2
1999 Germany 2
2000 Italy 1

8 Pole positions
1996 Germany
1996 Italy
1997 USA
1997 Europe
1997 Austria
1998 South Africa
1998 Holland
1999 Great Britain

Last of the win-or-crash racers

If you were asked to define the ideal 'Boy's Own' style motorcycle racer you would come up with someone not a million miles from Frankie Chili. Dashing good looks and the ex-model wife are a good start, his tendency to wear his heart on his sleeve helps, but it's that win-or-crash attitude that has made him a favourite worldwide, especially in the UK. British fans know a real sportsman when they see one.

Chili has been a top-level racer for 15 years, winning on all three classes of Grand Prix bike before moving to Superbike, first as a privateer and then as a works rider on both Ducati and Suzuki, and winning at every stage.

Frankie first came to international prominence when he won the European 125 Championship on an MBA in 1985. From there it was straight into 500 GPs on the now-uncompetitive Suzuki. Nevertheless, Frankie finished equal tenth overall with a best finish of sixth at Spa – in the wet. He got a more-forgiving Honda triple for 1987 and scored his first rostrum at World Championship level in France with second place – in the wet. Then came the transition to the V4 Honda, and a highest finish of seventh towards the end of the season as he absorbed the lessons of the NSR500. This was also the year of his first of a hat trick of Italian 500 titles.

But Frankie really came to prominence in 1989, mainly for the wrong reasons. Chili was now ranked alongside Christian Sarron as Europe's only challenger to American and Australian dominance. The fact that some of the established stars occasionally bitched about him was a sure sign he was becoming a contender, but after the Italian GP he became a hate figure. Misano is a tricky track at the best of times, in the wet it is impossible. When it rained on race day, nearly all the works riders decided not to race. The exception was Chili. He raced for an Italian team, used Italian tyres – Pirellis – and was therefore under extreme pressure to race. He did, and he won, but the famous smile was not apparent on the rostrum and Pirelli never mentioned the 'victory' in their advertising.

Frankie's first Superbike forays were on a Ducati.

One more year in 500s saw a downturn in form and the end of Frankie's full-time 500 career. In 1991 Frankie joined Aprilia's 250 effort, won at Assen and finished seventh in the championship. 'My first real win,' he said. Next year he won three rounds and finished third in the championship, although Frankie, Max Biaggi and Loris Reggiani played Aprilia's three little pigs to Cadalora's Honda-mounted big bad wolf. Frankie never won another GP. The next move was to Yamaha as team-mate to GP newboy Tetsuya Harada but it was the Japanese who took the title without Frankie even getting on the rostrum.

A year of unemployment followed, but in 1995 Frankie Chili found his spiritual home: he joined the World Superbike Championship. With a private Ducati that was at least a match for the works bikes and with the benefit of works support after mid-season, Frankie took just three rounds to get on the rostrum with second place in Race 2 at Donington. Typically, he had crashed in the first race. Next time out, at Monza, he crashed out of the first race at high speed before winning the second amid scenes that amounted to national rejoicing. An Italian winning an Italian World Championship round (strictly speaking, it was the San Marino round) on an Italian motorcycle is a very good way to instigate a few parties.

Ducati's owners, the Castiglioni brothers, were impressed; the Cagiva 500 GP bike was brought out of mothballs and Chili got a wild-card entry for the Mugello GP. Five years after he last raced a 500 Frankie qualified third but a bad start and an excursion into a gravel trap meant tenth was the best he could do. Nevertheless, Frankie had made a point on behalf of himself specifically and Superbike riders in general. He ended his first Superbike season in eighth, stayed with the semi-private Gattolone team for 1996 and ended that year in sixth. As well as his two wins, he set pole on the fastest two tracks of the year – Hockenheim and Monza.

Chili and Gattolone got their reward in 1997 with full works bikes. The start of the season summed up Frankie to perfection: a crash in the first race of the year put him out of the second, then came that win at Misano followed by retirement due to mechanical failure. Conventional wisdom had it that Frankie could win races but was unlikely to be a championship contender. With fellow Ducati man Carl Fogarty engaged in a bitter struggle for the title with John Kocinski, the Italian and the Englishman became friends. It was noticeable that the only man Carl was happy to see beside him on the rostrum, apart from best mate James Whitham, was Frankie. He had reason to be grateful to him at Assen after he had been beaten at the Dutch track for the first time in nine races, by Kocinski in Race 1. In the second race, Frankie shepherded Carl home and pointedly remarked that he hoped Ducati would remember this at contract time.

They did. Frankie was in the factory team the following year alongside Troy Corser with Virginio Ferrari as manager. It was his best season as five wins including a dominant double in South Africa show, but the events of Assen are what everyone remembers. Up until that point Frankie, for once, was a genuine championship contender and still was after Race 1 when he shadowed Fogarty before mugging him on the last lap. King Carl was not best pleased and Race 2 went down to the last corner, this time Chili fell. It looked like a simple mistake on the brakes but when the pair got back to the pit-lane Frankie took a swing at Carl accusing him of dirty riding on the flat-out approach to the chicane. Now, a bout of fisticuffs when helmets and leathers are still on and the blood is up is understandable if not praiseworthy. What Chili did next was neither. Wearing an

After years in the doldrums, Chili resurrected Suzuki's Superbike fortunes.

Whatever the conditions, you just know Frankie will be a contender.

uncharacteristically unstylish towelling dressing gown, he gatecrashed the winner's press conference and again accused Carl of foul play, issued some threats of his own about what would happen next time they met and tried to throw another punch.

What caused this outburst? No other racer could see anything wrong with Fogarty's riding, but what was not known generally was that as well as losing any chance of the title Chili had also lost the chance of getting a factory Ducati for 1999. To keep his ride, Frankie had to finish the season in the top three. That could not happen now, also Virginio Ferrari and Fogarty's manager Davide Tardozzi were in competition to manage the works team in 1999. Chili's outburst was a result of all these factors and guaranteed one thing and one thing only; he would not be on a Ducati in 1999.

Predictably, Frankie found a good home. The Suzuki team changed management from Harris Performance to Alstare and new boss Francis Batta signed Chili to head the effort. It was a tall order: the Harris squad had managed three rostrums in three years.

His determination to revenge himself on Ducati was dented at the start of the season when he finished 30 seconds behind the front men, and thoughts of retirement crossed his mind. But Frankie knew what was needed and with Dunlop he set about developing it. By Round 3 at Donington he had a good enough qualifier to take SuperPole, Suzuki's first since Polen at Sugo in 1989. The races showed they had a long way to go but it was the moment that hope appeared. Two races later the old Frankie Chili reappeared at Monza, scoring two rostrums on a bike palpably down on speed compared with the opposition. He got the GSX-R750 home just half-a-second behind double-winner Fogarty both times and even led the second race for a while just to show the top guys he was back. Two more rostrums followed before victory arrived at a sodden A1-Ring. It should have been a double, for Frankie fell in Race 1 while leading by the proverbial street. He did not make the same mistake twice: the Race 2 win was Suzuki's first ever outside Japan, the first since Alstare took over, and Frankie's first on a four-cylinder bike. The first dry-weather win came at Hockenheim in Race 2 after Fogarty had secured his fourth crown in Race 1. And a little gem it was, too. Down on pace, Frankie had to use all his experience to hang in the slipstream of the leaders, position himself precisely going into the final chicane, slipstream Slight and then outbrake Fogarty going into the stadium.

Proof positive that a 750cc four could mix it with the 1,000cc V-twins – provided you had a rider like Frankie Chili on it.

Equally surprisingly, Frankie's popularity with his British fans did not suffer one jot after his bust-up with Foggy, one female fan at Brands Hatch proudly showed Frankie her tattoo of his tiger's head helmet design on her shoulder, and Suzuki brought him over to the British bike show at the Birmingham NEC in November. In the paddock he assumed the role of elder statesman, standing up for the riders on matters like safety and prize money. Mind you, said some of the riders, he always was fond of the folding stuff.

He may never win a World Championship, but not many riders have had as long and as distinguished a career as Frankie Chili, even fewer have had success on such a variety of bikes, and none has been as popular.

Troy Corser

Born
27 November 1971
Wollongong,
New South Wales,
Australia

First win
1995 Round 6/Race 2
Salzburgring, Austria
Ducati 916

1 Championship
1994 11th
1995 2nd
1996 Champion
1998 3rd
1999 3rd
2000 3rd

21 Race wins
1995 Austria 2
1995 USA 2
1995 Japan 1
1995 Australia 1
1996 Great Britain 1 and 2
1996 Czech Rep 1 and 2
1996 Europe 2
1996 Spain 1 and 2
1998 USA 1
1998 Europe 2
1999 Australia 1 and 2
1999 Germany 2
2000 Australia 2
2000 San Marino 1 and 2
2000 Spain 1
2000 USA 2

Another product of what seemed to be the never-ending golden age of Australian domestic racing in the late-1980s and mid-'90s, Troy Gordon Corser's career path right up to the point of winning the World Superbike Championship in 1996 at the tender (and record breaking) age of 24 was an almost vertical climb.

From his first ventures on the tarmac at Oran Park in 1989 right through to lifting the World Superbike Championship trophy at his home venue of Phillip Island only eight years later, the upslope of Corser's career has been the model of near perfection, with the smart and ambitious Australian moving from each new field of battle to the next like some reincarnated Alexander the Great.

In fact, because of his gypsy-like trail of consistent but wandering career advancement, Corser's journey to the top was hardly route one, unlike Mick Doohan for example (a man who was proddie racing one day and 500 GP racing the next, even if it took him just as long to win his first world title as it did Corser).

Corser's method of career advancement was, however, hardly less impressive, to the point where even if he retired tomorrow a list of his achievements would still read favourably.

Many riders who went on to international success have won early in their careers, and Corser is no different, scooping State Championship honours on an RGV250, a feat which along with some other impressive rides, got him an *Australian Motorcycle News*-sponsored ride on a TZ250 at Phillip Island. He would take the Australian National 250 proddie championship in 1990 on the same Suzuki, and also get his first taste of Superbike racing on a slick-tyred GSX-R750 in a support race at the Phillip Island GP.

After sixth place in the National 250 GP Championship in 1991, Corser's first full season in Superbikes in 1992 ended with a creditable fourth place riding an OW01.

Learning his craft swiftly, Corser switched to the Winfield Honda team in 1993, giving them the Aussie Superbike title on the theoretically outpaced RC30 and propelling him inexorably towards a bigger pond.

His new chosen place of work, the American Superbike Championship, always was a tough neighbourhood in which to be the new boy, despite being mounted on competitive Ducati 888s run by former World Superbike Champions, Fast By Ferracci.

In addition to being the first ever non-American to win the crown, never mind win it in his rookie year, Corser was also allowed to compete in four World Championship events in 1994, with a smattering of podiums as his reward, the first of which came in the very first round at Donington Park.

A change of team to Alfred Inzinger's Promotor squad for his first real assault on the World Championship in 1995 would have been a complete success from the off, had it not been for the dominant Carl Fogarty who was on a record-breaking rampage towards title number two.

Four race wins and 15 podium finishes gave Corser second overall, albeit lightyears behind Fogarty on the official works machine. Impressive on an industrial scale, Corser was the hottest property in the paddock, as much for his eminent promotability and obvious smarts as his ability to set up and then successfully race motorcycles.

The youngest Champion

With Fogarty embracing the unpredictable charms of the still-enigmatic RC45 in 1996, and with star Ducati man John Kocinski soon going through interminable political dramas in the official works Ducati squad, the playing surface had never been smoother for a kid on the make like Corser.

With his mix of youthful exuberance and an on-bike maturity frighteningly well-developed for one of 24 years, Corser set about the championship with relish, becoming the first Australian to win the title and scoring a more-than-respectable seven wins in the 24-race series. His style was so different to Foggy's, so smooth that you needed a stopwatch to tell whether he was going fast or not.

The young Corser could do no wrong, and with sponsorship still fuelled by Power Horse the Promotor squad went and crossed the yawning chasm which separated World Superbike from the GP paddock.

Works YZR Yamahas or not, the financial collapse of Inzinger's empire marked the end of what had been a faltering GP introduction for Corser, with or without the intervention of Red Bull as a new sugary caffeine supplier early in the season.

Recriminations about lack of payment for both 1996 and '97, an inability to agree terms with the new team owners WCM, and a rake of confidence-destroying crashes meant Corser was in limbo land, his career in tatters and he had a bad taste in his mouth from GP racing.

His performances on track in the seven races before his final meltdown were unquestionably affected by his off-track problems (12th at Mugello being his best finish) but nevertheless, as some had found before him, a full-blown 500 GP bike was a demanding beast to tame, especially in so short a space of time. And for a rider like Corser, a reigning World Champion no less, it came as something of an unpleasant surprise. It was the sort of trauma that could send a career into free fall.

Rescue, emotional and otherwise, appeared when Virginio Ferrari brought him back into World Superbike with the AD-VF Ducati factory team for 1998, alongside Pierfrancesco Chili; the pair of them sharing machinery specification if little else with the Ducati Performance team specially created for the prodigal Carl Fogarty.

A potential World Championship win was now famously snatched from him when a crash in morning warm-up for the three-way title decider at the final Sugo round wrote Corser out of the reckoning, with a suspected ruptured spleen sending him to hospital. The cruellest possible outcome for Corser handed Fogarty a third World crown and relegated Corser to third.

Healed up and back to full fitness, Corser was then handed a golden chalice once more – a full factory team ride in the Davide Tardozzi-operated Ducati Performance team, which had taken over the Ducati mantle from the sacked Ferrari and his AD-VF team.

The only problem was his new team-mate, Carl Fogarty. Always the dominant partner in any team they had been drafted into, the only pair of men in the 1999 series who knew what it took to win the World Championship first-hand were now both in the same team. Shades of Rainey and Lawson in the 1990 Marlboro Yamaha squad. The word internecine was coined for just such a conflict, and it was Corser who was forced to play Abel to Fogarty's Cain.

The record books show a record points win for Fogarty, with Corser uncharacteristically toiling with poor tyre choices in several races and many

Troy's trademark standing wheelie celebration.

In 2000, the Aussie flag was flown from an Aprilia (below) rather than a Ducati (above).

a rumour about preferential treatment for the World Champ from his old mate Tardozzi doing the rounds.

This point of view conveniently and inexplicably ignores the fact that Tardozzi was Corser's influential team boss the year that he won the title, and Tardozzi's subsequent comments that 'I am a Troy Corser fan' are borne out by the fact that Tardozzi is still first to congratulate Troy after a successful race, and had to be strong-armed into finally ditching Corser in the first place. But nonetheless, Corser was the man toiling against an early season tweaked shoulder while Fogarty, free of injury, was romping away with the title lead.

Sugo, Troy's nemesis the previous season, once more proved his bogey circuit, in something less than the life-threatening way it had in 1998. Tied with Honda's Colin Edwards on 361 points, a countback of wins and podium positions gave Edwards, not Corser, the right to run the number-two plate in 2000. With second place being first loser in any ordinary circumstance, and therefore unimportant, Corser's third was to prove to be his undoing. It transpired that only second place in the championship, giving Ducati a one-two whitewash, would have absolutely guaranteed a year 2000 Ducati ride for Corser.

Perceived by some as too much of a party animal, Corser's curious and unexplained habit of fading in the middle of any race he was not leading was put down to either a lack of fitness or a lack of motivation, and in the increasingly ruthless world of the newly streamlined Ducati Corse operation, anything less than 100 per cent adherence to the new Red Order was deemed reason for dismissal. Ask Frankie Chili, Virginio Ferrari or even Franco Farne.

According to Corser, however, it was the way he was let go, very late in the cycle of contract negotiations and after all the other plum saddles had been occupied, that most rankled. His late jump into the job market gave him little choice but to accept a ride on the factory Aprilia which had impressed not at all in its maiden season.

It was this initial stroke of bad luck which turned Troy Corser's career around once more. His greatest talents always lay in his ability to not just go fast, but to maximise the machine at his disposal to go even faster, an attribute which makes him easily the most successful World Superbike pole position setter of all time and the undisputed king of the single-lap SuperPole discipline.

So much so that in his first competitive outing on the Aprilia he won SuperPole, a feat of arms which no-one, especially the all-new Aprilia WSB team or Corser himself, could have realistically expected so soon. From man to Superman and from bike to Superbike.

And so the story for the rest of the 2000 season unfolded. A weather-influenced win at Phillip Island was almost as weird as Gobert's on the Bimota, but a clean run of three wins (both races at Misano and race one in Valencia) proved that even the title itself was not beyond Corser's reach. It would not be hyperbole to state that of all the great riders in the paddock today, only Corser's mix of setup and racing ability could have delivered half as much in double the time.

Still not yet 30, Corser has a fair few years to drive home his revenge on those who doubted him, not to mention setting a total of pole positions (26 and counting) which may never be beaten.

John **Kocinski**

Born
20 March 1968
Little Rock, Arkansas,
USA

First win
1996 Round 1/Race 1
Misano, San Marino
Ducati 916

1 Championship
1996 3rd
1997 Champion

14 Race wins
1996 San Marino 1 and 2
1996 USA 1
1996 Indonesia 1 and 2
1997 Australia 1
1997 San Marino 2
1997 Italy 1
1997 USA 1 and 2
1997 Holland 1
1997 Spain 1 and 2
1997 Indonesia 1

6 Pole positions
1996 San Marino
1996 USA
1996 Holland
1997 Holland
1997 Spain
1997 Indonesia

Strange but fast, very fast

Of all the characters that have inhabited the World Superbike Championship, John Kocinski is the most difficult to understand or analyse. He came to Superbike having already won the GP 250 world title and four 500 GPs competing with men like Lawson, Rainey and Schwantz and stayed for just two years. He left without a backward glance having won for Honda the title the company so badly wanted for its RC45. In between, he took the most impressive victory ever seen in the Championship and in his last meeting almost knocked off his team-mate in Race 1 before crashing on the last lap in Race 2 while knocking Simon Crafar off. All this despite the fact he had already won the title.

Kocinski had not raced bikes in 1995 when no 500 team was willing to take a risk on his undoubted talent after Cagiva pulled out of the Grands

Prix. But the Castiglioni brothers, owners of the Cagiva group, needed a replacement for Carl Fogarty and were willing to pay John what he needed to ride their Ducati. And John needed a way back into top-level racing. Why would the 1990 250cc World Champion, a man who then won four 500cc GPs on two different makes of bike, be out of work? A good question.

The answer is in Kocinski's complex, infuriating and sometimes genuinely worrying character. On a motorcycle, the guy can be a sublime genius. Off it, he has trouble with team-mates, trouble with team members, trouble with the press, and – it seems – trouble with life in general. He can be charm incarnate for most of a race meeting then say something so insensitive or downright crass your jaw hits the floor. Neil Hodgson noticed it all too often as Kocinski's team-mate in the Ducati year. 'I used to think "John, why do you let yourself down like that?"' He is not the only one to have asked that question. And that is before we get on to the subject of Kocinski's legendary cleanliness fetish, a source of wonder and amusement to the rest of the paddock.

John's career started on the oval dirt-tracks at the tender age of five – he finished last in his first race. By the age of ten he was riding in five or six

Little John came to Superbike on a Ducati (below) but won the title on a Honda (right).

classes twice a weekend. After ranking third in the whole country by 12 years of age he felt burnt out, so he switched to the tarmac. He first raced Superbikes in 1984 and two years later had a works Yamaha contract. This was when Kenny Roberts Senior first noticed John and invited him to train with him over the winter. In 1987, Kocinski rode a 250 for Roberts in the AMA Championship, beating Kork Ballington and Alan Carter for the title. He also finished third in the Suzuka 8 Hours. It was now time for the world stage.

At the opening GP of 1988, Kocinski harassed multiple World Champion Anton Mang before his bike slowed and he finished fifth. The GP establishment understood what it had seen; the genuine article. In 1989 he entered two 250 GPs and won them both, the following year he was 250

champion, then it was up to the 500s where he drove Roberts and his team to distraction altering the bike trying to get it to behave like a 250. His habit of winning the last race of the year also sent Roberts ballistic.

Kocinski was rapidly becoming unemployable and started 1993 with Suzuki's uncompetitive 250. That relationship came to an end at Assen after Kocinski was mugged for second place on the last lap by Testsuya Harada and did not appear on the rostrum. He said the bike broke, the team said he revved it into oblivion.

The next stop was a bike nearly as ill-favoured as the 250 Suzuki, Cagiva's 500. This was John's most impressive year, he ended up third overall and took the marque's first dry-weather win. But when Cagiva pulled out of the GPs, John sat out the 1995 season.

This was the strange character that came to World Superbike and – typically – won his first race. Actually, he did the double after Anthony Gobert took the flag first but was later disqualified for a technical infringement. Kocinski ended the year third overall, in front of Carl Fogarty, but by two-thirds distance he had fallen out terminally with team manager Virginio Ferrari who took to begging his old charge Fogarty to beat the American.

No-one was surprised to see Kocinski move to Honda for 1997. As with Cagiva, he always had fans high up in the company. What emerged late in the year was that there would be a reward if John won the World Superbike title that had evaded Honda's flagship RC45 since 1994: a 500 Honda for the 1998 season. With Fogarty back home with Ducati, he and Kocinski had effectively swapped motorcycles. It would be a fascinating year.

The Honda took some getting used to and wet weather at the start of the year helped the American acclimatise. It was interesting, his rivals remarked, how close he stuck to Japanese members of the team. Team manager Neil Tuxworth had not just to keep the quirky (to put it mildly) Kocinski happy, he had to appease Aaron Slight who had to suffer in silence as the usual team practice of sharing information was jettisoned. Not an easy job. As usual, Carl Fogarty's opinion was pithy and to the point. He thought Kocinski was a great rider, one of the few who raced to win, but he hadn't got much time for him as a human being.

Just how hard Kocinski raced was evident at Assen where Fogarty had won every race since 1992 and where Carl had humbled him in the greatest finish the Championship had ever seen the previous year. In Race 1 Kocinski had a terrible start then proceeded to pass every other works bike in the field as if they weren't there, finally ghosting past Fogarty on the penultimate lap. There has never been a better ride in the Championship.

It followed two rounds where Foggy had crashed with Kocinski in front of him, and at the round before Kocinski had taken the double. When Kocinski took both wins at the next round, Carl's struggle with the recalcitrant Ducati was effectively over. Kocinski duly claimed the crown in Japan as Foggy crashed again, but if anyone thought the American's capacity to amaze was finished they should have waited for the last round. In Race 1 he rode through team-mate Slight's front wheel to take the win and when he tried to do the same to Simon Crafar in Race 2 both men fell.

It was a suitably strange and alienating ending to John Kocinski's World Superbike career. Unless, of course, he finds another convoluted route back to a works ride.

Kocinksi was always happy to tell journalists how happy he was to be on a Honda. Honda was pretty chuffed too.

Yuichi Takeda

Born
*29 November 1977
Saetama Prefecture,
Japan*

First win
*1996 Round 9/Race 1
Sugo, Japan
Honda RC45*

Championships
*1996 20th
1997 35th
1998 41st
1999 55th
2000 45th*

1 Race win
1996 Japan 1

The youngest winner

Minibike racing at the Akigase track in Saetama Prefecture north west of Tokyo must have been pretty intense in the late 1980s and early '90s. Among the young hopefuls getting their first taste of competition on their local track were current works Grand Prix riders Norifumi Abe and Daijiro Katoh as well as the Takeda brothers. Yuichi Takeda, who would go on to become the youngest ever winner of a World Superbike race, started minibike competition when he was just ten years old and he stayed in this breeding ground for future stars for six years before moving up to 250s when he was 16 years old.

It was not long before he made his mark on big bikes. In his second year of 250 racing, Yuichi became All-Japan Novice Champion on a Honda RS250. That was in 1994; in '95 he took the big step of leaving Japan and competing in Thunderbike, the Supersport 600 series that ran as a support class at the Grands Prix in 1995. Yuichi and his Honda CBR600 did not set the world on fire with 13th place overall. Officially, his year in Europe had nothing to do with the factory, but HRC, the Honda Racing Corporation, was obviously keeping track of Takeda's progress and he was drafted into the works Superbike team for the 1996 All-Japan Superbike Championship.

At 18 years old Yuichi fought off the challenge of Yamaha's local hero to win Race 1 in the Japanese round of the World Championship. The man he beat? – Noriyuki Haga. Amazingly, it was his first win on Honda's Superbike. Add in seventh overall in the All-Japan Championship and it could be said that at the time, Honda's faith was justified.

Things were even better for young Takeda-san in 1997. He finished third in the All-Japan Superbike Championship and, much more importantly, had a really good Suzuka 8 Hours. Teamed with his old minibike rival Daijiro Katoh, he qualified in pole position and finished the race in ninth. It is necessary to understand just how important the 8 Hours is to all the Japanese factories, especially Honda who own the Suzuka circuit. Oguma-san, for many years the head of HRC's racing efforts, used to say the race was an exam which any aspiring works rider had to pass, and Yuichi most certainly graduated in 1997. However, so far, this was the high point of his careeer. In 1998, he and Katoh qualified a respectable fourth for the 8 Hours but retired from the race itself. Takeda's All-Japan Championship performance also slipped, he finished the year in sixth place. Honda kept faith with him for another season and he was partnered with no less a rider than John Kocinski for the 8 Hours, finishing seventh.

Unfortunately, Takeda's loss of form resulted in Honda deciding not to employ him for the 2000 season. It was not only Yuichi who was disappointed as Honda had had high hopes for him and they were not realised. Compare Takeda's career path with that of his exact contemporary, Katoh: two Grand Prix wins as a wild card followed by a full-time Grand Prix ride and an 8 Hours victory in 2000 teamed with Tohru Ukawa. With Ukawa and other top 250 men moving up to the 500cc class for the 2001 season, Katoh was hot favourite for the title six months before the season started! He is definitely part of Honda's long-term plans. Sadly, the same cannot be said of Yuichi Takeda.

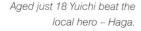

Aged just 18 Yuichi beat the local hero – Haga.

Takuma**Aoki**

Born
24 February 1974,
Gumma Prefecture,
Japan

First win
1996 Round 9/Race 2
Sugo, Japan
Honda RC45

Championships
1995 13th
1996 19th

1 Race win
1996 Japan 2

Japan's lost champion

When the middle one of Japan's 'Fireball Brothers' ran away with the second race at Sugo in 1996, it should not have been a surprise, but it was, even though his young team-mate Takeda won the first race of the day. When Takuma scorched his way to an even more comprehensive win a few hours later it completed only the second World Superbike double for the Honda RC45. Victories had been hard to come by for Honda's flagship but both Takeda and Aoki's wins were comprehensive.

There was nothing lucky about the win. The surprise is that he qualified nowhere and had a dreadful first race in which he collided with Yanagawa, who crashed, and then came home a lowly 11th, a humiliatingly lowly position for the reigning All-Japan Superbike Champion.

Takuma knew exactly what the problem was. Before the meeting he had decided, along with his chief mechanic Iwano-san (later in 500 GPs with Sete Gibernau), that they needed to try something radical to keep up with the World Superbike regulars. It was quickly apparent that they were wrong and between the races the team went back to the standard settings Takuma always used in All-Japan Championship races. As Japanese Champion he also realised something else: 'Deep down in my mind I know I have to win.' Which is exactly what he did: comprehensively. He lapped consistently faster than he had done all weekend and set the fastest lap of the round.

What's more, Takuma is adamant he did it on the bike he rode all season in his domestic championship. Unlike the visiting Castrol Honda riders, Fogarty and Slight, he had no new parts to use that weekend. He also remembers that his bike's settings were 'not so different' from theirs. Like them he was on Michelin tyres, not always the best at Sugo, but Takuma points out that they were the only tyres he used right through his career so he did not know the relative merits of the two makes and just got on with the job.

Ask Takuma about that race now and he will tell you that it was without doubt one of the highlights of his career, 'one of the most memorable races of my life.' And with characteristic politeness he adds that he was 'really delighted to beat Fogarty.' But the overwhelming memory of his first win at World Championship level is the extreme heights of concentration he had to maintain to make up for the first race. He not only won the race, he went on to retain his Japanese Superbike Championship and progress into the Grands Prix in the Repsol Honda team, albeit on the V-twin 500. Like all promising young Japanese riders, he had already been blooded in GPs

Sadly, this was the only time Takuma was to fly the victory flag at a World Championship race.

as a wild card at home at Suzuka in 1995 when he got a V4 on the rostrum in a wet race after only having an afternoon's testing before the event. That and the two All-Japan Superbike Championships marked him out as a true star of the future, more so even than older brother Nobuatsu and younger brother Haruchika who were already in the GPs.

Takuma's versatility was underlined by his fifth overall on the little V-twin in his first full World Championship season. Winning on the little twin was not possible, but heroically he did get it into the top three more than once. Sadly, we never got to find out if Takuma's astonishing versatility could give him a shot at being Japan's first 500 GP champion. He was paralysed from the waist down in a testing accident in the winter of 1997–8.

Akira Yanagawa

Born
15 July 1973
Kagoshima, Japan

First win
1997 Round 8/Race 2
A1-Ring, Austria
Kawasaki ZX-7R

Championships
1997 4th
1998 7th
1999 5th
2000 5th

3 Race wins
1997 Austria 2
1997 Japan 1
1999 Japan 2

2 Pole positions
1997 San Marino
1997 Japan

Kawasaki's consistent contender

Akira Yanagawa has his own little place in history as the first Japanese rider to win a World Superbike race away from the home tarmac of Sugo. The anti-Haga as some have called him, not in any unkind way, but to describe his off-track persona and lifestyle; Akira-san is pretty much everything that Nori-chan is not.

A family man, relatively gregarious in the paddock, with pretty good English skills, always super-fit, and happily settled in Europe for the entire racing season, Yanagawa goes about his business in an almost anonymous manner – until the flag drops, when he goes through the same horns'n'tail metamorphosis as every other racer on the World Superbike grid.

His three-years-and-counting tenure as the number-one rider in Harald Eckl's factory Kawasaki team has delivered little in the way of outright wins (only three career victories to date) but in terms of being a near permanent fixture in the championship top five to eight, race-on-race, season-on-season, Akira is a true contender.

His machinery, the long-in-the-tooth ZX-7R, the only bike out there still using carburettors as opposed to fuel injection, may be the prime reason that no-one ever seems to pick him as their favourite for a top-three championship finish, and indeed his run of fourth, seventh and fifth since his first full time season in 1997, would seem to bear this out.

An unusually late starter, Yanagawa was fully 16 years old before achieving his childhood ambition and hitting the circuits on a Honda NSR250SP production racer. In a strange case of growing backwards, Yanagawa then moved into the minibike racing class, with great success.

Back into the full-size world a year later, Akira blitzed his way round the Japanese Clubman series, winning a host of 250 and 400 production titles in 1989 and '90. An assault on the national 250 GP title the year after gave some good results, enough to warrant Suzuki signing him to ride their (still en vogue) TT F1 machines in the National Championships for two years, 1992 and '93.

Being dragged along in a Superbike-friendly tsunami in 1994, Akira joined Suzuki's Superbike race team. Tenth place overall and eighth in the Suzuka 8 Hours impressed Kawasaki enough to sign him to their All-Japan Superbike team, with Akira giving them two podium finishes and – far more importantly – a podium at the 8 Hours, when teamed with his recent World Superbike rival Katsuaki Fujiwara.

The first of Akira's many major injury bugbears, a broken wrist in 1996, once more saw him manage only two podium finishes when much more was expected. A major change in the way Kawasaki went World Superbike racing, sacking the under performing Muzzy squad and bringing in Harald Eckl to operate a full factory Kawasaki Race Team effort, was good news for Yanagawa. As unconvinced as the rest of the world at that time, Eckl nonetheless signed him to partner Simon Crafar.

By qualifying second at Phillip Island and racing with the top men, Yanagawa started to prove the doubters to be at least half wrong. Five podiums, including two race wins (two more than the highly rated Crafar) slotted Akira right into the top echelon of Superbike racing.

Teamed up with Ducati refugee Neil Hodgson in 1998, Akira struggled against the same handling problems as the young Briton, making a slightly better fist of it before being injured horribly in a massive Laguna Seca accident. Relegated to seventh in the title race, and without a win in 1998, the tough Japanese was back to top form in 1999, scoring a highly-respectable nine podium finishes and took Kawasaki's first World Superbike win for what seemed like decades rather than two years, in the very last race of the season at Sugo.

In 2000 his form was once more blighted by early season injury (collarbone and ankle this time), and the ZX-7R was not getting any younger. Often fastest through the speed trap, most obviously at Hockenheim (318kph no less …) the old Kwak had some uncharacteristic engine blow ups in 2000, aiding Yanagawa's cause not at all.

Despite these obvious problems, in terms of trying one's best with what is available, Yanagawa is as good as they come. In fact, many have been heard to ask the question of just how much better would be Fogarty, Edwards or Corser with the ZX-7R than Yanagawa. But like all other questions in motorcycle racing, we'll never know the answer unless we get to experiment a little.

Since Scott Russell left Kawasaki, only Akira Yanagawa has kept the green flag flying.

Noriyuki Haga

Born
2 March 1975
Aichi Prefecture, Japan

First win
1997 Round 11/Race 2
Sugo, Japan
Yamaha YZF750

Championships
1998 6th
1999 7th
2000 2nd

11 Race wins
1997 Japan 2
1998 Australia 2
1998 Great Britain 1 and 2
1998 USA 2
1998 Japan 2
1999 Spain 1
2000 Germany 2
2000 Spain 2
2000 USA 1
2000 Holland 2

1 Pole position
1998 Spain

The Samurai of Slide

In many ways Noriyuki Haga is the most remarkable man in World Superbike racing today. There are more successful riders, more consistent riders, and certainly more communicative riders (in any language), but Noriyuki Haga is a priceless commodity in one unique way.

He is the only Japanese rider that any non-Japanese fan really gives a hoot about. All others before him, with the possible exception of Nobby Ueda in GPs, have been prototypically Nipponese – restrained, polite, eager to learn English, and taking their responsibility as an ambassador for their homeland to a stiflingly serious degree. To Western eyes, they were and even now still are, kamikaze on the machine but soulless automatons off a bike.

We're speaking in generalities here, of course, but in terms of being a hero to fans outside their own borders, even most of the Europeans and Americans have a smaller following than the Nagoya-based Haga.

Up until his recent (and fair-to-say occasionally ill-advised 15kg weight loss programme) Haga was an unreconstructed womaniser, curry-nosher and lager swiller – never points against any rider in the eyes of the fans even in these more sophisticated and politically correct times. Bikers, frankly, love his anti-establishment reputation and sheer lust for life.

His on-bike charms are also difficult to miss, his nickname 'Samurai of Slide' describing his style to a perfectly crossed-up Tee. His first tastes of gravel rash and speed started, as seems a Japanese rule, with a present of a minibike at the tender age of four. At the age of 17 he turned professional road racer, competing in the All-Japan 250 championship for a season, finishing 13th overall.

A couple of hard years in the Superbike series in Japan, a notoriously

It is impossible to over-exaggerate the impact this man had on the Championship in general and Yamaha's fortunes in particular.

competitive world thanks to the massive presence of factory machines, delivered him only one podium finish. Hardly the stuff of legend, but for a man just into his 20s, much better was in store. An early win in the All-Japan series predated the greatest possible achievement for any Japanese rider, winning the Suzuka 8 Hours.

Best of all, his team-mate for that most-important race on the world racing calendar (if you come from the Japanese home islands at least) was the equally ambitious Colin Edwards, who was reported to have hand-picked Haga after watching his sliding style in a pre-8 Hours test session.

Now deified by his home factory, his lowly 8th place in the Japanese title race was as nothing that particular year, and Haga found himself the most favoured son at the beginning of the 1997 Championship year.

It is quite unusual to see Nori-chan touch the same piece of tarmac twice during a race.

It is quite unusual to see Nori-chan touch the same piece of tarmac twice during a race.

Yamaha's faith in him was more than justified as the charging 'Nori-chan' (loosely translated as Nori the Lad, and the mode of address he prefers to the more formal Haga-san or Mr Haga) won no fewer than seven races and the title itself. No mean feat on the YZF750, now considered well beyond its sell-by date as a world-championship level racer.

A full season of WSB championship racing beckoned, with many tipping Haga for ultimate success after he won one of the four World Superbike races he took part in as a replacement for his old mate Colin Edwards, who was out injured. Just to underline that his Sugo win was not a home-town fluke, he took second in the other race and finished third and fifth in his first overseas event at Sentul in Indonesia. All of which paled into nothingness after the first four races of Haga's first full season of World Superbike Championship racing in 1998.

Three wins from the first four races put Haga up there with the best of them, as he pushed the allegedly outpaced Yamaha YZF750 to the limit on its forgiving Dunlop tyres. And all on circuits unknown to him to boot. There was a new kid in town and he knew how to fight.

His lack of track intimacy and the general rigours of taking on the best in the world every weekend, usually on superior machinery to Haga's YZF, made the rest of the season a tough slog. His total of five race wins was only matched by Aaron Slight and Pierfrancesco Chili and helped put him sixth overall. Not too shabby, especially as he comprehensively outperformed his team-mate Scott Russell on the other Michelin-shod Yamaha.

Proof of his pure and unbridled ability also came with his chance to jump sideways into the GP world for a weekend, running at the front of the Japanese GP for the whole race and finishing third, only losing second place to Okada at the final chicane. 'It was easy', quoth Haga, astonishing riders and press alike.

The biggest challenge of his career so far came with the new R7 Yamaha in 1999, of which Haga had been central in the development of. Running stickier but less forgiving Michelin tyres, Haga was outgunned and out of luck in terms of challenging for the title win. His sheer brilliance alone gave him a solitary race win on the slowly improving R7, at the Lilliputian go-kart track of Albacete, but a couple of mechanical DNFs and too many crashes left him drowning down in seventh at season end, failing to score even 200 points when his talent demanded 300.

He was, of course, not applying himself enough to the self-acknowledged need to get fitter, train harder and maximise all his abilities at this stage. Drastic action was called for and in return for his favoured Dunlops on the rims for 2000, Haga was sent to the fat farm to lose pounds. Successfully as it turned out, if a little too rapidly.

Still the subject of appeal and counter appeal at the end of the 2000 season, Haga's post-race urine sample from the Kyalami round was found to contain an excess of the performance enhancing drug ephedrine.

The message on the back of the leathers says 'I'm gone!' And he usually is.

With the the threat of a ban hanging over his head like a Damoclean sword, Haga has shown true nervelessness and an ability to concentrate his mind to beautiful effect in every race since then. Still fallible, still unpredictable, Nori was the revelation of the 2000 series. In the season when anything without two cylinders was seen as just so much cannon fodder, Haga showed that four-cylinder machines cannot only defend themselves, but even carry the fight to the opposition with ruthless intent – something of a shock for Colin Edwards in the year he was supposed to have things all his way once Fogarty exited stage left humerus.

And there is even more to Haga than simply an ability to override his machine at will. His wild slides and tyre-hopping braking style may suggest a rider who just goes out and rides whatever he is given as hard as he can (like a Fogarty of old for instance) but in reality Haga is a valued development rider for Yamaha, and as his GP podium has demonstrated, he's not simply a monotone singer.

Nor is he anything less than big box office – in any country on the World Superbike calendar.

Colin **Edwards**

Born
27 February 1974
Houston, Texas, USA

First win
1998 Round 3/Race 1
Monza, Italy
Honda RC45

1 Championship
1995 11th
1996 5th
1997 12th
1998 5th
1999 2th
2000 Champion

16 Race wins
1998 Italy 1 and 2
1998 Europe 1
1999 Great Britain 2
1999 Spain 2
1999 Europe 1 and 2
1999 Austria 1
2000 South Africa 1 and 2
2000 Great Britain 1
2000 Italy 2
2000 Holland 1
2000 Germany II 1 and 2
2000 Great Britain II 2

10 Pole positions
1996 Indonesia
1996 Austria
1999 Italy
1999 Austria
2000 Japan
2000 Great Britain I
2000 Italy
2000 Germany I
2000 Holland
2000 Germany II

The Texas Tornado

If you were ever set the task of building the perfect racing beast in some Frankenstein-inspired attempt to win world titles, whatever it took, then you could do worse than combine human DNA from the North American and Australasian continents. The reasons are there for all to see if you consider the recent history of the World Superbike and 500 GP Championships, and care to take note of the nationalities of riders who have finished at the sharp end of those competitions in the last few years.

Colin Edwards is one such man, and with an Australian father and an American mother, the template for potential greatness has been there since his first ventures into the world of motocross racing as a kid. Burned out on the smell of two-stroke, the pubescent Texan turned his back on bike sport for a while before picking up a motorised cudgel again, this time on tarmac. And with no little success.

In 1991, Edwards had a reputation for literally winning every National race he actually finished, as his spark of competitiveness was fanned into a full-blown bonfire. Going pro in 1992, the AMA 250cc Championship was a reward for winning five out of the nine races, beating the fledgling Kenny Roberts Junior, plus experienced men like Jimmy Filice and Rich Oliver along the way and – more significantly – bringing him to the attention of the racing world across the Atlantic.

His first proper AMA Superbike season in 1993 halted his stellar career climb, however, bringing little in the way of success for him or his Vance & Hines Yamaha outfit. A running hat trick of wins in 1994 proved that Edwards had what it took after all. So much so that Yamaha's Belgarda-run Superbike team snapped him up to partner Yasutomo Nagai for a crack at the increasingly prestigious World Superbike Championship.

His introduction to global racing was a harsh one, partly because 1995 was something of a vintage year for full-time World Superbike inductees, with the Yamaha boys joining the other young guns Troy Corser (Ducati) and Anthony Gobert (Kawasaki) in a communal attempt to overthrow the established stars like Fogarty, Russell and Slight.

In any measurable sense it was a horrid year for Edwards, made nightmarish by the death of Yasu at the Dutch circuit of Assen and the subsequent withdrawal of the entire team from the rest of the season, dropping Edwards to 11th in the title race.

His salvation came the next season in what could be considered to be no less than perfect fashion. A win at the all-important Suzuka 8 Hours, something a rider can dine out on for at least a couple of years, catapulted him and his fellow Yamaha charger Noriyuki Haga to blue-eyed boy status back in Japan. The world, or at least that one lined by Yamaha logos, lay at his (curiously tiny) feet.

Colin's first win did not mark, as expected, an opening of the floodgates to more victories, but a few near misses and podium finishes proved that it would only be a matter of time.

But thanks to a wildly aggressive move by Jean-Philippe Ruggia during free practice for the Monza event the following year, Edwards' career took another clunk into reverse. A badly broken wrist, requiring an operation, left the young Texan broken in heart and body, especially after undergoing further restorative surgery to what turned out to be a rebroken collarbone, and then further scalpel work on his bad knees.

With his career in free-fall, and his long-held ambition to go GP racing

a seemingly impossible dream, Edwards looked to be waiting in oblivion's ante-room, unless something dramatic happened.

The second major salvage operation of his career came courtesy of John Kocinski, who had been given the chance to go GP racing with Honda as a reward for winning the Superbike world title the previous year. A nice Edwards-sized hole developed in the Castrol Honda squad, especially as Honda's dictum of 'Honda races, Honda wins' seemed to suit Colin's natural self-belief.

Lining up alongside the much more experienced Honda man Aaron Slight, Edwards had to wait until 1998's fifth round for his first race win of a then five-year old World Superbike career. And the irony of winning a double at a circuit his previous team had regarded as home soil, helping erase any memories of his run-in with Ruggia, was not lost on anyone.

A jubilant Edwards had to wait just a few hours for his second win, making his first sup at the font of the Gods a quenching double dose. (Not to mention leaving the serious statistical aberration that despite being a works Yamaha rider for three years, Edwards never did win a race for his long-time employer.)

Another win on the fast but flighty RC45 at Brands Hatch later in the year, and Edwards, fifth overall, was becoming something of an unofficial team number-one in the Castrol squad – or at least the coming man as once more Slight failed to win the World title at the final hurdle in Sugo.

Come 1999, and Edwards must have fancied his chances at taking the championship win – if his sometimes recalcitrant Honda V4 would let him. Almost always the fastest, and sometimes the sharpest tool in the Superbike box, the RC45 was just as often a monster to set up as Slight and Edwards would alternate between challenging for wins and then riding their hearts out to recover even some semblance of respectability.

In the final analysis, Edwards may have failed in his much-publicised boast of winning 10 races in the 1999 season, winning only half that number, but even then he still managed to take a narrow second overall after tying on points with Troy Corser.

The man most likely to depose Carl Fogarty had truly come of age in the world's premier four-stroke championship, and the only focus he had in the build up to the 2000 season was to dethrone Fogarty – and therefore

When they first became team-mates, Edwards and Aaron Slight were good friends. It didn't last.

obviously win the World Championship. Luck, or his own impatience, eradicated Fogarty from the battle after two races, leaving Edwards (by his own admission) rudderless, as he went from strong early season favourite to a long term but unconvincing championship leader, hounded by the unfancied Troy Corser, Frankie Chili and, most especially, Noriyuki Haga.

Part of Edwards's undoing is his typically American talent for telling everyone exactly what he is going to do, and yet too often not being able to deliver.

So it has been throughout his World Superbike career, but to his eternal credit, he also has the most un-American ability to eat humble pie in a dignified manner. Clearly trounced on-track by Fogarty during the height of their feud in the press several years ago, Edwards still had the gumption to make a special journey over to Fogarty's motorhome and congratulate him in person. A gesture which went a long way towards Fogarty naming Edwards as the next man to have to beat every week, especially now he has a big V-twin of his own to exploit to the max.

In some ways, Colin Edwards could be thought of as much a child of World Superbike as the Fogartys and Slights of this world. Coming from a two-stroke background, and with his sights fully set on the 500cc World Championship, Edwards has now come to the realisation that racing in post-Doohan 500 GPs is no longer the be all and end all of any upwardly-mobile racer's ambitions.

He may have faltered in the middle of the season under the pressure of testing for the 8 Hours, but the way he came back, especially the double in Germany and the final race at Brands Hatch, was the stuff of champions.

At 27 years old at the end of the 2000 season, Edwards is only now the same age as Fogarty was when he seized his first full factory World Superbike ride way back in 1994. That's an uncomfortable fact for the opposition to contemplate.

Keiichi Kitagawa

Born
24 March 1967
Kyoto, Japan

First win
1998 Round 12/Race 1
Sugo, Japan
Suzuki GSX-R750

Championships
1993 20th
1994 24th
1995 17th
1996 29th
1997 32nd
1998 16th
1999 22nd
2000 31st

1 Race win
1998 Japan 1

At last, another Suzuki winner

Before October 1998, Suzuki had not won a World Superbike race for over nine years. In fact they had only won two in total, both in the early days of the Championship, both at Sugo, and both in the wet. It could even be argued that Suzuki, or rather a factory Suzuki team, had never won a World Superbike race as those two wins came from the Don Knit Sugano and Yoshimura teams.

The long-awaited dry-weather win by a GSX-R also came at Sugo, and it took one of the old hands of the All-Japan Superbike Championship to do it. Keiichi Kitagawa has never been Japanese Superbike Champion but he was the last All-Japan F1 Champion, the formula that preceded Superbike as the blue-riband class in domestic Japanese racing after the last domestic 500cc championship in the world came to an end.

Luck was never with Kitagawa in the domestic championship. Injuries stopped him making a consistent challenge although in 1998 it took Shinichi Itoh and Honda until the last round to subdue the Suzuki rider's challenge. But luck has certainly been with him at Sugo over the years. As a Kawasaki rider he took a brace of second places at Sugo in 1993, handily beating the Kawasaki-mounted World Champion Scott Russell in the first race on a patently much faster motorcycle, much to the American's disgust. He got another rostrum in 1994 and a fourth in '95 before moving to Suzuki for the 1996 season, which is when injuries started to dog his progress.

However, his luck held at Sugo, his favourite circuit. In 1997 he only won one race in the All-Japan Championship and the following year he again only won one race and that was at – you guessed – Sugo, where he took his World Superbike win. Kitagawa-san says that the characteristics of the GSX-R750 were perfectly suited to Sugo, a circuit that puts a premium on high corner speed rather than hard braking followed by hard acceleration. He remembers that the combination of bike and tyres was

Previous Suzuki wins were by sponsored teams. This was the first by a GSX-R in factory colours.

perfect on the day and with characteristic Japanese understatement, says he was 'very happy' to win. He also remembers that he did his normal trick of switching from his usual cool, calm, calculating self to full-on combat mode. He says he can do it when necessary and he knows he did it at Sugo – he just cannot remember exactly when. He must have remembered something though, as he got among the Championship regulars again in 1999 with another rostrum finish.

Kitagawa-san was already over 30 years old when he took his World Championship victory and is now unlikely to get a full-time ride at that level. He does, however, have some ambitions left. First, he wants to avoid falling off and getting hurt and secondly, 'I want that All-Japan Championship.'

Ben Bostrom

Born
7 May 1974
Redding, California, USA

First win
1999 Round 8/Race 2
Laguna Seca, USA
Ducati 996

Championships
1999 15th
2000 7th

1 Race win
1999 USA 2

Evel Knievel rides again

Don't let the Evel Knievel leathers and chameleon-like haircolour changes fool you. World Superbike's very own Captain America may be wearing his vulgarly coloured Superhero underpants on the outside but he is also a deadly serious motorcycle racer in the fine American tradition. That is, he was born with a set of handlebars in his paws and digging sand with the rear tyre before he could safely handle a bucket and spade at the seaside.

His All-Americanism continued as per the usual star-spangled template, with his early races taking place on the dirt ovals around his Californian home. Just like the other greats who had preceded him across the pond of course.

Always intent on pavement racing even after his 'Rookie of the Year' accolade in the 600 AMA Grand National dirt track series of 1993,

Bostrom went on to become a roadracer exclusively in 1995 when he won his first AMA national road race.

Riding Zero Gravity Hondas in the AMA 600, Superbike and 750 Supersport championships for the next two years, but never quite winning championships, Bostrom was finally signed to a works ride in 1998, for the American Honda team on their RC45s and CBR600s.

Fifth in the 600 series, Bostrom went out and won the AMA Superbike title but two points always recur when his otherwise impressive championship win is brought up in conversation. First, the more illustrious talents of Anthony Gobert and Miguel DuHamel were out of the series at crucial times; second, and just as contentiously, Bostrom won the series without ever actually winning a race. His devastatingly fast consistency gave him the title, but curiously Honda passed on the notion of running the number-one plate on his bike and dropped him in favour of his brother Eric. Undeterred, Ben made a no worse than sideways move into the Vance & Hines Ducati squad. It was to be his true making.

Just missing out on the title the year after, and falling out with his V&H team-mate Anthony Gobert terminally, Bostrom did have the novel experience of winning a Superbike race. Obviously, the boy possesses a fair sense of occasion.

Waiting until the second race of the World Superbike meeting at Laguna, Bostrom took full points and confirmed to the Ducati factory that he was a potential World Champion. Thus the factory team signed him to partner Fogarty for a Y2K assault on the crown.

Once Fogarty was out, however, the young Bostrom, struggling to come

to terms with being thrown into an unflattering spotlight, learning tracks unlike those in America, being told to race with this and that, and struggling with some personal relationship problems, was simply not performing as expected.

In these days of Ducati being a win-at-all-costs manufacturer just like Honda (well, nothing like Honda, but you understand the idea), Bostrom was ousted to the NCR team in exchange for the equally ineffective but politically

Red for the works team, black for the NCR team, but both bikes are Ducatis.

important Juan Borja, and eventually the more immediately rapid Troy Bayliss.

As it turned out, the factory equipment he took with him, plus the motivation to prove them all wrong, had an immediate and highly beneficial effect. Dropped just before Hockenheim, his next race performances were excellent at Misano, where he finished sixth and then a brilliant third. A pair of second places next time out at Valencia and a podium at home in Laguna have shown that Bostrom has indeed got steel in that chilled-out backbone.

It would surprise no-one if Ducati held their nerve and continued to invest many of their Superbike hopes for the future in their stylish American.

Akira Ryo

Born
20 October 1967
Kobe, Japan

First win
1999 Round 13/Race 1
Sugo, Japan
Suzuki GSX-R750

Championships
1996 25th
1997 38th
1998 17th
1999 15th
2000 29th

1 Race win
1999 Japan 1

Suzuki strike again

Another Suzuki wild card upset the regulars in general and the factory Suzuki team in particular in 1999. This time it was Akira Ryo, another experienced All-Japan Championship runner who had been third in the Japanese domestic Superbike Championship in 1998 and would go on to finish runner-up in 1999. Even more than his team-mate Keiichi Kitagawa who won the previous year, Ryo is considered a Sugo specialist.

Akira got into bikes through the influence of his older brother, Hitoshi, and when he was just 15 years old shared a 400cc four-stroke with him in a three-hour endurance race. Big brother never made it to stardom, and Akira himself spent five years in novice classes before a single year in the junior class, all of them on two-strokes. He then moved up to the international A-class and started his Superbike career, becoming a full-time professional racer in 1991 with Kawasaki at the age of 23.

Akira was one of the early beneficiaries of a new trend among the Japanese factories, changing employees. Instead of seeing out his career with Kawasaki, Ryo moved to Suzuki in 1998 and immediately started repaying their faith in him.

His World Championship win at Sugo came courtesy of his usual plan for the circuit: make an early break. 'This', he says succinctly, 'is my style at Sugo.' It also came courtesy of the main competition, Noriyuki Haga,

Ryo prepares to lead home the first ever one-two Suzuki finish in the history of the Championship.

crashing at the end of the front straight but that did not detract from a historic one–two finish for Suzuki – the factory's first in the 12 years of the World Superbike Championship. Ryo's team-mate on the Dunlop-shod works GSX-R750s, Keiichi Kitagawa, followed him home.

Many thought that despite the fact he was over 30, Ryo would now get his chance in the full World Superbike team, but when Katsuaki Fujiwara kept his job, Akira got his reward in a different class.

Over the winter of 1999/2000, Ryo tested the RG500 Gamma Grand Prix bike to some effect and became one of the riders in line for a call-up should Kenny Roberts or Nobuatsu Aoki be injured. His wild-card ride at the 2000 Japanese Grand Prix, where he qualified third, was as much preparation for that as a reward for his Sugo victory.

Hitoyasu Izutsu

Born
20 March 1971
Osaka, Japan

First win
2000 Round 3/Race 1
Sugo, Japan
Kawasaki ZX-7RR

Championships
1999 55th
2000 19th

2 Race wins
2000 Japan 1 and 2

Kawasaki's new hope

Wild-card riders are expected to do well at Sugo: Honda riders have won, Yamaha riders have won and so have Suzuki riders. Up to the 2000 season, no Kawasaki-mounted wild card had won, and given the poor form of Kawasaki in the 1999 All-Japan Championship, no Team Green man was thought likely to end that run. Which makes it even more surprising that the unheralded Hitoyasu Izutsu, a man who has been around the All-Japan Championship since 1996 with a highest season-end position of eighth, chose the Japanese round of the 2000 championship not just to win but to win both races.

Much like Neil Hodgson, who he had ridden with at the 1998 Suzuka 8 Hours, it was the start of a winning habit. He had never won a round of his domestic championship yet promptly went out at Tsukaba and put that right. Then he won the next four races as well. At Motegi, he led home the first Kawasaki one-two since 1994. Not surprisingly, this form put him to the top of the points standings and encouraged the factory to think about sending him to the World Superbike Championship in 2001.

Izutsu has been out of Japan previously, in 1998 he was sent to the European round at Brands Hatch as a reinforcement for the injury-ridden factory team. Unfortunately, Brands Hatch caught him out not once but twice and he did not make the grid. That was in character for a rider who has always been thought of at home as – to put not too fine a point on it – a crasher. Unfortunately, he always tended to get hurt when he crashed so his end-of-season standings in the points tables never looked as good as they should.

He joined Kawasaki as a professional in 1993 having won the Western Supercup Sports Production Championship, that is the class that mixes 400cc four-strokes with 250cc two-strokes. After that it was the F1 Championship which was the precursor of Superbike before the Superbikes became the top class in the All-Japan Championship in 1996. Izutsu's

Izutsu may have been a crasher, but from Sugo 2000 onwards he was a reformed character.

championship positions, 14th in 1996, 12th in '97 and 8th in '98, hardly set the world on fire and make his 2000 performance all the more remarkable.

The Japanese Championship wins may be understandable as the factories used the 2000 series as a testbed for the following year's regulations which would allow specified tuning kit parts only. Dunlop also did a lot of work over the winter to close the gap on Michelin, but the World Championship wins were a major surprise. Just as with Neil Hodgson, those wins seemed to unlock some hidden reserves of confidence and propel Izutsu to new heights of competitiveness. If some influential people in Japan get their way then that new-found fighting spirit will be on the world stage as Kawasaki try to keep their ageing ZX-7 at the front of the World Superbike pack.

Neil Hodgson

Born
20 November 1973
Burnley, Lancashire,
Great Britain

First win
2000 Round 4/Race 2
Donington Park, GB
Ducati 996

Championships
1996 10th
1997 9th
1998 11th
2000 12th

2 Race wins
2000 Great Britain 2
2000 Europe 2

3 Pole positions
1997 Great Britain
2000 Europe
2000 Great Britain II

Not just a pretty face

Something happened to Neil Hodgson at the start of the 2000 season – he became a winner. He had always been fast but something was missing, that vital ingredient that turns a good rider into a great one. British fans had watched with frustration as their 18-year-old 125cc Champion went to GPs where he proved himself capable of qualifying with the fast guys but not staying with them in the race. His size was some excuse, Neil was around a foot taller than German 125 World Champ Dirk Raudies, so the only thing to do was to go up to 500s. It took him most of his first year to score a point but 12 months later he put his private bike on the front row alongside Cadalora, Doohan and Beattie at the Argentine GP.

It was not a time when there were any vacancies on works 500s and Neil saw no reason to soldier on for a third year with a motorbike that would not allow him to improve. The situation in Superbike was quite different. For 1996, Carl Fogarty had left Ducati and Mauro Lucchiari was deemed not good enough, thus leaving two of the most desirable seats in the Championship vacant. Hodgson was top of the Italian shopping list and not surprisingly the money was good too. Compared with the money you can earn as a GP 500 privateer, it was very, very good.

Neil found out who his team-mate would be one lunchtime in a restaurant near the Ducati factory. He walked in and noticed a familiar face at another table: John Kocinski. All of a sudden he was Ducati's number-two rider. While his first year in Superbike wasn't bad, it wasn't earth-shattering either. He scored just one rostrum finish with a third place at Laguna Seca and finished the year behind all other factory bikes except the new Suzukis.

The following year, 1997, was supposed to be the season it all went right, after all he had his friend Carl Fogarty as his new team-mate. The second Hockenheim race tells you all you need to know. Neil led by three seconds at one point but coming into the stadium section on the last lap he was shouldered aside by Fogarty then ran wide at the next corner letting most of the rest of the leading group through. He ended up eighth in a race he should have won. Still, he had ridden better than ever before at World Championship level, so things could only get better. The following week he shattered his kneecap while out training on a motocrosser. At the end of the year he only finished in front of one of the Suzukis, and his friendship with Carl Fogarty didn't look too good either.

Kawasaki had faith though, and snapped him up to ride alongside Akira Yanagawa. It was another unhappy year, the low point of which was the Japanese rider's horrible crash at Laguna Seca. A traumatised Hodgson was one of the first on the scene. A series of mechanical problems and breakdowns plus the knife-edge behaviour of the bike only added to the misery.

Neil Hodgson, one of the bright young hopes of British racing, had had three years on works machinery and had just one top-three finish to show for it. As Neil had always been an articulate, good-looking lad who was not afraid to tell the media he was ready to win there were more than a few paddock jeremiahs all too ready – and happy – to write him off.

The first Brands meeting of 2000: the rest didn't see which way he went in Race 2.

Back to the British Championship for 1999, where Neil could either sink into the comfort zone or find the motivation to restart his career. He won the first race but that was it. Things did not look good. Then, in 2000, came the big change. At Donington in Race 2 he and Chris Walker made Haga look safe as they chased Chili, and when Chili's tyres were totally shot they passed him on the last lap. The European round at Brands Hatch showed it was no fluke: a rostrum in Race 1 and then a runaway win in Race 2. Then there was the small matter of a war with Walker in the British Championship including one astonishing race where Neil had to start from the back row of the grid and rode through the whole field in eight laps.

In those last two rides he looked like Carl Fogarty painted orange – and he was still only 27 years of age. No-one was sniggering behind their hands any more and the big international team managers were interested again, very interested.

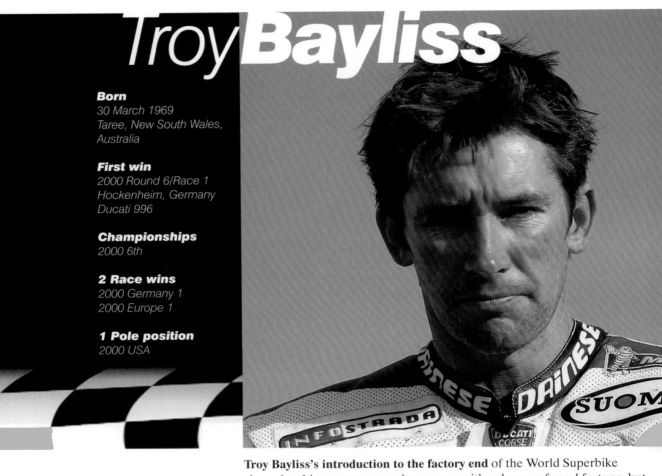

Troy Bayliss

Born
30 March 1969
Taree, New South Wales,
Australia

First win
2000 Round 6/Race 1
Hockenheim, Germany
Ducati 996

Championships
2000 6th

2 Race wins
2000 Germany 1
2000 Europe 1

1 Pole position
2000 USA

Another fast Aussie

Troy Bayliss's introduction to the factory end of the World Superbike championship spectrum may have come with a degree of good fortune, but no-one can deny the ever-smiling Bayliss his place at the top table after slogging away hard for the last ten years.

Starting out on the dirt as a kiddie in 1981, Bayliss took his first competitive tarmac steps at the advanced age of 23. His Kawasaki KR1-S exploits included a couple of national events, but his obvious speed was translated into results the following year. Sixth overall on a Kawasaki ZZ-R600 in the National Supersport Championship, followed up by a similar result the year after, made him a top contender for the following season.

His loyalty to Kawasaki's products made for a ZX-6R ride in 1995, a bike which delivered him a fine second place overall, with the added benefit of a competitive try out on a Team Kawasaki Superbike.

Finishing second after qualifying on pole impressed the Kawasaki Australia chiefs enough for them to offer him a full time Superbike berth in 1996 when he finished second in the more prestigious Shell Superbike Championship and third in the Shell Oils Championship.

The first meaningful non-Kawasaki rides of his career came in the following year, when he took an Ansett Air Freight GSX-R750 Suzuki to second in both national Superbike series. His real landmark performances in the grander scheme of things came at the World Superbike and GP rounds at Phillip Island. A fifth place in the rain in Superbike and an even more spectacular sixth on an unfancied Suzuki RGV 250 GP bike stamped him out as the next hot Aussie. The image of Troy riding around the outside of Olivier Jacque in Turn 2 and the Frenchman doing a double-take is the one that sticks in the memory.

The GSE team in the British Superbike Championship understood what they were looking at, hungry for success after a couple of tough Ducati years, they gambled on Bayliss as the man to turn their fortunes round.

An eighth place finish may not seem like much of a reward for their faith, but despite numerous breakdowns and a few crashes, Bayliss's loose (as in unscrewed and widely strewn) riding style won him praise from all. Learning each new circuit with his wheels out of line made the late-braking Bayliss popular as well as fast. The following year Bayliss kept his head while all around him were boiling theirs in engine oil or burying them in the sandtraps, all that experience was brought to bear and he won the British title.

British, American or World Superbike series, Dunlop or Michelin tyres, it made no difference: Bayliss and Ducati won.

His methodical off-track approach and full-blooded on-track style were a joy to watch, even if the crowd were obviously more behind the Chris Walkers of this world than some Aussie bloke. He wasn't disliked by any means, but it must still have been a hard year for Bayliss.

With the increasing status of the UK Superbike scene, many were surprised at Bayliss's decision to move to the AMA championships for 2000, but with the defection of both Vance & Hines Ducati riders to pastures new (for Bostrom) and potential oblivion (for Gobert) everyone in the UK knew that both V&H and Bayliss had made a good match, with lots of wins in prospect to bless their union.

Carl Fogarty's broken arm may have offered an unexpected World Superbike opportunity to Troy after a winter's preparation for AMA action, but it's not hyperbole to suggest that Bayliss had salvaged the factory Ducati team's fortunes almost single handedly by the end of the season.

Bayliss set about the best in the world, on unfamiliar circuits, in exactly the same fashion as he had in the UK two seasons earlier, and took his first World Championship victory at Hockenheim where novices aren't supposed to be able to win. Even being punted off the circuit twice in his first outing for the Infostrada Ducati team didn't faze him.

Rocketing into the top six despite missing three rounds, Bayliss looked like he had been riding at world level all his life, and despite his 31 years he may yet feature prominently in Ducati's future plans for world domination.

John **Reynolds**

Born
27 June 1965
Nottingham,
Great Britain

First win
2000 Round 13/Race 1
Brands Hatch,
Great Britain II
Ducati 996

Championships
1995 10th
1996 12th
2000 17th

1 Race win
2000 Great Britain II 1

Vindication at last

It's a cliché to say that you can never rationalise the off-track persona with the cut-throat on-track demeanour, but that describes John Reynolds perfectly. In action this polite, quiet family man is as tough as any of the young guns who have tried to beat him over the years.

John was another late comer to the tarmac after a successful career in schoolboy motocross. His first road race was on a classic Velocette! It was rapidly apparent that he was very good. Ron Haslam lent a hand early on but the fans really noticed John when he joined Kawasaki and fought an epic season-long Supersport battle with tough-guy Jim Moodie. In Superbike he won British Championships. But he suffered more than most from the lack of belief in British talent from the factory teams.

John went GP 500 racing for a year with Padgett's Harris Yamaha. But his chance for a serious campaign at world level came with help from Ben Atkins who set up the Reve Racing team to go World Superbike racing with semi-works Kawasakis. John's rostrum finishes at Brands and Assen were impressive enough to get him a ride on the new works Suzuki in 1996. The new-generation GSX-R750 suffered severe teething problems however and John returned to British Championship racing. Joining Atkins again, with multiple British Champion Roger Marshall as manager, John was a vital ingredient of the domestic scene's return to credibility.

For all these and other reasons the crowd was happy to see him get a World Championship win at last. In the re-arranged final round of the 2000 season, on a drying Brands Hatch track he led the first race for all but two laps, fighting off Troy Bayliss and Chris Walker. Champion Colin Edwards closed rapidly on intermediate tyres but fell before getting to grips with the leading group. Reynolds previously had his eye on a future in touring car racing – but now he has had a taste of the big time that just may have to wait.

Appendix:

Results

World Superbike Manufacturers' Championship

1988	Honda
1989	Honda
1990	Honda
1991	Ducati
1992	Ducati
1993	Ducati
1994	Ducati
1995	Ducati
1996	Ducati
1997	Honda
1998	Ducati
1999	Ducati
2000	Ducati

Daytona Superbike Race Winners

Year	Rider	Make
1976	S McLaughlin	BMW
1977	C Neilson	Ducati
1978	S McLaughlin	Suzuki
1979	R Pierce	Suzuki
1980	G Crosby	Suzuki
	F Spencer	Honda
1981	W Cooley	Suzuki
	F Spencer	Honda
1982	F Spencer	Honda
	M Baldwin	Honda
1983	F Spencer	Honda
	F Merkel	Honda
1984	F Spencer	Honda
	F Merkel	Honda
1985	*F Spencer	Honda
	F Merkel	Honda
1986	E Lawson	Yamaha
1987	W Rainey	Honda
1988	K Schwantz	Suzuki
1989	J Ashmead	Honda
1990	D Sadowski	Yamaha
1991	M DuHamel	Honda
1992	S Russell	Kawasaki
1993	E Lawson	Yamaha
1994	S Russell	Kawasaki
1995	S Russell	Kawasaki
1996	M DuHamel	Honda
1997	S Russell	Yamaha
1998	S Russell	Yamaha
1999	M DuHamel	Honda
2000	M Mladin	Suzuki

*Superbike became the Daytona 200 Mile formula in 1985

American Superbike Champions

Year	Rider	Make
1976	R Pridmore	BMW
1977	R Pridmore	Kawasaki
1978	R Pridmore	Kawasaki
1979	W Cooley	Suzuki
1980	W Cooley	Suzuki
1981	E Lawson	Kawasaki
1982	E Lawson	Kawasaki
1983	W Rainey	Kawasaki
1984	F Merkel	Honda
1985	F Merkel	Honda
1986	F Merkel	Honda
1987	W Rainey	Honda
1988	B Shobert	Honda
1989	J James	Suzuki
1990	D Chandler	Kawasaki
1991	T Stevens	Yamaha
1992	S Russell	Kawasaki
1993	D Polen	Ducati
1994	T Corser	Ducati
1995	M DuHamel	Honda
1996	D Chandler	Kawasaki
1997	D Chandler	Kawasaki
1998	B Bostrom	Ducati
1999	M Mladin	Suzuki
2000	M Mladin	Suzuki

German Pro-Superbike Champions

Year	Rider	Make
1991	U Mark	Yamaha
1992	E Weibel	Ducati
1993	E Weibel	Ducati
1994	U Mark	Ducati
1995	J Schmid	Kawasaki
1996	C Lindholm	Ducati
1997	C Lindholm	Yamaha
1998	A Meklau	Ducati
1999	C Lindholm	Yamaha

Australian Superbike Champions

Year	Rider	Make
1989	M Campbell	Honda
1990	M Campbell	Honda
1991	A Slight	Kawasaki
1992	M Mladin	Kawasaki
1993	T Corser	Honda
1994	A Gobert	Honda
1995	K McCarthy	Honda
1996	P Goddard	Suzuki
1997	M Craggill	Kawasaki
1998	M Craggill	Kawasaki
1999	S Martin	Ducati
2000	S Giles	Suzuki

British Superbike Champions

Year	Rider	Make
1995	S Hislop	Kawasaki
1996	N Mackenzie	Yamaha
1997	N Mackenzie	Yamaha
1998	N Mackenzie	Yamaha
1999	T Bayliss	Ducati
2000	N Hodgson	Ducati

Japanese Superbike Champions

Year	Rider	Make
1994	W Yoshikawa	Yamaha
1995	T Aoki	Honda
1996	T Aoki	Honda
1997	N Haga	Yamaha
1998	W Yoshikawa	Yamaha
1999	S Itoh	Honda

1988 SEASON

Round 1 – Great Britain
Donington Park, 3 April
Race 1 & 2, aggregate result
1 M Lucchinelli, Ita, Ducati
2 F Merkel, USA, Honda
3 J Dunlop, GB, Honda
4 R Marshall, GB, Suzuki
5 F Pirovano, Ita, Yamaha
6 K Irons, GB, Honda
7 J Suhonen, Fin, Yamaha
8 A McGladdery, GB, Suzuki
9 S Williams, GB, Bimota
10 M Farmer, GB, Suzuki
11 D Leach, GB, Yamaha
12 T Douglas, Can, Yamaha
13 J Lofthouse, GB, Suzuki
14 A Moyce, GB, Kawasaki
15 E Kuparinen, Fin, Kawasaki

Standings – 1 Lucchinelli 20;
2 Merkel 17; 3 Dunlop 15;
4 Marshall 13; 5 Pirovano 11;
6 Irons 10

Round 2 – Hungary
Hungaroring, 30 April
Race 1
1 F Merkel, USA, Honda
2 D Tardozzi, Ita, Bimota
3 S Mertens, Bel, Bimota
4 A Morillas, Fra, Kawasaki
5 F Pirovano, Ita, Yamaha
6 J Dunlop, GB, Honda
7 R Rasmussen, Den, Suzuki
8 R Burnett, GB, Honda
9 M Lucchinelli, Ita, Ducati
10 E Gschwender, Ger, Suzuki
11 E Delcamp, Fra, Kawasaki
12 P Iddon, GB, Bimota
13 M Galinski, Ger, Bimota
14 J Suhonen, Fin, Yamaha
15 A McGladdery, GB, Suzuki

Race 2
1 A Morillas, Fra, Kawasaki
2 S Mertens, Bel, Bimota
3 D Tardozzi, Ita, Bimota
4 R Burnett, GB, Honda
5 F Merkel, USA, Honda
6 F Pirovano, Ita, Yamaha
7 R Rasmussen, Den, Suzuki
8 P Iddon, GB, Bimota
9 E Gschwender, Ger, Suzuki
10 J Suhonen, Fin, Yamaha
11 V Ferrari, Ita, Honda
12 A Andersson, Swe, Suzuki
13 E Delcamp, Fra, Kawasaki
14 P Rubatto, Ger, Bimota
15 J-L Guignabodet, Fra, Honda

Standings – 1 Merkel 32.5;
2 Lucchinelli 23.5; 3 Pirovano 21.5;
4 Dunlop 20; 5 Morillas 16.5;
6 Mertens & Tardozzi 16

Round 3 – Germany
Hockenheim, 8 May
Race 1
1 D Tardozzi, Ita, Bimota
2 C Bouheben, Fra, Honda
3 A Vieira, Fra, Honda
4 E Weibel, CH, Honda
5 R Burnett, GB, Honda
6 M Lucchinelli, Ita, Ducati
7 J Dunlop, GB, Honda
8 A Hofmann, Ger, Honda
9 E Delcamp, Fra, Kawasaki
10 V Ferrari, Ita, Honda
11 F Pirovano, Ita, Yamaha
12 P Iddon, GB, Bimota

13 S Mertens, Bel, Bimota
14 K Irons, GB, Honda
15 P Rubatto, Ger, Bimota

Race 2
1 D Tardozzi, Ita, Bimota
2 S Mertens, Bel, Bimota
3 A Vieira, Fra, Honda
4 R Burnett, GB, Honda
5 J Dunlop, GB, Honda
6 E Delcamp, Fra, Kawasaki
7 K Irons, GB, Honda
8 F Pirovano, Ita, Yamaha
9 V Ferrari, Ita, Honda
10 A Hofmann, Ger, Honda
11 M Lucchinelli, Ita, Ducati
12 B Schmidt, Ger, Bimota
13 P Iddon, GB, Bimota
14 P Rubatto, Ger, Bimota
15 M Galinski, Ger, Bimota

Standings – 1 Tardozzi 36;
2 Merkel 32.5; 3 Lucchinelli 31;
4 Dunlop 30; 5 Pirovano 28;
6 Mertens 26

Round 4 – Austria
Osterreichring, 3 July
Race 1
1 M Lucchinelli, Ita, Ducati
2 F Pirovano, Ita, Yamaha
3 M Campbell, Aus, Honda
4 A Vieira, Fra, Honda
5 D Tardozzi, Ita, Bimota
6 E Weibel, CH, Honda
7 A Morillas, Fra, Kawasaki
8 R Phillis, Aus, Kawasaki
9 A Andersson, Swe, Suzuki
10 E Gschwender, Ger, Suzuki
11 K-H Reigl, Aut, Bimota
12 D Kemter, Aut, Honda
13 U Mark, Ger, Bimota
14 D Heinen, Bel, Honda
15 M Ricci, Ita, Ducati

Race 2
1 D Tardozzi, Ita, Bimota
2 C Bouheben, Fra, Honda
3 A Vieira, Fra, Honda
4 E Weibel, CH, Honda
5 A Morillas, Fra, Kawasaki
6 M Campbell, Aus, Honda
7 F Pirovano, Ita, Yamaha
8 F Merkel, USA, Honda
9 M Fabbri, Ita, Bimota
10 E Gschwender, Ger, Suzuki
11 P Ramon, Bel, Honda
12 A Andersson, Swe, Suzuki
13 J Suhonen, Fin, Yamaha
14 U Mark, Ger, Bimota
15 D Kemter, Aut, Honda

Standings – 1 Tardozzi 51.5;
2 Lucchinelli & Pirovano 41;
4 Merkel 36.5; 5 Dunlop 30;
6 Vieira 29

Round 5 – Japan
Sugo, 28 August
Race 1
1 G Goodfellow, Can, Suzuki
2 F Merkel, USA, Honda
3 Y Oshima, Jap, Suzuki
4 S Mertens, Bel, Bimota
5 M Watanabe, Jap, Yamaha
6 R Phillis, Aus, Kawasaki
7 A Slight, NZ, Bimota
8 T Hanamura, Jap, Honda
9 K Kobayashi, Jap, Honda
10 V Ferrari, Ita, Honda
11 T Kaneko, Jap, Yamaha

12 M Lucchinelli, Ita, Ducati
13 H Nakamura, Jap, Suzuki
14 S Endo, Jap, Honda
15 A Andersson, Swe, Suzuki

Race 2
1 M Doohan, Aus, Yamaha
2 K Iwahashi, Jap, Honda
3 G Goodfellow, Can, Suzuki
4 D Tardozzi, Ita, Bimota
5 E Weibel, CH, Honda
6 R Phillis, Aus, Kawasaki
7 B Morrison, GB, Honda
8 V Ferrari, Ita, Honda
9 T Hanamura, Jap, Honda
10 F Pirovano, Ita, Yamaha
11 F Merkel, USA, Honda
12 K Kobayashi, Jap, Honda
13 Y Oshima, Jap, Suzuki
14 A Slight, NZ, Bimota
15 M Campbell, Aus, Honda

Standings – 1 Tardozzi 58;
2 Merkel 47.5; 3 Pirovano 44;
4 Lucchinelli 43; 5 Mertens 32.5;
6 Dunlop 30

Round 6 – France
Le Mans, 4 September
Race 1
1 F Pirovano, Ita, Yamaha
2 E Delcamp, Fra, Kawasaki
3 S Mertens, Bel, Bimota
4 A Vieira, Fra, Honda
5 C Bouheben, Fra, Honda
6 F Merkel, USA, Honda
7 R Burnett, GB, Honda
8 T Rymer, GB, Honda
9 M Fabbri, Ita, Bimota
10 M Lucchinelli, Ita, Ducati
11 J Suhonen, Fin, Yamaha
12 D Tardozzi, Ita, Bimota
13 A Andersson, Swe, Suzuki
14 J-Y Mounier, Fra, Yamaha
15 M Linscott, GB, Honda

Standings – 1 Pirovano 64;
2 Tardozzi 62; 3 Merkel 57.5;
4 Lucchinelli 49; 5 Mertens 47.5;
6 Vieira 42

Round 7 – Portugal
Estoril, 11 September
Race 1
1 D Tardozzi, Ita, Bimota
2 S Mertens, Bel, Bimota
3 M Lucchinelli, Ita, Ducati
4 F Merkel, USA, Honda
5 T Rymer, GB, Honda
6 F Pirovano, Ita, Yamaha
7 P Rubatto, Ger, Bimota
8 A Andersson, Swe, Suzuki
9 P Iddon, GB, Bimota
10 R Dunlop, GB, Honda
11 M Ricci, Ita, Ducati
12 E Gschwender, Ger, Suzuki
13 A Grushka, Ger, Honda
14 J-L Guignabodet, Fra, Honda
15 A McGladdery, GB, Honda

Race 2
1 S Mertens, Bel, Bimota
2 D Tardozzi, Ita, Bimota
3 T Rymer, GB, Honda
4 M Lucchinelli, Ita, Ducati
5 F Merkel, USA, Honda
6 F Pirovano, Ita, Yamaha
7 R Dunlop, GB, Honda
8 P Iddon, GB, Bimota
9 A Andersson, Swe, Suzuki
10 M Ricci, Ita, Ducati
11 M Fabbri, Ita, Bimota
12 A McGladdery, GB, Honda
13 J Suhonen, Fin, Yamaha
14 A Grushka, Ger, Honda
15 J-L Guignabodet, Fra, Honda

Standings – 1 Tardozzi 80.5;
2 Pirovano 74; 3 Merkel 69.5;
4 Mertens 66; 5 Lucchinelli 63;
6 Vieira 42

Round 8 – Australia
Oran Park, 25 September
Race 1
1 M Doohan, Aus, Yamaha
2 M Dowson, Aus, Yamaha
3 R Phillis, Aus, Kawasaki
4 F Merkel, USA, Honda
5 M Campbell, Aus, Honda
6 F Pirovano, Ita, Yamaha
7 S Mertens, Bel, Bimota
8 G Goodfellow, Can, Honda
9 R Scolyer, Aus, Honda
10 S Gallagher, Aus, Honda
11 D Tardozzi, Ita, Bimota
12 A McGladdery, GB, Honda
13 R Dunlop, GB, Honda
14 T Rymer, GB, Honda
15 I Pero, Aus, Suzuki

Race 2
1 M Doohan, Aus, Yamaha
2 M Dowson, Aus, Yamaha
3 F Merkel, USA, Honda
4 R Phillis, Aus, Kawasaki
5 G Goodfellow, Can, Honda
6 S Mertens, Bel, Bimota
7 F Pirovano, Ita, Yamaha
8 M Campbell, Aus, Honda
9 R Scolyer, Aus, Honda
10 D Tardozzi, Ita, Bimota
11 T Rymer, GB, Honda
12 S Gallagher, Aus, Honda
13 A McGladdery, GB, Honda
14 R Dunlop, GB, Honda
15 L Willing, Aus, Yamaha

Standings – 1 Tardozzi 86;
2 Merkel & Pirovano 83.5;
4 Mertens 75.5; 5 Lucchinelli 63;
6 Vieira 42

Round 9 – New Zealand
Manfeild Park, 2 October
Race 1
1 F Merkel, USA, Honda
2 F Pirovano, Ita, Yamaha
3 G Goodfellow, Can, Honda
4 R Phillis, Aus, Kawasaki
5 D Tardozzi, Ita, Bimota
6 S Mertens, Bel, Bimota
7 T Douglas, Can, Yamaha
8 R Scolyer, Aus, Honda
9 T Rymer, GB, Honda
10 G Williams, NZ, Ducati
11 M Campbell, Aus, Honda
12 M King, NZ, Ducati
13 A Stroud, NZ, Bimota
14 A McGladdery, GB, Honda
15 R Dunlop, GB, Honda

Race 2
1 S Mertens, Bel, Bimota
2 M Campbell, Aus, Honda
3 R Phillis, Aus, Kawasaki
4 R Scolyer, Aus, Honda
5 F Merkel, USA, Honda
6 G Goodfellow, Can, Honda
7 T Rymer, GB, Honda
8 G Williams, NZ, Ducati
9 A Stroud, NZ, Bimota
10 A McGladdery, GB, Honda
11 T Douglas, Can, Yamaha
12 R Dunlop, GB, Honda
13 F Pirovano, Ita, Yamaha
14 D Warren, NZ, Honda
15 M King, NZ, Ducati

Final Standings – 1 Merkel 99;
2 Pirovano 93.5; 3 Tardozzi 91.5;
4 Mertens 90.5; 5 Lucchinelli 63;
6 Phillis & Vieira 42

1989 SEASON
Round 1 – Great Britain
Donington Park, 27 March
Race 1
1 F Pirovano, Ita, Yamaha
2 R Burnett, GB, Honda
3 T Rymer, GB, Yamaha
4 F Merkel, USA, Honda
5 T Crine, Fra, Suzuki
6 A Andersson, Swe, Yamaha
7 C Fogarty, GB, Honda
8 B Morrison, GB, Honda
9 A Hofmann, CH, Honda
10 P Igoa, Fra, Kawasaki
11 E Gschwender, Ger, Suzuki
12 M Phillips, GB, Yamaha
13 P Rubatto, Ger, Bimota
14 H Moineau, Fra, Suzuki
15 C Bouheben, Fra, Kawasaki

Race 2
1 G Falappa, Ita, Bimota
2 T Rymer, GB, Yamaha
3 R Burnett, GB, Honda
4 S Hislop, GB, Honda
5 A Andersson, Swe, Yamaha
6 F Merkel, USA, Honda
7 E Gschwender, Ger, Suzuki
8 P Rubatto, Ger, Bimota
9 M Phillips, GB, Yamaha
10 P Igoa, Fra, Kawasaki
11 A McGladdery, GB, Honda
12 P Iddon, GB, Bimota
13 C Fogarty, GB, Honda
14 R Rasmussen, Den, Suzuki
15 R Delaby, Lux, Honda

Standings – 1 Burnett & Rymer 32;
3 Merkel 23; 4 Andersson 21;
5 Falappa & Pirovano 20

Round 2 – Hungary
Hungaroring, 30 April
Race 1
1 F Merkel, USA, Honda
2 R Roche, Fra, Ducati
3 F Pirovano, Ita, Yamaha
4 R McElnea, GB, Yamaha
5 S Mertens, Bel, Honda
6 A Andersson, Swe, Yamaha
7 T Rymer, GB, Yamaha
8 E Gschwender, Ger, Suzuki
9 G Falappa, Ita, Bimota
10 B Morrison, GB, Honda
11 A Hofmann, CH, Honda
12 R Rasmussen, Den, Suzuki
13 P Igoa, Fra, Kawasaki
14 J Suhonen, Fin, Yamaha
15 M Campbell, Aus, Honda

Race 2
1 F Merkel, USA, Honda
2 F Pirovano, Ita, Yamaha
3 R McElnea, GB, Yamaha
4 G Falappa, Ita, Bimota
5 B Monti, Ita, Ducati
6 S Mertens, Bel, Honda
7 A Andersson, Swe, Yamaha
8 R Rasmussen, Den, Suzuki
9 T Rymer, GB, Yamaha
10 P Rubatto, Ger, Bimota
11 J Suhonen, Fin, Yamaha
12 M Campbell, Aus, Honda
13 B Morrison, GB, Honda
14 A Hofmann, CH, Honda
15 P Igoa, Fra, Kawasaki

Standings – 1 Merkel 63;
2 Pirovano 52; 3 Rymer 48;
4 Andersson & Falappa 40;
6 Burnett 32

Round 3 – Canada
Mosport Park, 4 June
Race 1
1 F Merkel, USA, Honda
2 R Roche, Fra, Ducati
3 R McMurter, Can, Honda
4 S Mertens, Bel, Honda
5 S Crevier, Can, Yamaha
6 F Pirovano, Ita, Yamaha
7 J Suhonen, Fin, Yamaha
8 M Baldwin, USA, Bimota
9 A Andersson, Swe, Yamaha
10 T Douglas, Can, Yamaha
11 M Mercier, Can, Suzuki
12 P Iddon, GB, Bimota
13 R Rasmussen, Den, Suzuki
14 W von Muralt, CH, Honda
15 M Fabbri, Ita, Bimota

Race 2
1 G Falappa, Ita, Bimota
2 R McMurter, Can, Honda
3 F Merkel, USA, Honda
4 F Pirovano, Ita, Yamaha
5 S Mertens, Bel, Honda
6 M Baldwin, USA, Bimota
7 B Monti, Ita, Ducati
8 T Rymer, GB, Yamaha
9 J Suhonen, Fin, Yamaha
10 G Goodfellow, Can, Suzuki
11 A Andersson, Swe, Yamaha
12 F Biliotti, Ita, Bimota
13 D Tardozzi, Ita, Bimota
14 M Mercier, Can, Suzuki
15 R Rasmussen, Den, Suzuki

Standings – 1 Merkel 98;
2 Pirovano 75; 3 Falappa 60;
4 Rymer 56; 5 Andersson 52;
6 Mertens 45

Round 4 – USA
Brainerd International Raceway,
11 June
Race 1
1 R Roche, Fra, Ducati
2 F Pirovano, Ita, Yamaha
3 S Mertens, Bel, Honda
4 F Merkel, USA, Honda
5 T Rymer, GB, Yamaha
6 B Monti, Ita, Ducati
7 M Baldwin, USA, Bimota
8 A Andersson, Swe, Yamaha
9 T Douglas, Can, Yamaha
10 R Arnaiz, USA, Yamaha
11 R McMurter, Can, Honda
12 F Biliotti, Ita, Bimota
13 G Goodfellow, Can, Suzuki
14 M Fabbri, Ita, Bimota
15 R Delaby, Lux, Honda

Race 2
1 R Roche, Fra, Ducati
2 S Mertens, Bel, Honda
3 F Merkel, USA, Honda
4 F Pirovano, Ita, Yamaha
5 T Rymer, GB, Yamaha
6 B Monti, Ita, Ducati
7 A Andersson, Swe, Yamaha
8 F Biliotti, Ita, Bimota
9 T Douglas, Can, Yamaha
10 G Goodfellow, Can, Suzuki
11 D Tardozzi, Ita, Bimota
12 D Chandler, USA, Kawasaki
13 R Delaby, Lux, Honda
14 M Fabbri, Ita, Bimota
15 W von Muralt, CH, Honda

Standings – 1 Merkel 126; 2 Pirovano 105;
3 Rymer 78; 4 Mertens 77;
5 Roche 74; 6 Andersson 69

Round 5 – Austria
Osterreichring, 2 July
Race 1
1 A Vieira, Fra, Honda
2 R Roche, Fra, Ducati
3 S Mertens, Bel, Honda
4 M Broccoli, Ita, Ducati
5 F Pirovano, Ita, Yamaha
6 B Monti, Ita, Ducati
7 M Campbell, Aus, Honda
8 A Andersson, Swe, Yamaha
9 T Rymer, GB, Yamaha
10 J Suhonen, Fin, Yamaha
11 F Merkel, USA, Honda
12 P Igoa, Fra, Kawasaki
13 G Falappa, Ita, Bimota
14 P Bolle, Fra, Kawasaki
15 E Gschwender, Ger, Suzuki

Race 2
1 S Mertens, Bel, Honda
2 F Pirovano, Ita, Yamaha
3 F Merkel, USA, Honda
4 M Broccoli, Ita, Ducati
5 P Igoa, Fra, Kawasaki
6 M Campbell, Aus, Honda
7 J Suhonen, Fin, Yamaha
8 A Vieira, Fra, Honda
9 A Andersson, Swe, Yamaha
10 R Roche, Fra, Ducati
11 E Gschwender, Ger, Suzuki
12 D Tardozzi, Ita, Bimota
13 M Ricci, Ita, Kawasaki
14 B Monti, Ita, Ducati
15 R Delaby, Lux, Honda

Standings – 1 Merkel 146;
2 Pirovano 133; 3 Mertens 112;
4 Roche 97; 5 Rymer 85;
6 Andersson 84

Round 6 – France
Circuit Paul Ricard, 30 July
Race 1
1 S Mertens, Bel, Honda
2 M Baldwin, USA, Bimota
3 R Roche, Fra, Ducati
4 T Rymer, GB, Yamaha
5 G Falappa, Ita, Bimota
6 J-Y Mounier, Fra, Yamaha
7 B Monti, Ita, Ducati
8 F Merkel, USA, Honda
9 D Tardozzi, Ita, Bimota
10 A Andersson, Swe, Yamaha
11 P Bolle, Fra, Kawasaki
12 R Rasmussen, Den, Suzuki
13 J de Vries, Nl, Yamaha
14 M Coq, Fra, Yamaha
15 D Handi, Fra, Yamaha

Race 2
1 G Falappa, Ita, Bimota
2 R Roche, Fra, Ducati
3 S Mertens, Bel, Honda
4 F Merkel, USA, Honda
5 M Baldwin, USA, Bimota
6 B Monti, Ita, Ducati
7 A Andersson, Swe, Yamaha
8 D Tardozzi, Ita, Bimota
9 P Bolle, Fra, Kawasaki
10 P Iddon, GB, Bimota
11 M Coq, Fra, Yamaha
12 R Rasmussen, Den, Suzuki
13 J-Y Mounier, Fra, Yamaha
14 E Weibel, CH, Kawasaki
15 E Delcamp, Fra, Yamaha

Standings – 1 Merkel 167;
2 Mertens 147; 3 Pirovano 133;
4 Roche 129; 5 Andersson 99;
6 Rymer 98

Round 7 – Japan
Sugo, 27 August
Race 1
1 D Polen, USA, Suzuki
2 M Dowson, Aus, Yamaha
3 R Phillis, Aus, Kawasaki
4 G Falappa, Ita, Bimota
5 T Arata, Jap, Yamaha
6 K Iwahashi, Jap, Honda
7 F Pirovano, Ita, Yamaha
8 S Mertens, Bel, Honda
9 A Slight, NZ, Kawasaki
10 N Abe, Jap, Honda
11 S Tsukamoto, Jap, Kawasaki
12 D Tardozzi, Ita, Bimota
13 R Roche, Fra, Ducati
14 S Doohan, Aus, Bimota
15 M Campbell, Aus, Honda

Race 2
1 M Dowson, Aus, Yamaha
2 K Iwahashi, Jap, Honda
3 G Falappa, Ita, Bimota
4 D Polen, USA, Suzuki
5 T Sohwa, Jap, Kawasaki
6 R Phillis, Aus, Kawasaki
7 A Slight, NZ, Kawasaki
8 S Mertens, Bel, Honda
9 T Arata, Jap, Yamaha
10 M Campbell, Aus, Honda
11 S Tsukamoto, Jap, Kawasaki
12 F Merkel, USA, Honda
13 T Rymer, GB, Yamaha
14 K Kobayashi, Jap, Honda
15 K Takeuchi, Jap, Yamaha

Standings – 1 Merkel 171;
2 Mertens 163; 3 Pirovano 142;
4 Roche 132; 5 Falappa 122;
6 Rymer 101

Round 8 – Germany
Hockenheim, 17 September
Race 1
1 R Roche, Fra, Ducati
2 S Mertens, Bel, Honda
3 A Vieira, Fra, Honda
4 F Pirovano, Ita, Yamaha
5 A Andersson, Swe, Yamaha
6 M Baldwin, USA, Bimota
7 A Hofmann, CH, Honda
8 F Merkel, USA, Honda
9 P Igoa, Fra, Kawasaki
10 J Suhonen, Fin, Yamaha
11 B Schmidt, Ger, Yamaha
12 R Burnett, GB, Honda
13 E Weibel, CH, Kawasaki
14 J-Y Mounier, Fra, Yamaha
15 G McGregor, Aus, Honda

Race 2
1 R Roche, Fra, Ducati
2 G Falappa, Ita, Bimota
3 S Mertens, Bel, Honda
4 F Merkel, USA, Honda
5 A Andersson, Swe, Yamaha
6 F Pirovano, Ita, Yamaha
7 M Baldwin, USA, Bimota
8 A Vieira, Fra, Honda
9 P Igoa, Fra, Kawasaki
10 M Lucchinelli, Ita, Ducati
11 B Schmidt, Ger, Yamaha
12 A Hofmann, CH, Honda
13 U Mark, Ger, Yamaha
14 J Suhonen, Fin, Yamaha
15 C Bouheben, Fra, Kawasaki

Standings – 1 Mertens 195;
2 Merkel 192; 3 Roche 172;
4 Pirovano 165; 5 Falappa 139;
6 Andersson 121

Round 9 – Italy
Pergusa, 24 September
Race 1
1 S Mertens, Bel, Honda
2 F Merkel, USA, Honda
3 F Pirovano, Ita, Yamaha
4 B Monti, Ita, Ducati
5 A Andersson, Swe, Yamaha
6 J Suhonen, Fin, Yamaha
7 P Igoa, Fra, Kawasaki
8 D Tardozzi, Ita, Bimota
9 M Lucchinelli, Ita, Ducati
10 P Bontempi, Ita, Honda
11 A Harmati, Hun, Honda
12 C Manici, Ita, Ducati
13 A Presciutti, Ita, Honda
14 S Ricchetti, Ita, Honda
15 A Narducci, Ita, Honda

Race 2
1 R Roche, Fra, Ducati
2 F Merkel, USA, Honda
3 B Monti, Ita, Ducati
4 F Pirovano, Ita, Yamaha
5 J Suhonen, Fin, Yamaha
6 P Igoa, Fra, Kawasaki
7 S Mertens, Bel, Honda
8 C Bouheben, Fra, Kawasaki
9 M Fabbri, Ita, Bimota
10 M dall'Aglio, Ita, Yamaha
11 A Harmati, Hun, Honda
12 P Bontempi, Ita, Honda
13 A Presciutti, Ita, Honda
14 C Manici, Ita, Ducati
15 O La Ferla, Ita, Yamaha

Standings – 1 Merkel 226;
2 Mertens 224; 3 Pirovano 193;
4 Roche 192; 5 Falappa 139;
6 Andersson 132

Round 10 – Australia
Oran Park, 12 November
Race 1
1 P Goddard, Aus, Yamaha
2 R Phillis, Aus, Kawasaki
3 F Pirovano, Ita, Yamaha
4 R Roche, Fra, Ducati
5 A Slight, NZ, Kawasaki
6 A Andersson, Swe, Yamaha
7 M Dowson, Aus, Yamaha
8 S Mertens, Bel, Honda
9 R Bongers, Aus, Yamaha
10 S Doohan, Aus, Suzuki
11 F Merkel, USA, Honda
12 J Suhonen, Fin, Yamaha
13 J Richards, Aus, Yamaha
14 T Sohwa, Jap, Kawasaki
15 S Martin, Aus, Suzuki

Race 2
1 M Dowson, Aus, Yamaha
2 R Roche, Fra, Ducati
3 R Phillis, Aus, Kawasaki
4 S Mertens, Bel, Honda
5 F Merkel, USA, Honda
6 A Slight, NZ, Kawasaki
7 T Sohwa, Jap, Kawasaki
8 R Bongers, Aus, Yamaha
9 M Blair, Aus, Suzuki
10 G Morris, Aus, Ducati
11 R Scolyer, Aus, Honda
12 S Crevier, Can, Yamaha
13 A Roberts, Aus, Yamaha
14 A McGladdery, GB, Honda
15 J Richards, Aus, Yamaha

Standings – 1 Mertens 245;
2 Merkel 242; 3 Roche 222;
4 Pirovano 208; 5 Andersson 142;
6 Falappa 139

Round 11 – New Zealand
Manfeild Park, 19 November
Race 1
1 T Rymer, GB, Yamaha
2 A Slight, NZ, Kawasaki
3 F Merkel, USA, Honda
4 M Dowson, Aus, Yamaha
5 R Phillis, Aus, Kawasaki
6 J Suhonen, Fin, Yamaha
7 A Andersson, Swe, Yamaha
8 G Williams, NZ, Ducati
9 T Sohwa, Jap, Kawasaki
10 S Crafar, NZ, Yamaha
11 E Kattenberg, NZ, Suzuki
12 R Josiah, NZ, Kawasaki
13 A McGladdery, GB, Honda
14 B Bernard, NZ, Suzuki
15 A Stroud, NZ, Yamaha

Race 2
1 S Mertens, Bel, Honda
2 M Campbell, Aus, Honda
3 F Merkel, USA, Honda
4 T Rymer, GB, Yamaha
5 R Phillis, Aus, Kawasaki
6 A Stroud, NZ, Yamaha
7 J Suhonen, Fin, Yamaha
8 A Andersson, Swe, Yamaha
9 T Sohwa, Jap, Kawasaki
10 S Crafar, NZ, Yamaha
11 A McGladdery, GB, Honda
12 G Ramage, NZ, Suzuki
13 E Kattenberg, NZ, Suzuki
14 R Josiah, NZ, Kawasaki
15 G Williams, NZ, Ducati

Final Standings – 1 Merkel 272;
2 Mertens 265; 3 Roche 222;
4 Pirovano 208; 5 Andersson 159;
6 Falappa 139

1990 SEASON
Round 1 – Spain
Jerez, 18 March
Race 1
1 R Roche, Fra, Ducati
2 F Merkel, USA, Honda
3 S Mertens, Bel, Honda
4 R Phillis, Aus, Kawasaki
5 G Falappa, Ita, Ducati
6 F Pirovano, Ita, Yamaha
7 T Rymer, GB, Yamaha
8 R McElnea, GB, Yamaha
9 A Andersson, Swe, Yamaha
10 E Gschwender, Ger, Suzuki
11 D Tardozzi, Ita, Ducati
12 J Lopez Mella, Spa, Honda
13 B Morrison, GB, Honda
14 C Fogarty, GB, Honda
15 E Weibel, CH, Kawasaki

Race 2
1 R Roche, Fra, Ducati
2 G Falappa, Ita, Ducati
3 F Merkel, USA, Honda
4 S Mertens, Bel, Honda
5 R Phillis, Aus, Kawasaki
6 R McElnea, GB, Yamaha
7 T Rymer, GB, Yamaha
8 F Pirovano, Ita, Yamaha
9 E Gschwender, Ger, Suzuki
10 D Amatriain, Spa, Honda
11 B Monti, Ita, Honda
12 A Andersson, Swe, Yamaha
13 A Hofmann, Ger, Honda
14 J de Vries, Nl, Yamaha
15 U Mark, Ger, Yamaha

Standings – 1 Roche 40; 2 Merkel 32;
3 Mertens & Falappa 28; 5 Phillis 24;
6 Rymer, McElnea & Pirovano 18

Round 2 – Great Britain
Donington Park, 16 April
Race 1
1 F Merkel, USA, Honda
2 R Roche, Fra, Ducati
3 S Mertens, Bel, Honda
4 R Phillis, Aus, Kawasaki
5 F Pirovano, Ita, Yamaha
6 C Fogarty, GB, Honda
7 G Falappa, Ita, Ducati
8 D Tardozzi, Ita, Ducati
9 U Mark, Ger, Yamaha
10 B Monti, Ita, Ducati
11 R Stringer, GB, Yamaha
12 J Whitham, GB, Honda
13 N Mackenzie, GB, Yamaha
14 B Morrison, GB, Honda
15 E Gschwender, Ger, Suzuki

Race 2
1 G Falappa, Ita, Ducati
2 R Roche, Fra, Ducati
3 F Merkel, USA, Honda
4 N Mackenzie, GB, Yamaha
5 F Pirovano, Ita, Yamaha
6 C Fogarty, GB, Honda
7 R Phillis, Aus, Kawasaki
8 S Mertens, Bel, Honda
9 A Andersson, Swe, Yamaha
10 U Mark, Ger, Yamaha
11 B Monti, Ita, Honda
12 E Gschwender, Ger, Suzuki
13 E Weibel, CH, Kawasaki
14 J de Vries, Nl, Yamaha
15 B Morrison, GB, Honda

Standings – 1 Roche 74;
2 Merkel 67; 3 Falappa 57;
4 Mertens 51; 5 Phillis 46;
6 Pirovano 40

Round 3 – Hungary
Hungaroring, 30 April
Race 1
1 F Merkel, USA, Honda
2 R Roche, Fra, Ducati
3 F Pirovano, Ita, Yamaha
4 M Campbell, Aus, Honda
5 R McElnea, GB, Yamaha
6 S Mertens, Bel, Honda
7 A Andersson, Swe, Yamaha
8 T Rymer, GB, Yamaha
9 B Monti, Ita, Honda
10 R Phillis, Aus, Kawasaki
11 D Amatriain, Spa, Honda
12 J Lopez Mella, Spa, Honda
13 E Gschwender, Ger, Suzuki
14 J de Vries, Nl, Yamaha
15 B Morrison, GB, Honda

Race 2
1 R Roche, Fra, Ducati
2 M Campbell, Aus, Honda
3 S Mertens, Bel, Honda
4 R McElnea, GB, Yamaha
5 T Rymer, GB, Yamaha
6 F Merkel, USA, Honda
7 G Falappa, Ita, Ducati
8 F Pirovano, Ita, Yamaha
9 D Tardozzi, Ita, Ducati
10 E Weibel, CH, Kawasaki
11 B Monti, Ita, Honda
12 D Amatriain, Spa, Honda
13 J de Vries, Nl, Yamaha
14 J Suhonen, Fin, Yamaha
15 M Galinski, Ger, Kawasaki

Standings – 1 Roche 111;
2 Merkel 97; 3 Mertens 76;
4 Falappa 66; 5 Pirovano 63;
6 Phillis 52

Round 4 – Germany
Hockenheim, 5 May
Race 1
1 F Merkel, USA, Honda
2 R McElnea, GB, Yamaha
3 G Falappa, Ita, Ducati
4 J Suhonen, Fin, Yamaha
5 A Hofmann, Ger, Honda
6 U Mark, Ger, Yamaha
7 A Andersson, Swe, Yamaha
8 F Pirovano, Ita, Yamaha
9 C Lindholm, Swe, Yamaha
10 R Stringer, GB, Yamaha
11 J Lopez Mella, Spa, Honda
12 J de Vries, Nl, Yamaha
13 H Meier, CH, Honda
14 W Moeckel, Ger, Honda
15 M Rudroff, Ger, Bimota

Race 2
1 S Mertens, Bel, Honda
2 R Roche, Fra, Ducati
3 F Merkel, USA, Honda
4 G Falappa, Ita, Ducati
5 F Pirovano, Ita, Yamaha
6 R McElnea, GB, Yamaha
7 T Rymer, GB, Yamaha
8 A Hofmann, Ger, Honda
9 M Campbell, Aus, Honda
10 J Suhonen, Fin, Yamaha
11 U Mark, Ger, Yamaha
12 A Andersson, Swe, Yamaha
13 E Weibel, CH, Kawasaki
14 B Monti, Ita, Honda
15 J de Vries, Nl, Yamaha

Standings – 1 Merkel 132;
2 Roche 128; 3 Mertens 96;
4 Falappa 94; 5 Pirovano 82;
6 McElnea 69

Round 5 – Canada
Mosport, 3 June
Race 1
1 R Roche, Fra, Ducati
2 J James, USA, Ducati
3 F Merkel, USA, Honda
4 T Rymer, GB, Yamaha
5 F Merkel, USA, Honda
6 S Mertens, Bel, Honda
7 B Monti, Ita, Honda
8 M Mercier, Can, Yamaha
9 J Suhonen, Fin, Yamaha
10 A Andersson, Swe, Yamaha
11 R McElnea, GB, Yamaha
12 M DuHamel, Can, Suzuki
13 P Picotte, Can, Yamaha
14 T Kipp, USA, Yamaha
15 R Delaby, Lux, Honda

Race 2
1 R Roche, Fra, Ducati
2 J James, USA, Ducati
3 S Mertens, Bel, Honda
4 M Mercier, Can, Yamaha
5 F Pirovano, Ita, Yamaha
6 R McElnea, GB, Yamaha
7 T Rymer, GB, Yamaha
8 R Phillis, Aus, Kawasaki
9 B Monti, Ita, Honda
10 F Merkel, USA, Honda
11 A Andersson, Swe, Yamaha
12 P Picotte, Can, Yamaha
13 J Suhonen, Fin, Yamaha
14 T Kipp, USA, Yamaha
15 M DuHamel, Can, Suzuki

Standings – 1 Roche 168;
2 Merkel 149; 3 Mertens 121;
4 Pirovano 108; 5 Falappa 94;
6 McElnea 84

Round 6 – USA
Brainerd International Raceway,
10 June
Race 1
1 S Mertens, Bel, Honda
2 R Roche, Fra, Ducati
3 D Chandler, USA, Kawasaki
4 T Rymer, GB, Yamaha
5 R McElnea, GB, Yamaha
6 R Phillis, Aus, Kawasaki
7 F Merkel, USA, Honda
8 F Pirovano, Ita, Yamaha
9 D Sadowski, USA, Yamaha
10 S Russell, USA, Kawasaki
11 B Monti, Ita, Honda
12 J Suhonen, Fin, Yamaha
13 D Tardozzi, Ita, Ducati
14 T Kipp, USA, Yamaha
15 B Bonhuil, Fra, Honda

Race 2
1 D Chandler, USA, Kawasaki
2 S Mertens, Bel, Honda
3 T Rymer, GB, Yamaha
4 R Roche, Fra, Ducati
5 R McElnea, GB, Yamaha
6 F Pirovano, Ita, Yamaha
7 S Russell, USA, Kawasaki
8 J Suhonen, Fin, Yamaha
9 T Stevens, USA, Yamaha
10 F Merkel, USA, Honda
11 B Monti, Ita, Honda
12 A Andersson, Swe, Yamaha
13 T Kipp, USA, Yamaha
14 R Delaby, Lux, Honda
15 B Bonhuil, Fra, Honda

Standings – 1 Roche 198; 2 Merkel 164;
3 Mertens 158; 4 Pirovano 126;
5 McElnea 106; 6 Rymer 96

Round 7 – Austria
Osterreichring, 1 July
Race 1
1 F Pirovano, Ita, Yamaha
2 S Mertens, Bel, Honda
3 R Phillis, Aus, Kawasaki
4 A Andersson, Swe, Yamaha
5 E Gschwender, Ger, Suzuki
6 R McElnea, GB, Yamaha
7 F Merkel, USA, Honda
8 R Roche, Fra, Ducati
9 B Monti, Ita, Honda
10 D Amatriain, Spa, Honda
11 J-M Mattioli, Fra, Honda
12 S Caracchi, Ita, Ducati
13 M Ricci, Ita, Kawasaki
14 J-Y Mounier, Fra, Yamaha
15 R Delaby, Lux, Honda

Race 2
1 S Mertens, Bel, Honda
2 R Roche, Fra, Ducati
3 F Pirovano, Ita, Yamaha
4 F Merkel, USA, Honda
5 B Monti, Ita, Honda
6 R McElnea, GB, Yamaha
7 A Vieira, Fra, Honda
8 J-Y Mounier, Fra, Yamaha
9 A Andersson, Swe, Yamaha
10 U Mark, Ger, Yamaha
11 J Suhonen, Fin, Yamaha
12 J-M Mattioli, Fra, Honda
13 R Delaby, Lux, Honda
14 E Gschwender, Ger, Suzuki
15 C Zwedorn, Aut, Honda

Standings – 1 Roche 223;
2 Mertens 195; 3 Merkel 186;
4 Pirovano 161; 5 McElnea 126;
6 Rymer 96

Round 8 – Japan
Sugo, 26 August
Race 1
1 R Roche, Fra, Ducati
2 B Monti, Ita, Honda
3 D Chandler, USA, Kawasaki
4 F Pirovano, Ita, Yamaha
5 P Goddard, Aus, Yamaha
6 R Phillis, Aus, Kawasaki
7 J James, USA, Ducati
8 D Polen, USA, Suzuki
9 K Osaka, Jap, Yamaha
10 S Kato, Jap, Yamaha
11 S Mertens, Bel, Honda
12 R McElnea, GB, Yamaha
13 M Saito, Jap, Yamaha
14 K Kobayashi, Jap, Yamaha
15 U Mark, Ger, Yamaha

Race 2
1 D Chandler, USA, Kawasaki
2 P Goddard, Aus, Yamaha
3 B Monti, Ita, Honda
4 F Pirovano, Ita, Yamaha
5 R Phillis, Aus, Kawasaki
6 R Roche, Fra, Ducati
7 J James, USA, Ducati
8 S Mertens, Bel, Honda
9 M Saito, Jap, Yamaha
10 B Morrison, GB, Honda
11 J Suhonen, Fin, Yamaha
12 S Miwa, Jap, Honda
13 U Mark, Ger, Yamaha
14 T Hanamura, Jap, Yamaha
15 M Campbell, Aus, Honda

Standings – 1 Roche 253;
2 Mertens 208; 3 Pirovano 187;
4 Merkel 186; 5 McElnea 126;
6 Monti 106

Round 9 – France
Le Mans, 9 September
Race 1
1 R Roche, Fra, Ducati
2 J James, USA, Ducati
3 S Mertens, Bel, Honda
4 B Monti, Ita, Honda
5 R Phillis, Aus, Kawasaki
6 R McElnea, GB, Yamaha
7 C Lavieille, Fra, Honda
8 J-M Mattioli, Fra, Honda
9 S Caracchi, Ita, Ducati
10 J Suhonen, Fin, Yamaha
11 A Andersson, Swe, Yamaha
12 E Weibel, CH, Honda
13 J de Vries, Nl, Yamaha

Round 10 – Italy

Race 2
1 F Pirovano, Ita, Yamaha
2 B Monti, Ita, Honda
3 R McElnea, GB, Yamaha
4 R Phillis, Aus, Kawasaki
5 F Merkel, USA, Honda
6 R Roche, Fra, Ducati
7 J Suhonen, Fin, Yamaha
8 J James, USA, Ducati
9 B Morrison, GB, Honda
10 J de Vries, Nl, Yamaha
11 A Andersson, Swe, Yamaha
12 H Meier, CH, Honda

14 A Hofmann, Ger, Honda
15 M Coq, Fra, Yamaha

Race 2
1 R Roche, Fra, Ducati
2 F Pirovano, Ita, Yamaha
3 S Mertens, Bel, Honda
4 B Monti, Ita, Honda
5 R McElnea, GB, Yamaha
6 R Phillis, Aus, Kawasaki
7 J-Y Mounier, Fra, Yamaha
8 C Fogarty, GB, Honda
9 E Weibel, CH, Honda
10 S Caracchi, Ita, Ducati
11 A Hofmann, Ger, Honda
12 J-M Mattioli, Fra, Honda
13 A Vieira, Fra, Honda
14 J Suhonen, Fin, Yamaha
15 B Morrison, GB, Honda

Standings – 1 Roche 293;
2 Mertens 238; 3 Pirovano 204;
4 Merkel 186; 5 McElnea 151;
6 Monti 132

Round 10 – Italy
Monza, 7 October
Race 1
1 F Pirovano, Ita, Yamaha
2 S Mertens, Bel, Honda
3 R Roche, Fra, Ducati
4 R Phillis, Aus, Kawasaki
5 R McElnea, GB, Yamaha
6 J Suhonen, Fin, Yamaha
7 J James, USA, Ducati
8 B Morrison, GB, Honda
9 A Andersson, Swe, Yamaha
10 E Weibel, CH, Honda
11 A Vieira, Fra, Honda
12 F Biliotti, Ita, Kawasaki
13 M Rudroff, Ger, Bimota
14 A Bosshard, CH, Honda
15 J de Vries, Nl, Yamaha

13 A Bosshard, CH, Honda
14 A Vieira, Fra, Honda
15 C Monsch, CH, Honda

Standings – 1 Roche 318;
2 Mertens 255; 3 Pirovano 244;
4 Merkel 197; 5 McElnea 177;
6 Phillis 152

Round 11 – Malaysia
Shah Alam, 4 November
Race 1
1 F Pirovano, Ita, Yamaha
2 R Phillis, Aus, Kawasaki
3 S Mertens, Bel, Honda
4 R Roche, Fra, Ducati
5 R McElnea, GB, Yamaha
6 P Goddard, Aus, Yamaha
7 T Rymer, GB, Yamaha
8 M Campbell, Aus, Honda
9 J Suhonen, Fin, Yamaha
10 R Bongers, Aus, Yamaha
11 J Knight, Aus, Kawasaki
12 A Andersson, Swe, Yamaha
13 S Crafar, NZ, Yamaha
14 S Kooi Tai, Mal, Honda
15 C Nattavude, Tld, Kawasaki

Race 2
1 F Pirovano, Ita, Yamaha
2 R Phillis, Aus, Kawasaki
3 R Roche, Fra, Ducati
4 S Mertens, Bel, Honda
5 R McElnea, GB, Yamaha
6 P Goddard, Aus, Yamaha
7 T Rymer, GB, Yamaha
8 J Suhonen, Fin, Yamaha
9 M Campbell, Aus, Honda
10 R Bongers, Aus, Yamaha
11 J Knight, Aus, Kawasaki

12 A Andersson, Swe, Yamaha
13 S Crafar, NZ, Yamaha
14 M Dowson, Aus, Yamaha
15 C Nattavude, Tld, Kawasaki

Standings – 1 Roche 346;
2 Pirovano 284; 3 Mertens 283;
4 McElnea 199; 5 Merkel 197;
6 Phillis 152

Round 12 – Australia
Phillip Island, 11 November
Race 1
1 P Goddard, Aus, Yamaha
2 F Pirovano, Ita, Yamaha
3 M Dowson, Aus, Yamaha
4 M Campbell, Aus, Honda
5 R Roche, Fra, Ducati
6 R Bongers, Aus, Yamaha
7 S Doohan, Aus, Honda
8 A Slight, NZ, Kawasaki
9 T Rymer, GB, Yamaha
10 J Suhonen, Fin, Yamaha
11 S Martin, Aus, Suzuki
12 R McElnea, GB, Yamaha
13 B Morrison, GB, Honda
14 P Guest, Aus, Yamaha
15 I Short, Aus, Suzuki

Race 2
1 R Phillis, Aus, Kawasaki
2 P Goddard, Aus, Yamaha
3 M Campbell, Aus, Honda
4 M Dowson, Aus, Yamaha
5 F Pirovano, Ita, Yamaha
6 S Doohan, Aus, Honda
7 A Slight, NZ, Kawasaki
8 R Roche, Fra, Ducati
9 S Mertens, Bel, Honda
10 S Martin, Aus, Suzuki

11 B Morrison, GB, Honda
12 P Guest, Aus, Yamaha
13 M O'Connor, Aus, Honda
14 A Roberts, Aus, Yamaha
15 A Andersson, Swe, Yamaha

Standings – 1 Roche 365;
2 Pirovano 312; 3 Mertens 290;
4 Phillis 206; 5 McElnea 203;
6 Merkel 197

Round 13 – New Zealand
Manfeild Park, 18 November
Race 1
1 T Rymer, GB, Yamaha
2 R Roche, Fra, Ducati
3 R McElnea, GB, Yamaha
4 D Beattie, Aus, Honda
5 R Phillis, Aus, Kawasaki
6 S Mertens, Bel, Honda
7 A Andersson, Swe, Yamaha
8 A Stroud, NZ, Yamaha
9 T Rees, NZ, Yamaha
10 B Morrison, GB, Honda
11 R Josiah, NZ, Kawasaki
12 R Lewis, NZ, Kawasaki
13 M Fissenden, Aus, Honda
14 B Billet, NZ, Honda
15 B Curtis, NZ, Suzuki

Race 2
1 R Phillis, Aus, Kawasaki
2 T Rymer, GB, Yamaha
3 A Slight, NZ, Kawasaki
4 F Pirovano, Ita, Yamaha
5 J Suhonen, Fin, Yamaha
6 A Andersson, Swe, Yamaha
7 A Stroud, NZ, Yamaha
8 B Morrison, GB, Honda
9 T Rees, NZ, Yamaha
10 R Josiah, NZ, Kawasaki
11 R Lewis, NZ, Kawasaki
12 M King, NZ, Ducati
13 B Billet, NZ, Honda
14 B Curtis, NZ, Suzuki
15 M Fissenden, Aus, Honda

Final Standings – 1 Roche 382;
2 Pirovano 325; 3 Mertens 300;
4 Phillis 237; 5 McElnea 218;
6 Merkel 197

1991 SEASON
Round 1 – Great Britain
Donington Park, 1 April
Race 1
1 D Polen, USA, Ducati
2 T Rymer, GB, Yamaha
3 F Pirovano, Ita, Yamaha
4 R Phillis, Aus, Kawasaki
5 R McElnea, GB, Yamaha
6 B Morrison, GB, Yamaha
7 N Mackenzie, GB, Honda
8 R Stringer, GB, Yamaha
9 J de Vries, Nl, Yamaha
10 J Reynolds, GB, Kawasaki
11 J Lopez Mella, Spa, Honda
12 C Lavieille, Fra, Ducati
13 E Weibel, CH, Honda
14 G Falappa, Ita, Ducati
15 S Manley, GB, Bimota

Race 2
1 S Mertens, Bel, Ducati
2 R Roche, Fra, Ducati
3 R Phillis, Aus, Kawasaki
4 T Rymer, GB, Yamaha
5 R McElnea, GB, Yamaha
6 B Morrison, GB, Yamaha
7 N Mackenzie, GB, Honda
8 F Pirovano, Ita, Yamaha

9 C Fogarty, GB, Honda
10 J de Vries, Nl, Yamaha
11 J Lopez Mella, Spa, Honda
12 C Lavieille, Fra, Ducati
13 D Amatriain, Spa, Honda
14 E Weibel, CH, Honda
15 L Maurel, Spa, Yamaha

Standings – 1 Rymer 30; 2 Phillis 28;
3 Pirovano 23; 4 McElnea 22;
5 Mertens, Morrison & Polen 20

Round 2 – Spain
Jarama, 28 April
Race 1
1 D Polen, USA, Ducati
2 R Phillis, Aus, Kawasaki
3 J Lopez Mella, Spa, Honda
4 D Amatriain, Spa, Honda
5 F Pirovano, Ita, Yamaha
6 B Monti, Ita, Honda
7 T Rymer, GB, Yamaha
8 U Mark, Ger, Yamaha
9 C Fogarty, GB, Honda
10 B Bonhuil, Fra, Yamaha
11 A Moreno, Spa, Honda
12 P Rubatto, Ger, Yamaha
13 W Amman, CH, Yamaha
14 A Presciutti, Ita, Kawasaki
15 J de Vries, Nl, Yamaha

Race 2
1 D Polen, USA, Ducati
2 S Mertens, Bel, Ducati
3 R Roche, Fra, Ducati
4 J Lopez Mella, Spa, Honda
5 F Pirovano, Ita, Yamaha
6 D Amatriain, Spa, Honda
7 U Mark, Ger, Yamaha
8 C Fogarty, GB, Honda
9 J Suhonen, Fin, Yamaha
10 L Maurel, Spa, Yamaha
11 A Moreno, Spa, Honda
12 B Bonhuil, Fra, Yamaha
13 D Sarron, Fra, Bimota
14 M Broccoli, Ita, Kawasaki
15 R Delaby, Lux, Honda

Standings – 1 Polen 60;
2 Pirovano & Phillis 45; 4 Rymer 39;
5 Mertens 37; 6 Roche 32

Round 3 – Canada
Mosport Park, 2 June
Race 1
1 P Picotte, Can, Yamaha
2 Y Brisson, Can, Honda
3 S Crevier, Can, Kawasaki
4 L Clarke, Can, Yamaha
5 M Taylor, Can, Kawasaki
6 B Pilon, Can, Yamaha
7 J Adamo, USA, Ducati
8 J Hopperstad, USA, Yamaha
9 C Gardner, USA, Yamaha
10 T Etherington, Can, Yamaha
11 C MacDonald, Can, Suzuki
12 M Walsh, Can, Yamaha
13 P Kress, USA, Kawasaki
14 F Mrazek, Can, Ducati
15 D Vance, Can, Suzuki

Race 2
1 T Kipp, USA, Yamaha
2 L Clarke, Can, Yamaha
3 R McMurter, Can, Honda
4 Y Brisson, Can, Honda
5 S Crevier, Can, Kawasaki
6 B Pilon, Can, Yamaha
7 J Hopperstad, USA, Yamaha
8 P Kress, USA, Kawasaki
9 T Etherington, Can, Yamaha

10 C Gardner, USA, Yamaha
11 C MacDonald, Can, Suzuki
12 M Walsh, Can, Yamaha
13 F Mrazek, Can, Ducati

Standings – 1 Polen 60;
2 Pirovano & Phillis 45; 4 Rymer 39;
5 Mertens 37; 6 Roche 32

Round 4 – USA
Brainerd, 9 June
Race 1
1 D Polen, USA, Ducati
2 S Russell, USA, Kawasaki
3 S Mertens, Bel, Ducati
4 R Phillis, Aus, Kawasaki
5 F Pirovano, Ita, Yamaha
6 F Merkel, USA, Honda
7 G Falappa, Ita, Ducati
8 B Monti, Ita, Honda
9 J Guenette, Can, Kawasaki
10 J de Vries, Nl, Yamaha
11 C Fogarty, GB, Honda
12 R McMurter, Can, Honda
13 J-Y Mounier, Fra, Yamaha
14 J Lopez Mella, Spa, Honda
15 N Mackenzie, GB, Honda

Race 2
1 D Polen, USA, Ducati
2 S Russell, USA, Kawasaki
3 S Mertens, Bel, Ducati
4 F Merkel, USA, Honda
5 R Phillis, Aus, Kawasaki
6 F Pirovano, Ita, Yamaha
7 B Monti, Ita, Honda
8 J Guenette, Can, Kawasaki
9 J-Y Mounier, Fra, Yamaha
10 J de Vries, Nl, Yamaha
11 C Fogarty, GB, Honda
12 B Bonhuil, Fra, Yamaha
13 B Turkington, USA, Suzuki
14 N Mackenzie, GB, Honda
15 A Narducci, Ita, Ducati

Standings – 1 Polen 100; 2 Phillis 69;
3 Mertens 67; 4 Pirovano 66;
5 Rymer 39; 6 Roche & Fogarty 32

Round 5 – Austria
Osterreichring, 30 June
Race 1
1 S Mertens, Bel, Ducati
2 D Polen, USA, Ducati
3 R Roche, Fra, Ducati
4 R Phillis, Aus, Kawasaki
5 D Tardozzi, Ita, Ducati
6 T Rymer, GB, Yamaha
7 U Mark, Ger, Yamaha
8 F Merkel, USA, Honda
9 J Suhonen, Fin, Yamaha
10 J-Y Mounier, Fra, Yamaha
11 J de Vries, Nl, Yamaha
12 D Amatriain, Spa, Honda
13 F Furlan, Ita, Honda
14 B Bammert, CH, Yamaha
15 P Rubatto, Ger, Yamaha

Race 2
1 D Polen, USA, Ducati
2 S Mertens, Bel, Ducati
3 R Roche, Fra, Ducati
4 R Phillis, Aus, Kawasaki
5 F Pirovano, Ita, Yamaha
6 D Tardozzi, Ita, Ducati
7 G Falappa, Ita, Ducati
8 F Merkel, USA, Honda
9 T Rymer, GB, Yamaha
10 U Mark, Ger, Yamaha
11 J Suhonen, Fin, Yamaha
12 J de Vries, Nl, Yamaha

13 P Rubatto, Ger, Yamaha
14 J-Y Mounier, Fra, Yamaha
15 R Wood, Zim, Bimota

Standings – 1 Polen 137;
2 Mertens 104; 3 Phillis 95;
4 Pirovano 77; 5 Roche 62;
6 Rymer 56

Round 6 – San Marino
Misano, 4 August
Race 1
1 D Polen, USA, Ducati
2 R Phillis, Aus, Kawasaki
3 D Tardozzi, Ita, Ducati
4 R Roche, Fra, Ducati
5 F Pirovano, Ita, Yamaha
6 S Mertens, Bel, Ducati
7 C Fogarty, GB, Honda
8 T Rymer, GB, Yamaha
9 F Merkel, USA, Honda
10 G Falappa, Ita, Ducati
11 U Mark, Ger, Yamaha
12 M Broccoli, Ita, Kawasaki
13 D Amatriain, Spa, Honda
14 R Wood, Zim, Bimota
15 J-M Mattioli, Fra, Yamaha

Race 2
1 D Polen, USA, Ducati
2 R Roche, Fra, Ducati
3 R Phillis, Aus, Kawasaki
4 F Pirovano, Ita, Yamaha
5 D Tardozzi, Ita, Ducati
6 G Falappa, Ita, Ducati
7 F Merkel, USA, Honda
8 C Fogarty, GB, Honda
9 T Rymer, GB, Yamaha
10 R Wood, Zim, Bimota
11 J Lopez Mella, Spa, Honda
12 M Broccoli, Ita, Kawasaki
13 D Amatriain, Spa, Honda
14 J-M Mattioli, Fra, Yamaha
15 J Suhonen, Fin, Yamaha

Standings – 1 Polen 177; 2 Phillis 127;
3 Mertens 114; 4 Pirovano 101;
5 Roche 92; 6 Rymer 71

Round 7 – Sweden
Anderstorp, 11 August
Race 1
1 D Polen, USA, Ducati
2 R Phillis, Aus, Kawasaki
3 F Pirovano, Ita, Yamaha
4 C Fogarty, GB, Honda
5 J Suhonen, Fin, Yamaha

6 G Falappa, Ita, Ducati
7 T Rymer, GB, Yamaha
8 F Merkel, USA, Honda
9 J-Y Mounier, Fra, Yamaha
10 U Mark, Ger, Yamaha
11 R McElnea, GB, Yamaha
12 J de Vries, Nl, Yamaha
13 P Rubatto, Ger, Yamaha
14 D Amatriain, Spa, Honda
15 R Rasmussen, Den, Yamaha

Race 2
1 D Polen, USA, Ducati
2 R Phillis, Aus, Kawasaki
3 R Roche, Fra, Ducati
4 C Fogarty, GB, Honda
5 C Lindholm, Swe, Yamaha
6 F Merkel, USA, Honda
7 J Suhonen, Fin, Yamaha
8 R McElnea, GB, Yamaha
9 J-Y Mounier, Fra, Yamaha
10 U Mark, Ger, Yamaha
11 D Amatriain, Spa, Honda
12 T Rymer, GB, Yamaha
13 G Falappa, Ita, Ducati
14 M Meregalli, Ita, Yamaha
15 C Guyot, Fra, Honda

Standings – 1 Polen 217; 2 Phillis 161;
3 Pirovano 116; 4 Mertens 114;
5 Roche 107; 6 Rymer 84

Round 8 – Japan
Sugo, 25 August
Race 1
1 D Polen, USA, Ducati
2 R Phillis, Aus, Kawasaki
3 A Slight, NZ, Kawasaki
4 P Goddard, Aus, Yamaha
5 K Magee, Aus, Yamaha
6 R Roche, Fra, Ducati
7 F Pirovano, Ita, Yamaha
8 S Russell, USA, Kawasaki
9 D Tardozzi, Ita, Ducati
10 G Falappa, Ita, Ducati
11 C Fogarty, GB, Honda
12 F Merkel, USA, Honda
13 R Tsuruta, Jap, Kawasaki
14 K Tada, Jap, Kawasaki
15 M Aoki, Jap, Suzuki

Race 2
1 D Polen, USA, Ducati
2 R Roche, Fra, Ducati
3 K Magee, Aus, Yamaha
4 A Slight, NZ, Kawasaki
5 S Russell, USA, Kawasaki

6 N Mackenzie, GB, Yamaha
7 F Pirovano, Ita, Yamaha
8 C Fogarty, GB, Honda
9 F Merkel, USA, Honda
10 D Tardozzi, Ita, Ducati
11 G Falappa, Ita, Ducati
12 R Tsuruta, Jap, Kawasaki
13 K Tada, Jap, Kawasaki
14 T Rymer, GB, Yamaha
15 M Aoki, Jap, Suzuki

Standings – 1 Polen 257; 2 Phillis 178;
3 Pirovano & Roche 134;
5 Mertens 114; 6 Rymer 86

Round 9 – Malaysia
Shah Alam, 1 September
Race 1
1 R Roche, Fra, Ducati
2 F Pirovano, Ita, Yamaha
3 D Tardozzi, Ita, Ducati
4 D Polen, USA, Ducati
5 R Phillis, Aus, Kawasaki
6 G Falappa, Ita, Ducati
7 A Slight, NZ, Kawasaki
8 C Fogarty, GB, Honda
9 S Mertens, Bel, Ducati
10 T Rymer, GB, Yamaha
11 A Stroud, NZ, Kawasaki
12 F Merkel, USA, Honda
13 J de Vries, Nl, Yamaha
14 J Lopez Mella, Spa, Honda
15 J Knight, Aus, Kawasaki

Race 2
1 R Roche, Fra, Ducati
2 S Mertens, Bel, Ducati
3 F Pirovano, Ita, Yamaha
4 A Slight, NZ, Kawasaki
5 D Polen, USA, Ducati
6 D Tardozzi, Ita, Ducati
7 C Fogarty, GB, Honda
8 S Crafar, NZ, Yamaha
9 F Merkel, USA, Honda
10 J Lopez Mella, Spa, Honda
11 J Knight, Aus, Kawasaki
12 J-Y Mounier, Fra, Yamaha
13 J de Vries, Nl, Yamaha
14 S Doohan, Aus, Yamaha
15 MH Kuan, Mal, Yamaha

Standings – 1 Polen 281; 2 Phillis 189;
3 Roche 174; 4 Pirovano 166;
5 Mertens 138; 6 Rymer 92

Round 10 – Germany
Hockenheim, 15 September
Race 1
1 D Polen, USA, Ducati
2 R Roche, Fra, Ducati
3 D Tardozzi, Ita, Ducati
4 R Phillis, Aus, Kawasaki
5 S Mertens, Bel, Ducati
6 G Falappa, Ita, Ducati
7 T Rymer, GB, Yamaha
8 U Mark, Ger, Yamaha
9 C Fogarty, GB, Honda
10 E Weibel, CH, Ducati
11 J-Y Mounier, Fra, Yamaha
12 T Franz, Ger, Honda
13 J de Vries, Nl, Yamaha
14 J Suhonen, Fin, Yamaha
15 D Amatriain, Spa, Honda

Race 2
1 R Roche, Fra, Ducati
2 D Polen, USA, Ducati
3 G Falappa, Ita, Ducati
4 R Phillis, Aus, Kawasaki
5 U Mark, Ger, Yamaha
6 S Mertens, Bel, Ducati

7 F Pirovano, Ita, Yamaha
8 D Tardozzi, Ita, Ducati
9 T Rymer, GB, Yamaha
10 C Fogarty, GB, Honda
11 E Weibel, CH, Ducati
12 J Suhonen, Fin, Yamaha
13 P Rubatto, Ger, Yamaha
14 B Caspers, Ger, Ducati
15 M Kellenberger, CH, Yamaha

Standings – 1 Polen 318; 2 Phillis 215; 3 Roche 211; 4 Pirovano 175; 5 Mertens 159; 6 Rymer 108

Round 11 – France
Magny-Cours, 29 September
Race 1
1 D Polen, USA, Ducati
2 R Roche, Fra, Ducati
3 F Merkel, USA, Honda
4 R Phillis, Aus, Kawasaki
5 T Rymer, GB, Yamaha
6 C Fogarty, GB, Honda
7 S Mertens, Bel, Ducati
8 B Morrison, GB, Yamaha
9 J Suhonen, Fin, Yamaha
10 B Bammert, CH, Yamaha
11 P Bontempi, Ita, Kawasaki
12 J de Vries, Nl, Yamaha
13 J-M Mattioli, Fra, Kawasaki
14 E Weibel, CH, Ducati
15 C Lindholm, Swe, Yamaha

Race 2
1 D Polen, USA, Ducati
2 R Roche, Fra, Ducati
3 S Mertens, Bel, Ducati
4 T Rymer, GB, Yamaha
5 R Phillis, Aus, Kawasaki
6 F Pirovano, Ita, Yamaha
7 C Fogarty, GB, Honda
8 G Falappa, Ita, Ducati
9 E Weibel, CH, Ducati
10 F Merkel, USA, Honda
11 B Morrison, GB, Yamaha
12 J Suhonen, Fin, Yamaha
13 D Amatriain, Spa, Honda
14 J de Vries, Nl, Yamaha
15 P Mouchet, Fra, Yamaha

Standings – 1 Polen 358; 2 Roche 245; 3 Phillis 239; 4 Pirovano 185; 5 Mertens 183; 6 Rymer 132

Round 12 – Italy
Mugello, 6 October
Race 1
1 D Polen, USA, Ducati
2 R Roche, Fra, Ducati
3 T Rymer, GB, Yamaha
4 S Mertens, Bel, Ducati
5 V Ferrari, Ita, Ducati
6 G Falappa, Ita, Ducati
7 C Fogarty, GB, Honda
8 F Merkel, USA, Honda
9 E Weibel, CH, Ducati
10 B Bammert, CH, Yamaha
11 M Broccoli, Ita, Kawasaki
12 V Scatola, Ita, Kawasaki
13 J Lopez Mella, Spa, Honda
14 F Furlan, Ita, Honda
15 J de Vries, Nl, Yamaha

Race 2
1 R Roche, Fra, Ducati
2 D Polen, USA, Ducati
3 T Rymer, GB, Yamaha
4 P Bontempi, Ita, Kawasaki
5 J de Vries, Nl, Yamaha
6 F Pirovano, Ita, Yamaha

7 E Weibel, CH, Ducati
8 S Manley, GB, Yamaha
9 V Scatola, Ita, Kawasaki
10 M Broccoli, Ita, Kawasaki
11 F Furlan, Ita, Honda
12 J Suhonen, Fin, Yamaha
13 P Rubatto, Ger, Yamaha
14 R Chesaux, CH, Honda
15 J Lopez Mella, Spa, Honda

Standings – 1 Polen 395; 2 Roche 282; 3 Phillis 239; 4 Mertens 196; 5 Pirovano 195; 6 Rymer 162

Round 13 – Australia
Phillip Island, 19 October
Race 1
1 K Magee, Aus, Yamaha
2 D Polen, USA, Ducati
3 A Slight, NZ, Kawasaki
4 R Phillis, Aus, Kawasaki
5 S Mertens, Bel, Ducati
6 M Campbell, Aus, Honda
7 S Doohan, Aus, Yamaha
8 S Martin, Aus, Suzuki
9 R Leslie, Aus, Ducati
10 M O'Connor, Aus, Honda
11 A Stroud, NZ, Kawasaki
12 S Giles, Aus, Honda
13 M Craggill, Aus, Honda
14 M Blair, Aus, Suzuki
15 E Kattenberg, NZ, Kawasaki

Race 2
1 D Polen, USA, Ducati
2 K Magee, Aus, Yamaha
3 R Phillis, Aus, Kawasaki
4 M Campbell, Aus, Honda
5 S Doohan, Aus, Yamaha
6 S Mertens, Bel, Ducati
7 S Martin, Aus, Suzuki
8 M O'Connor, Aus, Honda
9 D Pitman, Aus, Yamaha
10 P Guest, Aus, Yamaha
11 S Giles, Aus, Honda
12 M Craggill, Aus, Honda
13 I Short, Aus, Suzuki
14 T Rees, NZ, Yamaha
15 A Roberts, Aus, Yamaha

Final Standings – 1 Polen 432; 2 Roche 282; 3 Phillis 267; 4 Mertens 217; 5 Pirovano 195; 6 Rymer 162

1992 SEASON
Round 1 – Spain
Albacete, 5 April
Race 1
1 A Slight, NZ, Kawasaki
2 D Polen, USA, Ducati
3 F Pirovano, Ita, Yamaha
4 G Falappa, Ita, Ducati
5 D Amatriain, Spa, Ducati
6 B Monti, Ita, Honda
7 R Roche, Fra, Ducati
8 T Sohwa, Jap, Ducati
9 R Phillis, Aus, Kawasaki
10 J Lopez Mella, Spa, Honda
11 S Mertens, Bel, Ducati
12 C Fogarty, GB, Ducati
13 C Lindholm, Swe, Yamaha
14 T Rymer, GB, Kawasaki
15 J-Y Mounier, Fra, Yamaha

Race 2
1 R Roche, Fra, Ducati
2 R Phillis, Aus, Kawasaki
3 D Amatriain, Spa, Ducati
4 F Pirovano, Ita, Yamaha

5 G Falappa, Ita, Ducati
6 D Polen, USA, Ducati
7 S Russell, USA, Kawasaki
8 J Reynolds, GB, Kawasaki
9 T Rymer, GB, Kawasaki
10 C Fogarty, GB, Ducati
11 V Ferrari, Ita, Ducati
12 S Mertens, Bel, Ducati
13 F Furlan, Ita, Ducati
14 J Lopez Mella, Spa, Honda
15 C Lindholm, Swe, Yamaha

Standings – 1 Roche 29; 2 Pirovano 28; 3 Polen 27; 4 Amatriain 26; 5 Falappa & Phillis 24

Round 2 – Great Britain
Donington Park, 19 April
Race 1
1 R Roche, Fra, Ducati
2 F Pirovano, Ita, Yamaha
3 S Russell, USA, Kawasaki
4 R Phillis, Aus, Kawasaki
5 A Slight, NZ, Kawasaki
6 D Polen, USA, Ducati
7 S Mertens, Bel, Ducati
8 J-Y Mounier, Fra, Yamaha
9 R Stringer, GB, Kawasaki
10 B Monti, Ita, Honda
11 J Whitham, GB, Suzuki
12 D Amatriain, Spa, Ducati
13 J Reynolds, GB, Kawasaki
14 J de Vries, Nl, Yamaha
15 C Lindholm, Swe, Yamaha

Race 2
1 C Fogarty, GB, Ducati
2 R Roche, Fra, Ducati
3 S Russell, USA, Kawasaki
4 D Polen, USA, Ducati
5 F Pirovano, Ita, Yamaha
6 A Slight, NZ, Kawasaki
7 R Phillis, Aus, Kawasaki
8 G Falappa, Ita, Ducati
9 J Reynolds, GB, Kawasaki
10 D Amatriain, Spa, Ducati
11 T Sohwa, Jap, Kawasaki
12 R McElnea, GB, Yamaha
13 B Monti, Ita, Honda
14 J Whitham, GB, Suzuki
15 C Lindholm, Swe, Yamaha

Standings – 1 Roche 66; 2 Pirovano 56; 3 Polen 50; 4 Phillis 46; 5 Slight 41; Russell 39

Round 3 – Germany
Hockenheim, 10 May
Race 1
1 D Polen, USA, Ducati
2 R Phillis, Aus, Kawasaki
3 A Slight, NZ, Kawasaki
4 S Russell, USA, Kawasaki
5 R Roche, Fra, Ducati
6 S Mertens, Bel, Ducati
7 H Moineau, Fra, Suzuki
8 A Hofmann, Ger, Kawasaki
9 D Amatriain, Spa, Ducati
10 P Bontempi, Ita, Kawasaki
11 V Ferrari, Ita, Ducati
12 K Liegibel, Ger, Yamaha
13 A Meklau, Aut, Ducati
14 J-Y Mounier, Fra, Yamaha
15 S Seidel, Ger, Suzuki

Race 2
1 D Polen, USA, Ducati
2 R Phillis, Aus, Kawasaki
3 G Falappa, Ita, Ducati
4 R Roche, Fra, Ducati
5 A Slight, NZ, Kawasaki

6 F Pirovano, Ita, Yamaha
7 S Russell, USA, Kawasaki
8 J Reynolds, GB, Kawasaki
9 A Hofmann, Ger, Kawasaki
10 H Moineau, Fra, Suzuki
11 C Fogarty, GB, Ducati
12 E Weibel, D, Ducati
13 S Mertens, Bel, Ducati
14 M Broccoli, Ita, Kawasaki
15 V Ferrari, Ita, Ducati

Standings – 1 Polen & Roche 90; 3 Phillis 80; 4 Slight 67; 5 Pirovano 66; 6 Russell 61

Round 4 – Belgium
Spa-Francorchamps, 24 May
Race 1
1 R Phillis, Aus, Kawasaki
2 S Mertens, Bel, Ducati
3 S Russell, USA, Kawasaki
4 G Falappa, Ita, Ducati
5 D Polen, USA, Ducati
6 A Slight, NZ, Kawasaki
7 D Amatriain, Spa, Ducati
8 A Hofmann, Ger, Kawasaki
9 B Monti, Ita, Honda
10 V Ferrari, Ita, Ducati
11 J de Vries, Nl, Yamaha
12 C Lindholm, Swe, Yamaha
13 R Arnaiz, USA, Honda
14 P Bontempi, Ita, Kawasaki
15 S Crafar, NZ, Honda

Race 2
1 D Polen, USA, Ducati
2 G Falappa, Ita, Ducati
3 F Pirovano, Ita, Yamaha
4 R Roche, Fra, Ducati
5 R Phillis, Aus, Kawasaki
6 S Mertens, Bel, Ducati
7 A Slight, NZ, Kawasaki
8 C Fogarty, GB, Ducati
9 S Russell, USA, Kawasaki
10 H Moineau, Fra, Suzuki
11 D Amatriain, Spa, Ducati
12 D Tardozzi, Ita, Ducati
13 P Bontempi, Ita, Kawasaki
14 J de Vries, Nl, Yamaha
15 C Lindholm, Swe, Yamaha

Standings – 1 Polen 121; 2 Phillis 111; 3 Roche 103; 4 Slight 86; 5 Russell 83; 6 Pirovano 81

Round 5 – Andorra
Jerez, 21 June
Race 1
1 R Phillis, Aus, Kawasaki
2 R Roche, Fra, Ducati
3 G Falappa, Ita, Ducati
4 D Amatriain, Spa, Ducati
5 C Fogarty, GB, Ducati
6 A Slight, NZ, Kawasaki
7 C Lindholm, Swe, Yamaha
8 D Tardozzi, Ita, Ducati
9 B Monti, Ita, Honda
10 P Bontempi, Ita, Kawasaki
11 J d'Orgeix, Fra, Kawasaki
12 R Arnaiz, USA, Honda
13 J Suhonen, Fin, Yamaha
14 F Furlan, Ita, Ducati
15 J de Vries, Nl, Yamaha

Race 2
1 D Polen, USA, Ducati
2 R Phillis, Aus, Kawasaki
3 F Pirovano, Ita, Yamaha
4 S Mertens, Bel, Ducati
5 A Slight, NZ, Kawasaki
6 R Roche, Fra, Ducati

7 G Falappa, Ita, Ducati
8 F Furlan, Ita, Ducati
9 C Lindholm, Swe, Yamaha
10 B Monti, Ita, Honda
11 P Bontempi, Ita, Kawasaki
12 R Arnaiz, USA, Honda
13 J d'Orgeix, Fra, Kawasaki
14 J Suhonen, Fin, Yamaha
15 A Moreno, Spa, Yamaha

Standings – 1 Phillis 148; 2 Polen 141;
3 Roche 130; 4 Slight 107;
5 Falappa 101; 6 Pirovano 96

Round 6 – Austria
Osterreichring, 28 June
Race 1

1 G Falappa, Ita, Ducati
2 R Phillis, Aus, Kawasaki
3 D Polen, USA, Ducati
4 F Pirovano, Ita, Yamaha
5 D Tardozzi, Ita, Ducati
6 C Fogarty, GB, Ducati
7 A Slight, NZ, Kawasaki
8 D Amatriain, Spa, Ducati
9 F Merkel, USA, Yamaha
10 S Crafar, NZ, Honda
11 E Gschwender, Ger, Kawasaki
12 A Meklau, Aut, Ducati
13 J de Vries, Nl, Yamaha
14 P Bontempi, Ita, Kawasaki
15 V Ferrari, Ita, Ducati

Race 2

1 G Falappa, Ita, Ducati
2 S Mertens, Bel, Ducati
3 R Roche, Fra, Ducati
4 R Phillis, Aus, Kawasaki
5 D Polen, USA, Ducati
6 F Pirovano, Ita, Yamaha
7 C Fogarty, GB, Ducati
8 D Tardozzi, Ita, Ducati
9 D Amatriain, Spa, Ducati
10 F Merkel, USA, Yamaha
11 S Crafar, NZ, Honda
12 J de Vries, Nl, Yamaha
13 A Meklau, Aut, Ducati
14 J Suhonen, Fin, Yamaha
15 U Mark, Ger, Yamaha

Standings – 1 Phillis 178; 2 Polen 167;
3 Roche 145; 4 Falappa 141;
5 Pirovano 119; 6 Slight 116

Round 7 – San Marino
Mugello, 19 July
Race 1

1 R Roche, Fra, Ducati
2 D Polen, USA, Ducati
3 G Falappa, Ita, Ducati
4 S Mertens, Bel, Ducati
5 F Pirovano, Ita, Yamaha
6 A Morillas, Fra, Yamaha
7 C Fogarty, GB, Ducati
8 D Amatriain, Spa, Ducati
9 R Arnaiz, USA, Honda
10 C Lindholm, Swe, Yamaha
11 P Bontempi, Ita, Kawasaki
12 V Ferrari, Ita, Ducati
13 A Hofmann, Ger, Kawasaki
14 J de Vries, Nl, Yamaha
15 B Monti, Ita, Honda

Race 2

1 R Roche, Fra, Ducati
2 G Falappa, Ita, Ducati
3 D Polen, USA, Ducati
4 C Fogarty, GB, Ducati
5 R Phillis, Aus, Kawasaki
6 A Morillas, Fra, Yamaha
7 D Amatriain, Spa, Ducati

8 C Lindholm, Swe, Yamaha
9 P Bontempi, Ita, Kawasaki
10 J de Vries, Nl, Yamaha
11 A Hofmann, Ger, Kawasaki
12 R Arnaiz, USA, Honda
13 K Truchess, Aut, Kawasaki
14 F Furlan, Ita, Ducati
15 M Broccoli, Ita, Kawasaki

Standings – 1 Polen 199; 2 Phillis 189;
3 Roche 185; 4 Falappa 173;
5 Pirovano 130; 6 Slight 116

Round 8 – Malaysia
Johor, 23 August
Race 1

1 R Roche, Fra, Ducati
2 F Pirovano, Ita, Yamaha
3 R Phillis, Aus, Kawasaki
4 A Slight, NZ, Kawasaki
5 S Mertens, Bel, Ducati
6 G Falappa, Ita, Ducati
7 C Haldane, NZ, Yamaha
8 D Polen, USA, Ducati
9 P Bontempi, Ita, Kawasaki
10 A Morillas, Fra, Yamaha
11 F Merkel, USA, Yamaha
12 S Hislop, GB, Kawasaki
13 D Tardozzi, Ita, Ducati
14 T Jordan, Aus, Kawasaki
15 A Stroud, NZ, Kawasaki

Race 2

1 D Polen, USA, Ducati
2 R Roche, Fra, Ducati
3 A Slight, NZ, Kawasaki
4 G Falappa, Ita, Ducati
5 F Merkel, USA, Yamaha
6 F Pirovano, Ita, Yamaha
7 D Amatriain, Spa, Ducati
8 R Phillis, Aus, Kawasaki
9 T Jordan, Aus, Kawasaki
10 P Bontempi, Ita, Kawasaki
11 A Stroud, NZ, Kawasaki
12 C Haldane, NZ, Yamaha
13 A Morillas, Fra, Yamaha
14 V Ferrari, Ita, Ducati
15 J de Vries, Nl, Yamaha

Standings – 1 Polen 227;
2 Roche 222; 3 Phillis 212;
4 Falappa 196; 5 Pirovano 157;
6 Slight 144

Round 9 – Japan
Sugo, 30 August
Race 1

1 D Polen, USA, Ducati
2 K Magee, Aus, Yamaha
3 F Pirovano, Ita, Yamaha
4 S Tsukamoto, Jap, Kawasaki
5 R Roche, Fra, Ducati
6 A Slight, NZ, Kawasaki
7 K Kitagawa, Jap, Kawasaki
8 S Mertens, Bel, Ducati
9 P Bontempi, Ita, Kawasaki
10 M Mladin, Aus, Kawasaki
11 R Phillis, Aus, Kawasaki
12 S Imai, Jap, Kawasaki
13 D Tardozzi, Ita, Ducati
14 A Morillas, Fra, Yamaha
15 T Shirai, Jap, Honda

Race 2

1 D Polen, USA, Ducati
2 K Magee, Aus, Yamaha
3 F Pirovano, Ita, Yamaha
4 A Slight, NZ, Kawasaki
5 S Tsukamoto, Jap, Kawasaki
6 G Falappa, Ita, Ducati
7 K Kitagawa, Jap, Kawasaki

8 R Roche, Fra, Ducati
9 D Tardozzi, Ita, Ducati
10 R Phillis, Aus, Kawasaki
11 P Bontempi, Ita, Kawasaki
12 M Mladin, Aus, Kawasaki
13 F Merkel, USA, Yamaha
14 W Yoshikawa, Jap, Yamaha
15 B Monti, Ita, Honda

Standings – 1 Polen 267;
2 Roche 241; 3 Phillis 223;
4 Falappa 206; 5 Pirovano 187;
6 Slight 167

Round 10 – Holland
Assen, 13 September
Race 1

1 D Polen, USA, Ducati
2 S Mertens, Bel, Ducati
3 R Roche, Fra, Ducati
4 C Fogarty, GB, Ducati
5 R Phillis, Aus, Kawasaki
6 P Bontempi, Ita, Kawasaki
7 A Slight, NZ, Kawasaki
8 G Falappa, Ita, Ducati
9 F Pirovano, Ita, Yamaha
10 A Morillas, Fra, Yamaha
11 T Rymer, GB, Kawasaki
12 C Lindholm, Swe, Yamaha
13 F Merkel, USA, Yamaha
14 D Amatriain, Spa, Ducati
15 R Kellenberger, CH, Yamaha

Race 2

1 G Falappa, Ita, Ducati
2 C Fogarty, GB, Ducati
3 R Roche, Fra, Ducati
4 A Slight, NZ, Kawasaki
5 D Amatriain, Spa, Ducati
6 F Furlan, Ita, Ducati
7 A Morillas, Fra, Yamaha
8 F Pirovano, Ita, Yamaha
9 R Kellenberger, CH, Yamaha
10 J-Y Mounier, Fra, Yamaha
11 M Pajic, Nl, Yamaha
12 J Verwijst, Nl, Kawasaki
13 A Meklau, Aut, Ducati

14 J d'Orgeix, Fra, Kawasaki
15 F Ferracci, Fra, Ducati

Standings – 1 Polen 287;
2 Roche 271; 3 Phillis & Falappa 234;
5 Pirovano 202; 6 Slight 189

Round 11 – Italy
Monza, 4 October
Race 1

1 F Pirovano, Ita, Yamaha
2 S Mertens, Bel, Ducati
3 R Phillis, Aus, Kawasaki
4 P Bontempi, Ita, Kawasaki
5 V de Stefanis, Ita, Ducati
6 D Amatriain, Spa, Ducati
7 J d'Orgeix, Fra, Kawasaki
8 M Lucchiari, Ita, Ducati
9 J Suhonen, Fin, Yamaha
10 D Polen, USA, Ducati
11 V Ferrari, Ita, Ducati
12 G Falappa, Ita, Ducati
13 U Mark, Ger, Yamaha
14 P Igoa, Fra, Suzuki
15 V Scatola, Ita, Kawasaki

Race 2

1 F Pirovano, Ita, Yamaha
2 R Roche, Fra, Ducati
3 P Bontempi, Ita, Kawasaki
4 S Mertens, Bel, Ducati
5 D Polen, USA, Ducati
6 G Falappa, Ita, Ducati
7 J d'Orgeix, Fra, Kawasaki
8 D Amatriain, Spa, Ducati
9 V Ferrari, Ita, Ducati
10 J Suhonen, Fin, Yamaha
11 G Grassetti, Ita, Ducati
12 M Lucchiari, Ita, Ducati
13 P Igoa, Fra, Suzuki
14 M Amalric, Fra, Yamaha
15 R Phillis, Aus, Kawasaki

Standings – 1 Polen 304;
2 Roche 288; 3 Phillis 250;
4 Falappa 248; 5 Pirovano 242;
6 Slight 189

Round 12 – Australia
Phillip Island, 18 October
Race 1
1 K Magee, Aus, Yamaha
2 D Polen, USA, Ducati
3 S Mertens, Bel, Ducati
4 A Slight, NZ, Kawasaki
5 G Falappa, Ita, Ducati
6 R Phillis, Aus, Kawasaki
7 C Fogarty, GB, Ducati
8 P Bontempi, Ita, Kawasaki
9 M Campbell, Aus, Honda
10 F Merkel, USA, Yamaha
11 M O'Connor, Aus, Honda
12 F Pirovano, Ita, Yamaha
13 M Craggill, Aus, Kawasaki
14 J de Vries, Nl, Yamaha
15 P Guest, Aus, Yamaha

Race 2
1 R Roche, Fra, Ducati
2 K Magee, Aus, Yamaha
3 A Slight, NZ, Kawasaki
4 D Polen, USA, Ducati
5 M Mladin, Aus, Kawasaki
6 F Pirovano, Ita, Yamaha
7 P Bontempi, Ita, Kawasaki
8 M O'Connor, Aus, Honda
9 R Phillis, Aus, Kawasaki
10 S Doohan, Aus, Yamaha
11 M Craggill, Aus, Kawasaki
12 F Merkel, USA, Yamaha
13 J de Vries, Nl, Yamaha
14 T Corser, Aus, Yamaha
15 K McCarthy, Aus, Suzuki

*Standings – 1 Polen 334;
2 Roche 308; 3 Phillis 267;
4 Falappa 259; 5 Pirovano 256;
6 Slight 217*

Round 13 – New Zealand
Manfeild, 25 October
Race 1
1 D Polen, USA, Ducati
2 A Slight, NZ, Kawasaki
3 R Roche, Fra, Ducati
4 R Phillis, Aus, Kawasaki
5 F Pirovano, Ita, Yamaha
6 F Merkel, USA, Yamaha
7 P Bontempi, Ita, Kawasaki
8 S Doohan, Aus, Yamaha
9 D Amatriain, Spa, Ducati
10 T Corser, Aus, Yamaha
11 T Rees, NZ, Yamaha
12 R Josiah, NZ, Kawasaki
13 P McQuilkin, NZ, Suzuki
14 M King, NZ, Ducati
15 S Buckley, NZ, Yamaha

Race 2
1 G Falappa, Ita, Ducati
2 D Polen, USA, Ducati
3 A Slight, NZ, Kawasaki
4 R Roche, Fra, Ducati
5 F Pirovano, Ita, Yamaha
6 F Merkel, USA, Yamaha
7 R Phillis, Aus, Kawasaki
8 S Doohan, Aus, Yamaha
9 D Amatriain, Spa, Ducati
10 T Corser, Aus, Yamaha
11 C Lindholm, Swe, Yamaha
12 T Rees, NZ, Yamaha
13 P McQuilkin, NZ, Suzuki
14 R Josiah, NZ, Kawasaki
15 S Buckley, NZ, Yamaha

*Final Standings – 1 Polen 371;
2 Roche 336; 3 Phillis 289;
4 Falappa 279; 5 Pirovano 278;
6 Slight 249*

1993 SEASON
Round 1 – Ireland
9 April, Brands Hatch
Race 1
1 G Falappa, Ita, Ducati
2 S Russell, USA, Kawasaki
3 B Morrison, GB, Kawasaki
4 A Morillas, Fra, Kawasaki
5 A Slight, NZ, Kawasaki
6 S Mertens, Bel, Ducati
7 F Merkel, USA, Yamaha
8 M Farmer, GB, Kawasaki
9 D Jefferies, GB, Yamaha
10 T Nobles, USA, Honda
11 J Garriga, Spa, Ducati
12 V de Stefanis, Ita, Yamaha
13 M Lucchiari, Ita, Ducati
14 H Moineau, Fra, Suzuki
15 B Metzger, CH, Yamaha

Race 2
1 G Falappa, Ita, Ducati
2 S Russell, USA, Kawasaki
3 F Pirovano, Ita, Yamaha
4 S Mertens, Bel, Ducati
5 T Rymer, GB, Yamaha
6 A Slight, NZ, Kawasaki
7 F Merkel, USA, Yamaha
8 J Garriga, Spa, Ducati
9 V de Stefanis, Ita, Yamaha
10 E Gschwender, Ger, Kawasaki
11 A Morillas, Fra, Kawasaki
12 M Lucchiari, Ita, Ducati
13 B Monti, Ita, Ducati
14 D Jefferies, GB, Yamaha
15 D Amatriain, Spa, Ducati

*Standings – 1 Falappa 40;
2 Russell 34; 3 Mertens 23;
4 Slight 21; 5 Merkel & Morillas 18*

Round 2 – Germany
Hockenheim, 9 May
Race 1
1 G Falappa, Ita, Ducati
2 F Pirovano, Ita, Yamaha
3 C Fogarty, GB, Ducati
4 A Slight, NZ, Kawasaki
5 A Morillas, Fra, Kawasaki
6 S Russell, USA, Kawasaki
7 A Hofmann, Ger, Kawasaki
8 T Rymer, GB, Yamaha
9 C Lindholm, Swe, Yamaha
10 R Kellerman, Ger, Yamaha
11 J de Vries, Nl, Yamaha
12 E Weibel, CH, Ducati
13 D Sarron, Fra, Yamaha
14 U Mark, Ger, Yamaha
15 B Schick, Ger, Ducati

Race 2
1 S Russell, USA, Kawasaki
2 J Garriga, Spa, Ducati
3 G Falappa, Ita, Ducati
4 A Slight, NZ, Kawasaki
5 F Pirovano, Ita, Yamaha
6 S Mertens, Bel, Ducati
7 C Fogarty, GB, Ducati
8 A Morillas, Fra, Kawasaki
9 P Bontempi, Ita, Kawasaki
10 S Crafar, NZ, Ducati
11 E Weibel, CH, Ducati
12 F Merkel, USA, Yamaha
13 C Lindholm, Swe, Yamaha
14 R Kellerman, CH, Yamaha
15 D Amatriain, Spa, Ducati

*Standings – 1 Falappa 75;
2 Russell 64; 3 Slight 47;
4 Pirovano 43; 5 Morillas 37;
6 Mertens 33*

Round 3 – Spain
Albacete, 30 May
Race 1
1 C Fogarty, GB, Ducati
2 A Slight, NZ, Kawasaki
3 P Bontempi, Ita, Kawasaki
4 F Pirovano, Ita, Yamaha
5 D Amatriain, Spa, Ducati
6 J Garriga, Spa, Ducati
7 T Rymer, GB, Yamaha
8 S Crafar, NZ, Ducati
9 F Merkel, USA, Yamaha
10 R McElnea, GB, Yamaha
11 J Whitham, GB, Yamaha
12 M Lucchiari, Ita, Ducati
13 C Lindholm, Swe, Yamaha
14 F Furlan, Ita, Kawasaki
15 A Presciutti, Ita, Ducati

Race 2
1 C Fogarty, GB, Ducati
2 S Russell, USA, Kawasaki
3 A Slight, NZ, Kawasaki
4 S Mertens, Bel, Ducati
5 J Garriga, Spa, Ducati
6 P Bontempi, Ita, Kawasaki
7 F Pirovano, Ita, Yamaha
8 S Crafar, NZ, Ducati
9 T Rymer, GB, Yamaha
10 M Lucchiari, Ita, Ducati
11 J Whitham, GB, Yamaha
12 F Merkel, USA, Yamaha
13 A Morillas, Fra, Kawasaki
14 R McElnea, GB, Yamaha
15 J de Vries, Nl, Yamaha

*Standings – 1 Russell 81;
2 Slight 79; 3 Falappa 75;
4 Pirovano 65; 5 Fogarty 64;
6 Garriga 51*

Round 4 – San Marino
Misano, 27 June
Race 1
1 G Falappa, Ita, Ducati
2 M Lucchiari, Ita, Ducati
3 F Pirovano, Ita, Yamaha
4 S Russell, USA, Kawasaki
5 C Fogarty, GB, Ducati
6 A Slight, NZ, Kawasaki
7 J Garriga, Spa, Ducati
8 B Monti, Ita, Ducati
9 T Rymer, GB, Yamaha
10 F Merkel, USA, Yamaha
11 J de Vries, Nl, Yamaha
12 A Presciutti, Ita, Ducati
13 A Harmati, Hun, Yamaha
14 J-M Deletang, Fra, Yamaha
15 T Nobles, USA, Honda

Race 2
1 G Falappa, Ita, Ducati
2 S Russell, USA, Kawasaki
3 C Fogarty, GB, Ducati
4 M Lucchiari, Ita, Ducati
5 J Garriga, Spa, Ducati
6 A Slight, NZ, Kawasaki
7 P Bontempi, Ita, Kawasaki
8 B Monti, Ita, Ducati
9 T Rymer, GB, Yamaha
10 S Mertens, Bel, Ducati
11 F Pirovano, Ita, Yamaha
12 J de Vries, Nl, Yamaha
13 D Amatriain, Spa, Ducati
14 U Mark, Ger, Yamaha
15 J-M Deletang, Fra, Yamaha

*Standings – 1 Falappa 115;
2 Russell 111; 3 Slight 99;
4 Fogarty 90; 5 Pirovano 85;
6 Garriga 71*

Round 5 – Austria
Osterreichring, 11 July
Race 1
1 A Meklau, Aut, Ducati
2 A Slight, NZ, Kawasaki
3 S Russell, USA, Kawasaki
4 C Fogarty, GB, Ducati
5 P Bontempi, Ita, Kawasaki
6 G Falappa, Ita, Ducati
7 J de Vries, Nl, Yamaha
8 E Gschwender, Ger, Kawasaki
9 S Mertens, Bel, Ducati
10 F Furlan, Ita, Kawasaki
11 F Merkel, USA, Yamaha
12 C Lindholm, Swe, Yamaha
13 J-M Deletang, Fra, Yamaha
14 M Ernst, CH, Kawasaki
15 T Rogier, Fra, Ducati

Race 2
1 G Falappa, Ita, Ducati
2 F Merkel, USA, Yamaha
3 A Meklau, Aut, Ducati
4 C Fogarty, GB, Ducati
5 M Lucchiari, Ita, Ducati
6 E Gschwender, Ger, Kawasaki
7 S Russell, USA, Kawasaki
8 T Nobles, USA, Honda
9 J de Vries, Nl, Yamaha
10 J-M Deletang, Fra, Yamaha
11 T Rogier, Fra, Ducati
12 H Moineau, Fra, Suzuki
13 M Ernst, CH, Kawasaki
14 U Mark, Ger, Yamaha
15 P Bontempi, Ita, Kawasaki

Standings – 1 Falappa 135;
2 Russell 130.5; 3 Slight 116;
4 Fogarty 109.5; 5 Pirovano 85;
6 Garriga 71

Round 6 – Czech Republic
Brno, 18 July
Race 1
1 C Fogarty, GB, Ducati
2 S Russell, USA, Kawasaki
3 A Slight, NZ, Kawasaki
4 F Pirovano, Ita, Yamaha
5 G Falappa, Ita, Ducati
6 M Lucchiari, Ita, Ducati
7 P Bontempi, Ita, Kawasaki
8 E Weibel, CH, Ducati
9 T Rymer, GB, Yamaha
10 S Mertens, Bel, Ducati
11 A Hofmann, Ger, Kawasaki
12 B Monti, Ita, Ducati
13 A Presciutti, Ita, Ducati
14 J de Vries, Nl, Yamaha
15 E Gschwender, Ger, Kawasaki

Race 2
1 S Russell, USA, Kawasaki
2 C Fogarty, GB, Ducati
3 S Mertens, Bel, Ducati
4 F Pirovano, Ita, Yamaha
5 F Merkel, USA, Yamaha
6 P Bontempi, Ita, Kawasaki
7 C Lindholm, Swe, Yamaha
8 J de Vries, Nl, Yamaha
9 A Presciutti, Ita, Ducati
10 A Hofmann, Ger, Kawasaki
11 B Schick, Ger, Ducati
12 J-M Deletang, Fra, Yamaha
13 T Nobles, USA, Honda
14 E Gschwender, Ger, Kawasaki
15 M Kellenberger, CH, Kawasaki

Standings – 1 Russell 167.5;
2 Fogarty 146.5; 3 Falappa 146;
4 Slight 131; 5 Pirovano 111;
6 Mertens 80

Round 7 – Sweden
Anderstorp, 8 August
Race 1
1 C Fogarty, GB, Ducati
2 G Falappa, Ita, Ducati
3 F Pirovano, Ita, Yamaha
4 S Russell, USA, Kawasaki
5 J Whitham, GB, Yamaha
6 S Mertens, Bel, Ducati
7 P Bontempi, Ita, Kawasaki
8 A Slight, NZ, Kawasaki
9 C Lindholm, Swe, Yamaha
10 F Furlan, Ita, Kawasaki
11 J-M Deletang, Fra, Yamaha
12 F Merkel, USA, Yamaha
13 J de Vries, Nl, Yamaha
14 P Mouchet, Fra, Ducati
15 J-Y Mounier, Fra, Yamaha

Race 2
1 C Fogarty, GB, Ducati
2 S Russell, USA, Kawasaki
3 G Falappa, Ita, Ducati
4 F Pirovano, Ita, Yamaha
5 A Slight, NZ, Kawasaki
6 S Mertens, Bel, Ducati
7 F Furlan, Ita, Kawasaki
8 P Bontempi, Ita, Kawasaki
9 J de Vries, Nl, Yamaha
10 B Morrison, GB, Kawasaki
11 H Moineau, Fra, Suzuki
12 A Harmati, Hun, Yamaha
13 J-Y Mounier, Fra, Yamaha
14 R Valderhaug, Nor, Yamaha
15 C Rebuttini, Fra, Ducati

Standings – 1 Russell 197.5;
2 Fogarty 186.5; 3 Falappa 178;
4 Slight 150; 5 Pirovano 139;
6 Mertens 100

Round 8 – Malaysia
Johor, 22 August
Race 1
1 C Fogarty, GB, Ducati
2 S Russell, USA, Kawasaki
3 F Pirovano, Ita, Yamaha
4 A Slight, NZ, Kawasaki
5 S Mertens, Bel, Ducati
6 P Bontempi, Ita, Kawasaki
7 M Lucchiari, Ita, Ducati
8 C Lindholm, Swe, Yamaha
9 F Merkel, USA, Yamaha
10 F Furlan, Ita, Kawasaki
11 B Archibald, Aus, Yamaha
12 J-M Deletang, Fra, Yamaha
13 K Watson, Aus, Kawasaki
14 C Adi Haslam, Mal, Kawasaki
15 T Jordan, Aus, Kawasaki

Race 2
1 C Fogarty, GB, Ducati
2 S Russell, USA, Kawasaki
3 F Pirovano, Ita, Yamaha
4 P Bontempi, Ita, Kawasaki
5 S Mertens, Bel, Ducati
6 A Slight, NZ, Kawasaki
7 R Phillis, Aus, Kawasaki
8 T Rymer, GB, Yamaha
9 M Lucchiari, Ita, Ducati
10 C Lindholm, Swe, Yamaha
11 H Moineau, Fra, Suzuki
12 J de Vries, Nl, Yamaha
13 J-M Deletang, Fra, Yamaha
14 T Jordan, Aus, Kawasaki
15 B Archibald, Aus, Yamaha

Standings – 1 Russell 231.5;
2 Fogarty 226.5; 3 Falappa 178;
4 Slight 173; 5 Pirovano 169;
6 Mertens 122

Round 9 – Japan
Sugo, 29 August
Race 1
1 C Fogarty, GB, Ducati
2 K Kitagawa, Jap, Kawasaki
3 S Tsukamoto, Jap, Kawasaki
4 S Mertens, Bel, Ducati
5 G Falappa, Ita, Ducati
6 A Slight, NZ, Kawasaki
7 F Pirovano, Ita, Yamaha
8 S Russell, USA, Kawasaki
9 P Bontempi, Ita, Kawasaki
10 T Rymer, GB, Yamaha
11 T Arakaki, Jap, Ducati
12 K Takahashi, Jap, Yamaha
13 A Presciutti, Ita, Ducati
14 C Lindholm, Swe, Yamaha
15 M Suzuki, Jap, Ducati

Race 2
1 S Russell, USA, Kawasaki
2 K Kitagawa, Jap, Kawasaki
3 S Tsukamoto, Jap, Kawasaki
4 A Slight, NZ, Kawasaki
5 F Pirovano, Ita, Yamaha
6 T Arakaki, Jap, Ducati
7 T Rymer, GB, Yamaha
8 S Miyazaki, Jap, Kawasaki
9 M Suzuki, Jap, Ducati
10 S Imai, Jap, Kawasaki
11 F Furlan, Ita, Kawasaki
12 C Lindholm, Swe, Yamaha
13 M Nakada, Jap, Yamaha
14 M Mogi, Jap, Kawasaki
15 H Senmyo, Jap, Honda

Standings – 1 Russell 259.5;
2 Fogarty 246.5; 3 Slight 196;
4 Falappa & Pirovano 189;
6 Mertens 135

Round 10 – Holland
Assen, 12 September
Race 1
1 C Fogarty, GB, Ducati
2 S Russell, USA, Kawasaki
3 A Slight, NZ, Kawasaki
4 S Mertens, Bel, Ducati
5 J Whitham, GB, Yamaha
6 P Bontempi, Ita, Kawasaki
7 T Rymer, GB, Yamaha
8 A Hofmann, Ger, Kawasaki
9 C Lindholm, Swe, Yamaha
10 M Lucchiari, Ita, Ducati
11 F Merkel, USA, Yamaha
12 J de Vries, Nl, Yamaha
13 F Furlan, Ita, Kawasaki
14 C Lavieille, Fra, Ducati
15 E Gschwender, Ger, Kawasaki

Race 2
1 C Fogarty, GB, Ducati
2 S Russell, USA, Kawasaki
3 S Mertens, Bel, Ducati
4 F Pirovano, Ita, Yamaha
5 J Whitham, GB, Yamaha
6 A Slight, NZ, Kawasaki
7 G Falappa, Ita, Ducati
8 C Lindholm, Swe, Yamaha
9 T Rymer, GB, Yamaha
10 P Bontempi, Ita, Kawasaki
11 J de Vries, Nl, Yamaha
12 A Hofmann, Ger, Kawasaki
13 F Furlan, Ita, Kawasaki
14 M Pajic, Nl, Kawasaki
15 A Vieira, Fra, Yamaha

Standings – 1 Russell 293.5;
2 Fogarty 286.5; 3 Slight 221;
4 Pirovano 202; 5 Falappa 198;
6 Mertens 163

Round 11 – Italy
Monza, 26 September
Race 1
1 A Slight, NZ, Kawasaki
2 S Russell, USA, Kawasaki
3 F Pirovano, Ita, Yamaha
4 C Fogarty, GB, Ducati
5 T Nobles, USA, Honda
6 C Lindholm, Swe, Yamaha
7 A Vieira, Fra, Yamaha
8 B Morrison, GB, Kawasaki
9 F Furlan, Ita, Kawasaki
10 M Ernst, CH, Kawasaki
11 D Sarron, Fra, Yamaha
12 M Mastrelli, Ita, Yamaha
13 A Morillas, Fra, Kawasaki
14 H Moineau, Fra, Suzuki
15 D Bonoris, Fra, Kawasaki

Race 2
1 G Falappa, Ita, Ducati
2 A Slight, NZ, Kawasaki
3 F Pirovano, Ita, Yamaha
4 C Fogarty, GB, Ducati
5 S Russell, USA, Kawasaki
6 M Lucchiari, Ita, Ducati
7 S Mertens, Bel, Ducati
8 P Bontempi, Ita, Kawasaki
9 C Lindholm, Swe, Yamaha
10 T Nobles, USA, Honda
11 M Ernst, CH, Kawasaki
12 B Morrison, GB, Kawasaki
13 H Moineau, Fra, Suzuki
14 F Furlan, Ita, Kawasaki
15 B Mugues, CH, Kawasaki

Standings – 1 Russell 321.5;
2 Fogarty 312.5; 3 Slight 258;
4 Pirovano 232; 5 Falappa 218;
6 Mertens 172

Round 12 – Great Britain
Donington Park, 3 October
Race 1
1 S Russell, USA, Kawasaki
2 C Fogarty, GB, Ducati
3 A Slight, NZ, Kawasaki
4 F Pirovano, Ita, Yamaha
5 P Bontempi, Ita, Kawasaki
6 B Morrison, GB, Kawasaki
7 A Meklau, Aut, Ducati
8 A Hofmann, Ger, Kawasaki
9 C Lindholm, Swe, Yamaha
10 J McWilliams, GB, Ducati
11 C Lavieille, Fra, Ducati
12 S Hislop, GB, Ducati
13 M Rutter, GB, Kawasaki
14 R Stringer, GB, Kawasaki
15 M. Uedl, Ger, Kawasaki

Race 2
1 S Russell, USA, Kawasaki
2 A Slight, NZ, Kawasaki
3 J Whitham, GB, Yamaha
4 N Mackenzie, GB, Ducati
5 G Falappa, Ita, Ducati
6 F Pirovano, Ita, Yamaha
7 A Meklau, Aut, Ducati
8 P Bontempi, Ita, Kawasaki
9 B Morrison, GB, Kawasaki
10 C Lindholm, Swe, Yamaha
11 M Llewellyn, GB, Kawasaki
12 M Uedl, Ger, Kawasaki
13 C Lavieille, Fra, Ducati
14 D Bonoris, Fra, Kawasaki
15 A Vieira, Fra, Yamaha

Standings – 1 Russell 361.5;
2 Fogarty 329.5; 3 Slight 290;
4 Pirovano 255; 5 Falappa 229;
6 Mertens 172

Round 13 – Portugal
Estoril, 17 October
Race 1
1 F Pirovano, Ita, Yamaha
2 P Bontempi, Ita, Kawasaki
3 A Slight, NZ, Kawasaki
4 G Falappa, Ita, Ducati
5 T Rymer, GB, Yamaha
6 S Crafar, NZ, Ducati
7 A Meklau, Aut, Ducati
8 B Morrison, GB, Kawasaki
9 D Sarron, Fra, Yamaha
10 D Bonoris, Fra, Kawasaki
11 F Merkel, USA, Yamaha
12 J de Vries, NI, Yamaha
13 J-M Deletang, Fra, Yamaha
14 M Graziano, Fra, Suzuki
15 T Pereira, Por, Suzuki

Race 2
1 C Fogarty, GB, Ducati
2 S Russell, USA, Kawasaki
3 F Pirovano, Ita, Yamaha
4 G Falappa, Ita, Ducati
5 A Slight, NZ, Kawasaki
6 T Rymer, GB, Yamaha
7 A Meklau, Aut, Ducati
8 B Morrison, GB, Kawasaki
9 F Merkel, USA, Yamaha
10 P Bontempi, Ita, Kawasaki
11 D Sarron, Fra, Yamaha
12 C Lindholm, Swe, Yamaha
13 J-M Deletang, Fra, Yamaha
14 D Bonoris, Fra, Kawasaki
15 C Lavieille, Fra, Ducati

Final Standings – 1 Russell 378.5;
2 Fogarty 349.5; 3 Slight 316;
4 Pirovano 290; 5 Falappa 255;
6 Bontempi 184.5

1994 SEASON
Round 1 – Great Britain
Donington Park, 2 May,
Race 1
1 C Fogarty, GB, Ducati
2 A Slight, NZ, Honda
3 F Pirovano, Ita, Ducati
4 S Russell, USA, Kawasaki
5 G Falappa, Ita, Ducati
6 S Crafar, NZ, Honda
7 P Bontempi, Ita, Kawasaki
8 B Morrison, GB, Honda
9 D Polen, USA, Honda
10 M Moroni, Ita, Kawasaki
11 V de Stefanis, Ita, Ducati
12 J-Y Mounier, Fra, Ducati
13 M Rutter, GB, Ducati
14 J Moodie, GB, Yamaha
15 A Meklau, Aut, Ducati

Race 2
1 S Russell, USA, Kawasaki
2 C Fogarty, GB, Ducati
3 T Corser, Aus, Ducati
4 G Falappa, Ita, Ducati
5 S Crafar, NZ, Honda
6 B Morrison, GB, Honda
7 D Polen, USA, Honda
8 M Lucchiari, Ita, Yamaha
9 J-Y Mounier, Fra, Ducati
10 M Moroni, Ita, Kawasaki
11 N Hopkins, GB, Yamaha
12 A Vieira, Fra, Honda
13 J Kuhn, Fra, Honda
14 D Bonoris, Fra, Kawasaki
15 S Foti, Ita, Ducati

Standings – 1 Fogarty 37;
2 Russell 33; 3 Falappa 24;
4 Crafar 21; 5 Morrison 18; 6 Slight 17

Round 2 – Germany
Hockenheim, 8 May
Race 1
1 S Russell, USA, Kawasaki
2 A Slight, NZ, Honda
3 T Rymer, GB, Ducati
4 A Morillas, Fra, Kawasaki
5 D Polen, USA, Honda
6 J-Y Mounier, Fra, Ducati
7 S Crafar, NZ, Honda
8 E Weibel, CH, Ducati
9 R Phillis, Aus, Kawasaki
10 R Kellenberger, Ger, Yamaha
11 A Vieira, Fra, Honda
12 A Perselli, Ita, Ducati
13 M Paquay, Bel, Honda
14 B Morrison, GB, Honda
15 U Mark, Ger, Ducati

Race 2
1 S Russell, USA, Kawasaki
2 F Pirovano, Ita, Ducati
3 D Polen, USA, Honda
4 G Falappa, Ita, Ducati
5 K Kitagawa, Jap, Kawasaki
6 T Rymer, GB, Kawasaki
7 V de Stefanis, Ita, Ducati
8 E Weibel, CH, Ducati
9 U Mark, Ger, Ducati
10 A Meklau, Aut, Ducati
11 M Moroni, Ita, Kawasaki
12 C Lindholm, Swe, Yamaha
13 J Schmid, Ger, Kawasaki
14 J-Y Mounier, Fra, Ducati
15 D Bonoris, Fra, Kawasaki

Standings – 1 Russell 73;
2 Polen 42;
3 Falappa & Fogarty 37; 5 Slight 34;
6 Pirovano 32

Round 3 – Italy
Misano, 29 May
Race 1
1 S Russell, USA, Kawasaki
2 G Falappa, Ita, Ducati
3 A Slight, NZ, Honda
4 S Mertens, Bel, Ducati
5 M Lucchiari, Ita, Yamaha
6 V de Stefanis, Ita, Ducati
7 S Crafar, NZ, Honda
8 G Liverani, Ita, Honda
9 M Meregalli, Ita, Yamaha
10 A Meklau, Aut, Ducati
11 J Whitham, GB, Ducati
12 D Polen, USA, Honda
13 C Mariottini, Ita, Ducati
14 A Perselli, Ita, Ducati
15 M Moroni, Ita, Kawasaki

Race 2
1 G Falappa, Ita, Ducati
2 S Russell, USA, Kawasaki
3 M Lucchiari, Ita, Yamaha
4 A Slight, NZ, Honda
5 C Fogarty, GB, Ducati
6 F Pirovano, Ita, Ducati
7 P Bontempi, Ita, Kawasaki
8 V de Stefanis, Ita, Ducati
9 T Rymer, GB, Ducati
10 A Meklau, Aut, Ducati
11 S Crafar, NZ, Honda
12 M Meregalli, Ita, Yamaha
13 S Foti, Ita, Ducati
14 M Moroni, Ita, Kawasaki
15 D Polen, USA, Honda

Standings – 1 Russell 110;
2 Falappa 74; 3 Slight 62;
4 Fogarty 48; 5 Polen 47;
6 Crafar 44

Round 4 – Spain
Albacete, 19 June
Race 1
1 C Fogarty, GB, Ducati
2 A Slight, NZ, Honda
3 J Whitham, GB, Ducati
4 P Bontempi, Ita, Kawasaki
5 T Rymer, GB, Kawasaki
6 D Polen, USA, Honda
7 A Meklau, Aut, Ducati
8 S Crafar, NZ, Honda
9 S Mertens, Bel, Ducati
10 B Morrison, GB, Honda
11 S Foti, Ita, Ducati
12 A Morillas, Fra, Kawasaki
13 C Cardus, Spa, Ducati
14 S Caracchi, Ita, Ducati
15 M Paquay, Bel, Honda

Race 2
1 C Fogarty, GB, Ducati
2 A Slight, NZ, Honda
3 J Whitham, GB, Ducati
4 A Meklau, Aut, Ducati
5 T Rymer, GB, Kawasaki
6 P Bontempi, Ita, Kawasaki
7 D Polen, USA, Honda
8 C Cardus, Spa, Ducati
9 A Morillas, Fra, Kawasaki
10 S Mertens, Bel, Ducati
11 F Pirovano, Ita, Ducati
12 S Foti, Ita, Ducati
13 B Morrison, GB, Honda
14 S Crafar, NZ, Honda
15 G Liverani, Ita, Honda

Standings – 1 Russell 110;
2 Slight 96; 3 Fogarty 88;
4 Falappa 74;
5 Crafar & Rymer 54

Round 5 – Austria
Osterreichring, 17 July
Race 1
1 C Fogarty, GB, Ducati
2 A Meklau, Aut, Ducati
3 D Polen, USA, Honda
4 A Slight, NZ, Honda
5 S Mertens, Bel, Ducati
6 S Crafar, NZ, Honda
7 J Whitham, GB, Ducati
8 F Pirovano, Ita, Ducati
9 R Panichi, Ita, Ducati
10 R Phillis, Aus, Kawasaki
11 P Bontempi, Ita, Kawasaki
12 M Meregalli, Ita, Yamaha
13 S Foti, Ita, Ducati
14 S Russell, USA, Kawasaki
15 C Lindholm, Swe, Yamaha

Race 2
1 C Fogarty, GB, Ducati
2 A Meklau, Aut, Ducati
3 D Polen, USA, Honda
4 A Slight, NZ, Honda
5 S Mertens, Bel, Ducati
6 S Crafar, NZ, Honda
7 P Casoli, Ita, Yamaha
8 J Schmid, Ger, Kawasaki
9 P Bontempi, Ita, Kawasaki
10 S Foti, Ita, Ducati
11 T Rymer, GB, Kawasaki
12 S Russell, USA, Kawasaki
13 R Phillis, Aus, Kawasaki
14 C Lindholm, Swe, Yamaha
15 M Meregalli, Ita, Yamaha

Standings – 1 Fogarty 128;
2 Slight 122; 3 Russell 116;
4 Polen 96; 5 Meklau 75;
6 Crafar & Falappa 74

Round 6 – Indonesia
Sentul, 21 August
Race 1
1 J Whitham, GB, Ducati
2 A Slight, NZ, Honda
3 S Russell, USA, Kawasaki
4 D Polen, USA, Honda
5 S Crafar, NZ, Honda
6 A Meklau, Aut, Ducati
7 A Morillas, Fra, Kawasaki
8 T Rymer, GB, Kawasaki
9 S Mertens, Bel, Ducati
10 V de Stefanis, Ita, Ducati
11 P Bontempi, Ita, Kawasaki
13 B Morrison, GB, Honda
14 G Muteau, Fra, Ducati
15 A Vieira, Fra, Honda

Race 2
1 C Fogarty, GB, Ducati
2 A Slight, NZ, Honda
3 S Russell, USA, Kawasaki
4 J Whitham, GB, Ducati
5 A Meklau, Aut, Ducati
6 D Polen, USA, Honda
7 T Rymer, GB, Kawasaki
8 A Morillas, Fra, Kawasaki
9 S Mertens, Bel, Ducati
10 S Crafar, NZ, Honda
11 P Bontempi, Ita, Kawasaki
12 V de Stefanis, Ita, Ducati
13 B Morrison, GB, Honda
14 A Vieira, Fra, Honda
15 M Moroni, Ita, Kawasaki

Standings – 1 Slight 156;
2 Fogarty 148; 3 Russell 146;
4 Polen 119; 5 Meklau 96;
6 Crafar 91

Round 7 – Japan
Sugo, 28 August
Race 1
1 S Russell, USA, Kawasaki
2 F Pirovano, Ita, Ducati
3 Y Nagai, Jap, Yamaha
4 C Fogarty, GB, Ducati
5 W Yoshikawa, Jap, Yamaha
6 A Slight, NZ, Honda
7 T Aoki, Jap, Honda
8 A Gobert, Aus, Honda
9 A Meklau, Aut, Ducati
10 D Polen, USA, Honda
11 A Yanagawa, Jap, Suzuki
12 P Bontempi, Ita, Kawasaki
13 A Morillas, Fra, Kawasaki
14 A Vieira, Fra, Honda
15 K Iwahashi, Jap, Honda

Race 2
1 S Russell, USA, Kawasaki
2 C Fogarty, GB, Ducati
3 K Kitagawa, Jap, Kawasaki
4 W Yoshikawa, Jap, Yamaha
5 Y Nagai, Jap, Yamaha
6 A Gobert, Aus, Honda
7 A Slight, NZ, Honda
8 T Aoki, Jap, Honda
9 T Rymer, GB, Kawasaki
10 J Whitham, GB, Ducati
11 N Fujiwara, Jap, Yamaha
12 N Haga, Jap, Honda
13 T Tsukamoto, Jap, Kawasaki
14 S Crafar, NZ, Honda
15 S Takeishi, Jap, Honda

Standings – 1 Russell 186;
2 Fogarty 178; 3 Slight 175;
4 Polen 125; 5 Meklau 103;
6 Crafar 93

Round 8 – Holland
Assen, 11 September
Race 1
1 C Fogarty, GB, Ducati
2 P Casoli, Ita, Yamaha
3 A Slight, NZ, Honda
4 T Rymer, GB, Kawasaki
5 J Whitham, GB, Ducati
6 S Russell, USA, Kawasaki
7 S Crafar, NZ, Honda
8 J Schmid, Ger, Kawasaki
9 A Meklau, Aut, Ducati
10 S Mertens, Bel, Ducati
11 D Polen, USA, Honda
12 J-Y Mounier, Fra, Ducati
13 M Paquay, Bel, Honda
14 J de Vries, Nl, Yamaha
15 A Harmati, Hun, Yamaha

Race 2
1 C Fogarty, GB, Ducati
2 A Slight, NZ, Honda
3 M Lucchiari, Ita, Ducati
4 P Casoli, Ita, Yamaha
5 J Whitham, GB, Ducati
6 T Rymer, GB, Kawasaki
7 S Crafar, NZ, Honda
8 J Schmid, Ger, Kawasaki
9 S Russell, USA, Kawasaki
10 C Lindholm, Swe, Yamaha
11 F Pirovano, Ita, Ducati
12 A Meklau, Aut, Ducati
13 S Foti, Ita, Ducati
14 J-Y Mounier, Fra, Ducati
15 J de Vries, Nl, Yamaha

Standings – 1 Fogarty 218;
2 Slight 207; 3 Russell 203;
4 Polen 130; 5 Meklau 114;
6 Crafar 111

Round 9 – San Marino
Mugello, 25 September
Race 1
1 S Russell, USA, Kawasaki
2 C Fogarty, GB, Ducati
3 T Corser, Aus, Ducati
4 A Slight, NZ, Honda
5 F Pirovano, Ita, Ducati
6 A Meklau, Aut, Ducati
7 P Casoli, Ita, Yamaha
8 J Whitham, GB, Ducati
9 S Crafar, NZ, Honda
10 P Bontempi, Ita, Kawasaki
11 D Polen, USA, Honda
12 S Foti, Ita, Ducati
13 C Lindholm, Swe, Yamaha
14 M Meregalli, Ita, Yamaha
15 S Mertens, Bel, Ducati

Race 2
1 C Fogarty, GB, Ducati
2 A Slight, NZ, Honda
3 M Lucchiari, Ita, Ducati
4 J Whitham, GB, Ducati
5 F Pirovano, Ita, Ducati
6 P Bontempi, Ita, Kawasaki
7 D Polen, USA, Honda
8 J Schmid, Ger, Kawasaki
9 S Crafar, NZ, Honda
10 M Meregalli, Ita, Yamaha
11 B Morrison, GB, Honda
12 C Lindholm, Swe, Yamaha
13 J de Vries, Nl, Yamaha
14 S Mertens, Bel, Ducati
15 M Moroni, Ita, Kawasaki

Standings – 1 Fogarty 255;
2 Slight 237; 3 Russell 223;
4 Polen 144; 5 Whitham 126;
6 Crafar 125

Round 10 – Great Britain
Donington Park, 2 October
Race 1
1 S Russell, USA, Kawasaki
2 T Corser, Aus, Ducati
3 P Casoli, Ita, Yamaha
4 A Carter, GB, Ducati
5 S Crafar, NZ, Honda
6 P Bontempi, Ita, Kawasaki
7 A Meklau, Aut, Ducati
8 A Slight, NZ, Honda
9 B Morrison, GB, Honda
10 M Rutter, GB, Ducati
11 J Schmid, Ger, Kawasaki
12 D Polen, USA, Honda
13 V de Stefanis, Ita, Ducati
14 C Fogarty, GB, Ducati
15 M Meregalli, Ita, Yamaha

Race 2
1 S Russell, USA, Kawasaki
2 T Corser, Aus, Ducati
3 M Lucchiari, Ita, Ducati
4 P Casoli, Ita, Yamaha
5 C Fogarty, GB, Ducati
6 A Carter, GB, Ducati
7 P Bontempi, Ita, Kawasaki
8 B Morrison, GB, Honda
9 A Meklau, Aut, Ducati
10 A Slight, NZ, Honda
11 M Meregalli, Ita, Yamaha
12 F Pirovano, Ita, Ducati
13 J de Vries, Nl, Yamaha
14 M Llewellyn, GB, Ducati
15 S Crafar, NZ, Honda

Standings – 1 Fogarty 268;
2 Russell 263; 3 Slight 251;
4 Polen 148; 5 Meklau 140;
6 Crafar 137

Round 11 – Australia
Phillip Island, 30 October
Race 1
1 C Fogarty, GB, Ducati
2 S Russell, USA, Kawasaki
3 A Gobert, Aus, Kawasaki
4 A Slight, NZ, Honda
5 T Corser, Aus, Ducati
6 K McCarthy, Aus, Honda
7 M Mladin, Aus, Kawasaki
8 S Giles, Aus, Ducati
9 P Bontempi, Ita, Kawasaki
10 S Crafar, NZ, Honda
11 D Polen, USA, Honda
12 P Goddard, Aus, Suzuki
13 R Leslie, Aus, Ducati
14 A Meklau, Aut, Ducati
15 S Martin, Aus, Suzuki

Race 2
1 A Gobert, Aus, Kawasaki
2 C Fogarty, GB, Ducati
3 T Corser, Aus, Ducati
4 A Slight, NZ, Honda
5 K McCarthy, Aus, Honda
6 S Crafar, NZ, Honda
7 S Giles, Aus, Ducati
8 F Pirovano, Ita, Ducati
9 P Bontempi, Ita, Kawasaki
10 A Meklau, Aut, Ducati
11 D Polen, USA, Honda
12 S Mertens, Bel, Ducati
13 P Goddard, Aus, Suzuki
14 M Craggill, Aus, Kawasaki
15 S Martin, Aus, Suzuki

Final Standings – 1 Fogarty 305;
2 Russell 280; 3 Slight 277;
4 Polen 158; 5 Crafar 153;
6 Meklau 148

1995 SEASON
Round 1 – Germany
Hockenheim, 7 May
Race 1
1 C Fogarty, GB, Ducati
2 F Pirovano, Ita, Ducati
3 J Schmid, Ger, Kawasaki
4 Y Nagai, Jap, Yamaha
5 K Kitagawa, Jap, Kawasaki
6 A Slight, NZ, Honda
7 C Edwards, USA, Yamaha
8 S Russell, USA, Kawasaki
9 S Crafar, NZ, Honda
10 T Corser, Aus, Ducati
11 P Bontempi, Ita, Kawasaki
12 M Meregalli, Ita, Yamaha
13 A Morillas, Fra, Ducati
14 E Weibel, CH, Ducati
15 P Chili, Ita, Ducati

Race 2
1 C Fogarty, GB, Ducati
2 J Schmid, Ger, Kawasaki
3 A Slight, NZ, Honda
4 Y Nagai, Jap, Yamaha
5 C Edwards, USA, Yamaha
6 S Crafar, NZ, Honda
7 M Lucchiari, Ita, Ducati
8 T Corser, Aus, Ducati
9 P Chili, Ita, Ducati
10 S Russell, USA, Kawasaki
11 A Meklau, Aut, Ducati
12 K Kitagawa, Jap, Kawaaki
13 F Pirovano, Ita, Ducati
14 P Bontempi, Ita, Kawasaki
15 P Casoli, Ita, Yamaha

Standings – 1 Fogarty 50;
2 Schmid 36; 3 Nagai & Slight 26;
5 Pirovano 23; 6 Edwards 20

Round 2 – Italy
Misano, 21 May
Race 1
1 M Lucchiari, Ita, Ducati
2 C Fogarty, GB, Ducati
3 T Corser, Aus, Ducati
4 P Chili, Ita, Ducati
5 F Pirovano, Ita, Ducati
6 A Gobert, Aus, Kawasaki
7 J Reynolds, GB, Kawasaki
8 P Bontempi, Ita, Kawasaki
9 S Crafar, NZ, Honda
10 G Liverani, Ita, Ducati
11 A Meklau, Aut, Ducati
12 A Morillas, Fra, Ducati
13 Y Nagai, Jap, Yamaha
14 S Russell, USA, Kawasaki
15 J Schmid, Ger, Kawasaki

Race 2
1 M Lucchiari, Ita, Ducati
2 C Fogarty, GB, Ducati
3 T Corser, Aus, Ducati
4 P Chili, Ita, Ducati
5 P Bontempi, Ita, Kawasaki
6 F Pirovano, Ita, Ducati
7 A Meklau, Aut, Ducati
8 S Russell, USA, Kawasaki
9 J Reynolds, GB, Kawasaki
10 S Crafar, NZ, Honda
11 G Liverani, Ita, Ducati
12 J Schmid, Ger, Kawasaki
13 A Slight, NZ, Honda
14 A Morillas, Fra, Ducati
15 S Hislop, GB, Ducati

Standings – 1 Fogarty 90;
2 Lucchiari 59; 3 Corser 46;
4 Pirovano 44; 5 Schmid 41;
6 Chili 34

Round 3 – Great Britain
Donington Park, 28 May
Race 1
1 C Fogarty, GB, Ducati
2 T Corser, Aus, Ducati
3 J Whitham, GB, Ducati
4 A Slight, NZ, Honda
5 P Bontempi, Ita, Kawasaki
6 S Russell, USA, Kawasaki
7 J Reynolds, GB, Kawasaki
8 S Crafar, NZ, Honda
9 M Lucchiari, Ita, Ducati
10 A Gobert, Aus, Kawasaki
11 F Pirovano, Ita, Ducati
12 A Morillas, Fra, Ducati
13 J Schmid, Ger, Kawaski
14 Y Nagai, Jap, Yamaha
15 P Casoli, Ita, Yamaha

Race 2
1 C Fogarty, GB, Ducati
2 P Chili, Ita, Ducati
3 A Slight, NZ, Honda
4 P Bontempi, Ita, Kawasaki
5 F Pirovano, Ita, Ducati
6 S Crafar, NZ, Honda
7 Y Nagai, Jap, Yamaha
8 J Whitham, GB, Ducati
9 A Morillas, Fra, Ducati
10 M Lucchiari, Ita, Ducati
11 J Reynolds, GB, Kawasaki
12 C Edwards, USA, Yamaha
13 P Casoli, Ita, Yamaha
14 A Meklau, Aut, Ducati
15 M Llewellyn, GB, Ducati

Standings – 1 Fogarty 140;
2 Lucchiari 72; 3 Corser 66;
4 Pirovano 60; 5 Slight 58;
6 Chili 54

Round 4 – San Marino
Monza, 18 June
Race 1
1 C Fogarty, GB, Ducati
2 A Slight, NZ, Honda
3 C Edwards, USA, Yamaha
4 S Crafar, NZ, Honda
5 Y Nagai, Jap, Yamaha
6 M Lucchiari, Ita, Ducati
7 P Bontempi, Ita, Kawasaki
8 F Pirovano, Ita, Ducati
9 J Reynolds, GB, Kawasaki
10 G Liverani, Ita, Ducati
11 S Tsujimoto, Jap, Honda
12 M Gallina, Ita, Ducati
13 D Jefferies, GB, Kawasaki
14 J-Y Mounier, Fra, Ducati
15 F di Maso, Ita, Ducati

Race 2
1 P Chili, Ita, Ducati
2 C Fogarty, GB, Ducati
3 A Slight, NZ, Honda
4 Y Nagai, Jap, Yamaha
5 C Edwards, USA, Yamaha
6 M Lucchiari, Ita, Ducati
7 S Crafar, NZ, Honda
8 F Pirovano, Ita, Ducati
9 A Meklau, Aut, Ducati
10 J Reynolds, GB, Kawasaki
11 M Meregalli, Ita, Yamaha
12 A Gobert, Aus, Kawasaki
13 P Casoli, Ita, Yamaha
14 S Tsujimoto, Jap, Honda
15 F di Maso, Ita, Ducati

Standings – 1 Fogarty 185;
2 Slight 94; 3 Lucchiari 92;
4 Chili 79; 5 Pirovano 76;
6 Crafar 70

Round 5 – Spain
Albacete, 25 June
Race 1
1 A Slight, NZ, Honda
2 C Fogarty, GB, Ducati
3 T Corser, Aus, Ducati
4 P Chili, Ita, Ducati
5 P Bontempi, Ita, Kawasaki
6 F Pirovano, Ita, Ducati
7 A Gobert, Aus, Kawasaki
8 A Meklau, Aut, Ducati
9 Y Nagai, Jap, Yamaha
10 C Edwards, USA, Yamaha
11 S Crafar, NZ, Honda
12 J Reynolds, GB, Kawasaki
13 P Casoli, Ita, Yamaha
14 A Morillas, Fra, Ducati
15 G Liverani, Ita, Ducati

Race 2
1 C Fogarty, GB, Ducati
2 P Chili, Ita, Ducati
3 A Slight, NZ, Honda
4 F Pirovano, Ita, Ducati
5 T Corser, Aus, Ducati
6 Y Nagai, Jap, Yamaha
7 A Meklau, Aut, Ducati
8 J Reynolds, GB, Kawasaki
9 P Casoli, Ita, Yamaha
10 S Crafar, NZ, Honda
11 C Edwards, USA, Yamaha
12 M Meregalli, Ita, Yamaha
13 D Jefferies, GB, Kawasaki
14 G Liverani, Ita, Ducati
15 S Tsujimoto, Jap, Honda

Standings – 1 Fogarty 230;
2 Slight 135; 3 Chili 112;
4 Pirovano 99; 5 Corser 93;
6 Lucchiari 92

Round 6 – Austria
Salzburgring, 9 July
Race 1
1 C Fogarty, GB, Ducati
2 A Gobert, Aus, Kawasaki
3 T Corser, Aus, Ducati
4 A Slight, NZ, Honda
5 Y Nagai, Jap, Yamaha
6 A Meklau, Aut, Ducati
7 J Schmid, Ger, Kawasaki
8 F Pirovano, Ita, Ducati
9 C Edwards, USA, Yamaha
10 P Bontempi, Ita, Kawasaki
11 P Chili, Ita, Ducati
12 P Casoli, Ita, Yamaha
13 M Lucchiari, Ita, Ducati
14 S Crafar, NZ, Honda
15 G Liverani, Ita, Ducati

Race 2
1 T Corser, Aus, Ducati
2 C Fogarty, GB, Ducati
3 A Gobert, Aus, Kawasaki
4 A Slight, NZ, Honda
5 F Pirovano, Ita, Ducati
6 Y Nagai, Jap, Yamaha
7 M Lucchiari, Ita, Ducati
8 P Bontempi, Ita, Kawasaki
9 S Crafar, NZ, Honda
10 P Casoli, Ita, Yamaha
11 H Bradl, Ger, Kawasaki
12 M Liedl, Ger, Kawasaki
13 M Rudroff, Ger, Ducati
14 A Morillas, Fra, Ducati
15 M Meregalli, Ita, Yamaha

Standings – 1 Fogarty 275;
2 Slight 161; 3 Corser 134;
4 Pirovano 118; 5 Chili 117;
6 Lucchiari 104

Round 7 – USA
Laguna Seca, 23 July
Race 1
1 A Gobert, Aus, Kawasaki
2 T Corser, Aus, Ducati
3 M DuHamel, Can, Honda
4 M Hale, USA, Honda
5 C Fogarty, GB, Ducati
6 S Crafar, NZ, Honda
7 F Spencer, USA, Ducati
8 C Edwards, USA, Yamaha
9 A Slight, NZ, Honda
10 Y Nagai, Jap, Yamaha
11 M Smith, USA, Ducati
12 T Kipp, USA, Yamaha
13 P Bontempi, Ita, Kawasaki
14 M Lucchiari, Ita, Ducati
15 P Picotte, Can, Kawasaki

Race 2
1 T Corser, Aus, Ducati
2 A Gobert, Aus, Kawasaki
3 M Hale, USA, Honda
4 M DuHamel, Can, Honda
5 Y Nagai, Jap, Yamaha
6 S Crafar, NZ, Honda
7 C Fogarty, GB, Ducati
8 F Pirovano, Ita, Ducati
9 C Edwards, USA, Yamaha
10 P Picotte, Can, Kawasaki
11 P Bontempi, Ita, Kawasaki
12 S Crevier, Can, Kawasaki
13 T Kipp, USA, Yamaha
14 M Lucchiari, Ita, Ducati
15 P Casoli, Ita, Yamaha

Standings – 1 Fogarty 295;
2 Corser 179; 3 Slight 168;
4 Pirovano 126; 5 Nagai 119;
6 Chili 117

Round 8 – Europe
Brands Hatch, 6 August
Race 1
1 C Fogarty, GB, Ducati
2 T Corser, Aus, Ducati
3 A Gobert, Aus, Kawasaki
4 J Reynolds, GB, Kawasaki
5 C Edwards, USA, Yamaha
6 P Chili, Ita, Ducati
7 F Pirovano, Ita, Ducati
8 S Hislop, GB, Ducati
9 A Slight, NZ, Honda
10 S Crafar, NZ, Honda
11 M Lucchiari, Ita, Ducati
12 P Casoli, Ita, Yamaha
13 P Bontempi, Ita, Kawasaki
14 D Jefferies, GB, Kawasaki
15 G Liverani, Ita, Ducati

Race 2
1 C Fogarty, GB, Ducati
2 C Edwards, USA, Yamaha
3 J Reynolds, GB, Kawasaki
4 Y Nagai, Jap, Yamaha
5 A Gobert, Aus, Kawasaki
6 T Corser, Aus, Ducati
7 F Pirovano, Ita, Ducati
8 A Slight, NZ, Honda
9 S Hislop, GB, Ducati
10 S Crafar, NZ, Honda
11 M Lucchiari, Ita, Ducati
12 A Morillas, Fra, Ducati
13 P Casoli, Ita, Yamaha
14 P Bontempi, Ita, Kawasaki
15 D Jefferies, GB, Kawasaki

Standings – 1 Fogarty 345;
2 Corser 209; 3 Slight 183;
4 Pirovano 144; 5 Gobert 137;
6 Nagai 132

Round 9 – Japan
Sugo, 27 August
Race 1
1 T Corser, Aus, Ducati
2 A Slight, NZ, Honda
3 Y Nagai, Jap, Yamaha
4 K Kitagawa, Jap, Kawasaki
5 A Gobert, Aus, Kawasaki
6 C Edwards, USA, Yamaha
7 W Yoshikawa, Jap, Yamaha
8 N Fujiwara, Jap, Yamaha
9 J Reynolds, GB, Kawasaki
10 S Crafar, NZ, Honda
11 A Ryoh, Jap, Kawasaki
12 Y Nukumi, Jap, Ducati
13 F Pirovano, Ita, Ducati
14 P Bontempi, Ita, Kawasaki
15 P Chili, Ita, Ducati

Race 2
1 C Fogarty, GB, Ducati
2 Y Nagai, Jap, Yamaha
3 K Fujiwara, Jap, Kawasaki
4 A Slight, NZ, Honda
5 W Yoshikawa, Jap, Yamaha
6 K Kitagawa, Jap, Kawasaki
7 T Aoki, Jap, Honda
8 T Corser, Aus, Ducati
9 A Gobert, Aus, Kawasaki
10 C Edwards, USA, Yamaha
11 S Takeishi, Jap, Honda
12 J Reynolds, GB, Kawasaki
13 P Bontempi, Ita, Kawasaki
14 N Fujiwara, Jap, Yamaha
15 S Crafar, NZ, Honda

Standings – 1 Fogarty 370;
2 Corser 242; 3 Slight 216;
4 Nagai 168; 5 Gobert 155;
6 Pirovano 147

Round 10 – Holland
Assen, 10 September
Race 1
1 C Fogarty, GB, Ducati
2 S Crafar, NZ, Honda
3 T Corser, Aus, Ducati
4 A Slight, NZ, Honda
5 M Lucchiari, Ita, Ducati
6 J Reynolds, GB, Kawasaki
7 Y Nagai, Jap, Yamaha
8 P Casoli, Ita, Yamaha
9 A Gobert, Aus, Kawasaki
10 F Pirovano, Ita, Ducati
11 S Hislop, GB, Ducati
12 P Bontempi, Ita, Kawasaki
13 A Meklau, Aut, Ducati
14 J Schmid, Ger, Kawasaki
15 B Morrison, GB, Ducati

Race 2
1 C Fogarty, GB, Ducati
2 A Slight, NZ, Honda
3 J Reynolds, GB, Kawasaki
4 M Lucchiari, Ita, Ducati
5 Y Nagai, Jap, Yamaha
6 C Edwards, USA, Yamaha
7 A Gobert, Aus, Kawasaki
8 J Schmid, Ger, Kawasaki
9 P Bontempi, Ita, Kawasaki
10 P Casoli, Ita, Yamaha
11 B Morrison, GB, Ducati
12 J-Y Mounier, Fra, Ducati
13 M Pajic, Nl, Kawasaki
14 G Liverani, Ita, Ducati
15 R Kaufmann, Ger, Yamaha

Standings – 1 Fogarty 420;
2 Corser 258; 3 Slight 249;
4 Nagai 188; 5 Gobert 171;
6 Pirovano 153

Round 11 – Indonesia
Sentul, 15 October
Race 1
1 C Fogarty, GB, Ducati
2 T Corser, Aus, Ducati
3 A Slight, NZ, Honda
4 A Gobert, Aus, Kawasaki
5 F Pirovano, Ita, Ducati
6 M Hale, USA, Ducati
7 M Lucchiari, Ita, Ducati
8 A Meklau, Aut, Ducati
9 J Reynolds, GB, Kawasaki
10 B Morrison, GB, Ducati
11 P Bontempi, Ita, Kawasaki
12 P Goddard, Aus, Suzuki
13 J Schmid, Ger, Kawasaki
14 F Spencer, USA, Ducati
15 Y Briguet, CH, Honda

Race 2
1 A Slight, NZ, Honda
2 T Corser, Aus, Ducati
3 P Chili, Ita, Ducati
4 A Gobert, Aus, Kawasaki
5 S Crafar, NZ, Honda
6 F Pirovano, Ita, Ducati
7 M Hale, USA, Ducati
8 P Bontempi, Ita, Kawasaki
9 J Reynolds, GB, Kawasaki
10 A Meklau, Aut, Ducati
11 M Lucchiari, Ita, Ducati
12 J Schmid, Ger, Kawasaki
13 P Goddard, Aus, Suzuki
14 Y Briguet, CH, Honda
15 G Liverani, Ita, Ducati

Standings – 1 Fogarty 445;
2 Corser 298; 3 Slight 290;
4 Gobert 197; 5 Nagai 188;
6 Pirovano 174

Round 12 – Australia
Phillip Island, 29 October
Race 1
1 T Corser, Aus, Ducati
2 A Slight, NZ, Honda
3 S Crafar, NZ, Honda
4 C Fogarty, GB, Ducati
5 J Reynolds, GB, Kawasaki
6 P Chili, Ita, Ducati
7 F Spencer, USA, Ducati
8 K McCarthy, Aus, Honda
9 M Mladin, Aus, Kawasaki
10 S Giles, Aus, Ducati
11 J McEwen, NZ, Ducati
12 P Bontempi, Ita, Kawasaki
13 M Craggill, Aus, Kawasaki
14 M Hale, USA, Ducati
15 R Baird, Aus, Honda

Race 2
1 A Gobert, Aus, Kawasaki
2 C Fogarty, GB, Ducati
3 T Corser, Aus, Ducati
4 A Slight, NZ, Honda
5 S Crafar, NZ, Honda
6 M Hale, USA, Ducati
7 J Reynolds, GB, Kawasaki
8 P Bontempi, Ita, Kawasaki
9 S Giles, Aus, Ducati
10 P Chili, Ita, Ducati
11 B Morrison, GB, Ducati
12 F Pirovano, Ita, Ducati
13 M Craggill, Aus, Kawasaki
14 R Baird, Aus, Honda
15 J Schmid, Ger, Kawasaki

Final Standings – 1 Fogarty 478;
2 Corser 339; 3 Slight 323;
4 Gobert 222; 5 Nagai 188;
6 Crafar 187

1996 SEASON
Round 1 – San Marino
Misano, 14 April
Race 1
1 J Kocinski, USA, Ducati
2 T Corser, Aus, Ducati
3 P Chili, Ita, Ducati
5 S Crafar, NZ, Kawasaki
6 A Slight, NZ, Honda
7 C Fogarty, GB, Honda
8 C Lindholm, Swe, Ducati
9 W Yoshikawa, Jap, Yamaha
10 P Bontempi, Ita, Kawasaki
11 C Edwards, USA, Yamaha
12 N Hodgson, GB, Ducati
13 M Hale, USA, Ducati
14 B Morrison, GB, Ducati
15 M Paquay, Bel, Ducati

Race 2
1 J Kocinski, USA, Ducati
2 T Corser, Aus, Ducati
3 P Chili, Ita, Ducati
4 S Crafar, NZ, Kawasaki
5 A Slight, NZ, Honda
6 C Fogarty, GB, Honda
7 C Edwards, USA, Yamaha
8 M Hale, USA, Ducati
9 C Lindholm, Swe, Ducati
10 P Bontempi, Ita, Kawasaki
11 W Yoshikawa, Jap, Yamaha
12 K McCarthy, Aus, Suzuki
13 P Casoli, Ita, Ducati
14 J Schmid, Ger, Kawasaki
15 M Paquay, Bel, Ducati

Standings – 1 Kocinski 50;
2 Corser 40; 3 Chili 32;
4 Crafar 26; 5 Slight 21;
6 Fogarty 19

Round 2 – Great Britain
Donington Park, 28 April
Race 1
1 T Corser, Aus, Ducati
2 S Crafar, NZ, Kawasaki
3 A Gobert, Aus, Kawasaki
4 P Chili, Ita, Ducati
5 A Slight, NZ, Honda
6 C Edwards, USA, Yamaha
7 J Kocinski, USA, Ducati
8 C Fogarty, GB, Honda
9 W Yoshikawa, Jap, Yamaha
10 P Bontempi, Ita, Kawasaki
11 P Casoli, Ita, Ducati
12 J Schmid, Ger, Kawasaki
13 K McCarthy, Aus, Suzuki
14 M Hale, USA, Ducati
15 S Chambon, Fra, Ducati

Race 2
1 T Corser, Aus, Ducati
2 A Slight, NZ, Honda
3 A Gobert, Aus, Kawasaki
4 C Edwards, USA, Yamaha
5 P Chili, Ita, Ducati
6 J Kocinski, USA, Ducati
7 C Fogarty, GB, Honda
8 C Lindholm, Swe, Ducati
9 P Casoli, Ita, Ducati
10 J Whitham, GB, Yamaha
11 P Bontempi, Ita, Kawasaki
12 W Yoshikawa, Jap, Yamaha
13 N Mackenzie, GB, Yamaha
14 K McCarthy, Aus, Suzuki
15 S Chambon, Fra, Ducati

Standings – 1 Corser 90;
2 Kocinski 69; 3 Chili 56;
4 Slight 52; 5 Crafar 46;
6 Gobert 43

Round 3 – Germany
Hockenheim, 12 May
Race 1
1 A Slight, NZ, Honda
2 J Kocinski, USA, Ducati
3 C Edwards, USA, Yamaha
4 S Crafar, NZ, Kawasaki
5 C Fogarty, GB, Honda
6 A Gobert, Aus, Kawasaki
7 P Casoli, Ita, Ducati
8 C Lindholm, Swe, Ducati
9 J Schmid, Ger, Kawasaki
10 K McCarthy, Aus, Suzuki
11 R Kellenberger, CH, Honda
12 P Bontempi, Ita, Kawasaki
13 A Meklau, Aut, Ducati
14 S Chambon, Fra, Ducati
15 M Paquay, Bel, Ducati

Race 2
1 C Fogarty, GB, Honda
2 A Slight, NZ, Honda
3 J Kocinski, USA, Ducati
4 S Crafar, NZ, Kawasaki
5 C Edwards, USA, Yamaha
6 P Casoli, Ita, Ducati
7 C Lindholm, Swe, Ducati
8 M Hale, USA, Ducati
9 K McCarthy, Aus, Suzuki
10 R Kellenberger, CH, Honda
11 A Meklau, Aut, Ducati
12 U Mark, Ger, Yamaha
13 P Bontempi, Ita, Kawasaki
14 R Phillis, Aus, Kawasaki
15 F di Maso, Ita, Ducati

Standings – 1 Kocinski 105;
2 Slight 97; 3 Corser 90;
4 Crafar & Fogarty 72;
6 Edwards 64

Round 4 – Italy
Monza, 16 June
Race 1
1 C Fogarty, GB, Honda
2 A Slight, NZ, Honda
3 C Edwards, USA, Yamaha
4 P Chili, Ita, Ducati
5 T Corser, Aus, Ducati
6 N Hodgson, GB, Ducati
7 J Whitham GB, Yamaha
8 K McCarthy, Aus, Suzuki
9 S Crafar, NZ, Kawasaki
10 C Lindholm, Swe, Ducati
11 B Morrison, GB, Ducati
12 A Meklau, Aut, Ducati
13 S Giles, Aus, Ducati
14 I Jerman, Slo, Kawasaki
15 J Reynolds, GB, Suzuki

Race 2
1 P Chili, Ita, Ducati
2 A Slight, NZ, Honda
3 C Fogarty, GB, Honda
4 T Corser, Aus, Ducati
5 C Edwards, USA, Yamaha
6 J Whitham GB, Yamaha
7 J Reynolds, GB, Suzuki
8 K McCarthy, Aus, Suzuki
9 N Hodgson, GB, Ducati
10 A Gobert, Aus, Kawasaki
11 A Meklau, Aut, Ducati
12 B Morrison, GB, Ducati
13 M Paquay, Bel, Ducati
14 C Lindholm, Swe, Ducati
15 R Phillis, Aus, Kawasaki

Standings – 1 Slight 137;
2 Corser 114; 3 Fogarty 113;
4 Kocinski 105; 5 Chili 94;
6 Edwards 91

Round 5 – Czech Republic
Brno, 30 June
Race 1
1 T Corser, Aus, Ducati
2 C Fogarty, GB, Honda
3 A Slight, NZ, Honda
4 J Kocinski, USA, Ducati
5 J Reynolds, GB, Suzuki
6 C Edwards, USA, Yamaha
7 M Hale, USA, Ducati
8 P Chili, Ita, Ducati
9 W Yoshikawa, Jap, Yamaha
10 S Crafar, NZ, Kawasaki
11 N Hodgson, GB, Ducati
12 A Meklau, Aut, Ducati
13 J Schmid, Ger, Kawasaki
14 K McCarthy, Aus, Suzuki
15 R Phillis, Aus, Kawasaki

Race 2
1 T Corser, Aus, Ducati
2 A Slight, NZ, Honda
3 C Fogarty, GB, Honda
4 N Hodgson, GB, Ducati
5 M Hale, USA, Ducati
6 J Kocinski, USA, Ducati
7 C Edwards, USA, Yamaha
8 J Reynolds, GB, Suzuki
9 S Crafar, NZ, Kawasaki
10 P Chili, Ita, Ducati
11 W Yoshikawa, Jap, Yamaha
12 A Meklau, Aut, Ducati
13 C Lindholm, Swe, Ducati
14 P Casoli, Ita, Ducati
15 R Phillis, Aus, Kawasaki

Standings – 1 Slight 173;
2 Corser 164; 3 Fogarty 149;
4 Kocinski 128; 5 Edwards 110;
6 Chili 108

Round 6 – USA
Laguna Seca, 21 July
Race 1
1 J Kocinski, USA, Ducati
2 T Corser, Aus, Ducati
3 N Hodgson, GB, Ducati
4 C Edwards, USA, Yamaha
5 A Slight, NZ, Honda
6 M Hale, USA, Ducati
7 S Crafar, NZ, Kawasaki
8 C Fogarty, GB, Honda
9 W Yoshikawa, Jap, Yamaha
10 K McCarthy, Aus, Suzuki
11 P Casoli, Ita, Ducati
12 Larry Pegram, USA, Ducati
13 P Bontempi, Ita, Kawasaki
14 J Boustas, Gre, Ducati
15 M Smith, USA, Kawasaki

Race 2
1 A Gobert, Aus, Kawasaki
2 T Corser, Aus, Ducati
3 A Slight, NZ, Honda
4 C Fogarty, GB, Honda
5 S Crafar, NZ, Kawasaki
6 D Chandler, USA, Kawasaki
7 P Chili, Ita, Ducati
8 W Yoshikawa, Jap, Yamaha
9 N Hodgson, GB, Ducati
10 M Hale, USA, Ducati
11 P Casoli, Ita, Ducati
12 J Kocinski, USA, Ducati
13 K McCarthy, Aus, Suzuki
14 L Pegram, USA, Ducati
15 M Smith, USA, Kawasaki

Standings – 1 Corser 204;
2 Slight 200; 3 Fogarty 170;
4 Kocinski 157; 5 Edwards 123;
6 Chili 117

Round 7 – Europe
Brands Hatch, 4 August
Race 1
 1 P Chili, Ita, Ducati
 2 A Gobert, Aus, Kawasaki
 3 J Kocinski, USA, Ducati
 4 C Edwards, USA, Yamaha
 5 C Fogarty, GB, Honda
 6 A Slight, NZ, Honda
 7 J Reynolds, GB, Suzuki
 8 N Hodgson, GB, Ducati
 9 S Crafar, NZ, Kawasaki
10 W Yoshikawa, Jap, Yamaha
11 N Mackenzie, GB, Yamaha
12 M Hale, USA, Ducati
13 P Bontempi, Ita, Kawasaki
14 I Simpson, GB, Ducati
15 J Boustas, Gre, Ducati

Race 2
 1 T Corser, Aus, Ducati
 2 P Chili, Ita, Ducati
 3 C Edwards, USA, Yamaha
 4 A Gobert, Aus, Kawasaki
 5 A Slight, NZ, Honda
 6 W Yoshikawa, Jap, Yamaha
 7 P Casoli, Ita, Ducati
 8 J Reynolds, GB, Suzuki
 9 P Bontempi, Ita, Kawasaki
10 K McCarthy, Aus, Suzuki
11 M Hale, USA, Ducati
12 M Paquay, Bel, Ducati
13 J Moodie, GB, Ducati
14 S Giles, Aus, Ducati
15 I Jerman, Slo, Kawasaki

Standings – 1 Corser 229;
2 Slight 221; 3 Fogarty 181;
4 Kocinski 173; 5 Chili 162;
6 Edwards 152

Round 8 – Indonesia
Sentul, 18 August
Race 1
 1 J Kocinski, USA, Ducati
 2 C Fogarty, GB, Honda
 3 A Slight, NZ, Honda
 4 P Chili, Ita, Ducati
 5 C Edwards, USA, Yamaha
 6 T Corser, Aus, Ducati
 7 W Yoshikawa, Jap, Yamaha
 8 P Casoli, Ita, Ducati
 9 J Reynolds, GB, Suzuki
10 M Hale, USA, Ducati
11 P Bontempi, Ita, Kawasaki
12 S Crafar, NZ, Kawasaki
13 K McCarthy, Aus, Suzuki
14 D Thomas, Aus, Honda
15 R Phillis, Aus, Kawasaki

Race 2
 1 J Kocinski, USA, Ducati
 2 A Slight, NZ, Honda
 3 C Fogarty, GB, Honda
 4 C Edwards, USA, Yamaha
 5 T Corser, Aus, Ducati
 6 J Reynolds, GB, Suzuki
 7 W Yoshikawa, Jap, Yamaha
 8 N Hodgson, GB, Ducati
 9 M Hale, USA, Ducati
10 K McCarthy, Aus, Suzuki
11 S Crafar, NZ, Kawasaki
12 P Bontempi, Ita, Kawasaki
13 R Phillis, Aus, Kawasaki
14 J Boustas, Gre, Ducati
15 S Martin, Aus, Suzuki

Standings – 1 Slight 257;
2 Corser 250; 3 Kocinski 223;
4 Fogarty 217; 5 Edwards 176;
6 Chili 175

Round 9 – Japan
Sugo, 25 August
Race 1
 1 Y Takeda, Jap, Honda
 2 N Haga, Jap, Yamaha
 3 W Yoshikawa, Jap, Yamaha
 4 T Corser, Aus, Ducati
 5 J Kocinski, USA, Ducati
 6 A Slight, NZ, Honda
 7 N Fujiwara, Jap, Yamaha
 8 C Fogarty, GB, Honda
 9 A Ryo, Jap, Kawasaki
10 S Takeishi, Jap, Kawasaki
11 T Aoki, Jap, Honda
12 K Kitagawa, Jap, Suzuki
13 N Hodgson, GB, Ducati
14 J Reynolds, GB, Suzuki
15 T Serizawa, Jap, Suzuki

Race 2
 1 T Aoki, Jap, Honda
 2 J Kocinski, USA, Ducati
 3 A Slight, NZ, Honda
 4 C Fogarty, GB, Honda
 5 N Fujiwara, Jap, Yamaha
 6 A Ryo, Jap, Kawasaki
 7 S Takeishi, Jap, Kawasaki
 8 W Yoshikawa, Jap, Yamaha
 9 T Corser, Aus, Ducati
10 K Kitagawa, Jap, Suzuki
11 S Crafar, NZ, Kawasaki
12 J Reynolds, GB, Suzuki
13 Y Nukumi, Jap, Ducati
14 N Hodgson, GB, Ducati
15 T Serizawa, Jap, Suzuki

Standings – 1 Slight 283;
2 Corser 270; 3 Kocinski 254;
4 Fogarty 238; 5 Edwards 176;
6 Chili 175

Round 10 – Holland
Assen, 8 September
Race 1
 1 C Fogarty, GB, Honda
 2 P Chili, Ita, Ducati
 3 A Slight, NZ, Honda
 4 T Corser, Aus, Ducati
 5 J Kocinski, USA, Ducati
 6 J Whitham, GB, Yamaha
 7 N Hodgson, GB, Ducati
 8 S Crafar, NZ, Kawasaki
 9 C Lindholm, Swe, Ducati
10 W Yoshikawa, Jap, Yamaha
11 M Hale, USA, Ducati
12 J de Vries, Nl, Yamaha
13 J Reynolds, GB, Suzuki
14 K McCarthy, Aus, Suzuki
15 P Bontempi, Ita, Kawasaki

Race 2
 1 C Fogarty, GB, Honda
 2 T Corser, Aus, Ducati
 3 J Kocinski, USA, Ducati
 4 P Chili, Ita, Ducati
 5 A Slight, NZ, Honda
 6 N Hodgson, GB, Ducati
 7 W Yoshikawa, Jap, Yamaha
 8 S Crafar, NZ, Kawasaki
 9 K McCarthy, Aus, Suzuki
10 A Meklau, Aut, Ducati
11 P Casoli, Ita, Ducati
12 M Hale, USA, Ducati
13 J de Vries, Nl, Yamaha
14 J Whitham, GB, Yamaha
15 S Emmett, GB, Ducati

Standings – 1 Slight 310;
2 Corser 303; 3 Fogarty 288;
4 Kocinski 281; 5 Chili 208;
6 Edwards 176

Round 11 – Spain
Albacete, 6 October
Race 1
 1 T Corser, Aus, Ducati
 2 C Edwards, USA, Yamaha
 3 J Kocinski, USA, Ducati
 4 S Crafar, NZ, Kawasaki
 5 C Fogarty, GB, Honda
 6 W Yoshikawa, Jap, Yamaha
 7 J Reynolds, GB, Suzuki
 8 N Hodgson, GB, Ducati
 9 A Slight, NZ, Honda
10 M Hale, USA, Ducati
11 G Lavilla, Spa, Yamaha
12 S Emmett, GB, Ducati
13 P Bontempi, Ita, Kawasaki
14 P Casoli, Ita, Ducati
15 J Schmid, Ger, Kawasaki

Race 2
 1 T Corser, Aus, Ducati
 2 J Kocinski, USA, Ducati
 3 C Edwards, USA, Yamaha
 4 S Crafar, NZ, Kawasaki
 5 W Yoshikawa, Jap, Yamaha
 6 A Slight, NZ, Honda
 7 C Fogarty, GB, Honda
 8 N Hodgson, GB, Ducati
 9 J Reynolds, GB, Suzuki
10 J Schmid, Ger, Kawasaki
11 M Craggill, Aus, Kawasaki
12 G Lavilla, Spa, Yamaha
13 P Bontempi, Ita, Kawasaki
14 S Emmett, GB, Ducati
15 K McCarthy, Aus, Suzuki

Standings – 1 Corser 353;
2 Slight 327; 3 Kocinski 317;
4 Fogarty 308; 5 Edwards 212;
6 Chili 208

Round 12 – Australia
Phillip Island, 27 October
Race 1
 1 A Gobert, Aus, Kawasaki
 2 C Edwards, USA, Yamaha
 3 T Corser, Aus, Ducati
 4 C Fogarty, GB, Honda
 5 P Goddard, Aus, Suzuki
 6 W Yoshikawa, Jap, Yamaha
 7 J Kocinski, USA, Ducati
 8 P Chili, Ita, Ducati
 9 M Hale, USA, Ducati
10 K McCarthy, Aus, Suzuki
11 J Reynolds, GB, Suzuki
12 P Bontempi, Ita, Kawasaki
13 D Buckmaster, Aus, Suzuki
14 S Martin, Aus, Suzuki
15 D Thomas, Aus, Honda

Race 2
 1 A Gobert, Aus, Kawasaki
 2 A Slight, NZ, Honda
 3 C Edwards, USA, Yamaha
 4 M Hale, USA, Ducati
 5 J Kocinski, USA, Ducati
 6 C Fogarty, GB, Honda
 7 W Yoshikawa, Jap, Yamaha
 8 P Goddard, Aus, Suzuki
 9 P Chili, Ita, Ducati
10 J Reynolds, GB, Suzuki
11 S Crafar, NZ, Kawasaki
12 N Hodgson, GB, Ducati
13 C Connell, Aus, Ducati
14 D Thomas, Aus, Honda
15 K McCarthy, Aus, Suzuki

Final Standings – 1 Corser 369;
2 Slight 347; 3 Kocinski 337;
4 Fogarty 331; 5 Edwards 248;
6 Chili 223

1997 SEASON
Round 1 – Australia
Phillip Island, 23 March
Race 1
 1 J Kocinski, USA, Honda
 2 C Fogarty, GB, Ducati
 3 S Crafar, NZ, Kawasaki
 4 A Yanagawa, Jap, Kawasaki
 5 T Bayliss, Aus, Suzuki
 6 M Craggill, Aus, Kawasaki
 7 S Russell, USA, Yamaha
 8 A Meklau, Aut, Ducati
 9 S Giles, Aus, Honda
10 P Riba Cabana, Spa, Honda
11 J Love, Aus, Ducati
12 I Jerman, Slo, Kawasaki
13 B Archibald, Aus, Kawasaki
14 G Moss, Aus, Honda
15 C Stafford, Aus, Yamaha

Race 2
 1 A Slight, NZ, Honda
 2 C Edwards, USA, Yamaha
 3 S Crafar, NZ, Kawasaki
 4 C Fogarty, GB, Ducati
 5 T Bayliss, Aus, Suzuki
 6 S Russell, USA, Yamaha
 7 J Kocinski, USA, Honda
 8 D Buckmaster, Aus, Kawasaki
 9 M Craggill, Aus, Kawasaki
10 S Giles, Aus, Honda
11 C Connell, Aus, Ducati
12 P Bontempi, Ita, Kawasaki
13 J Whitham, GB, Suzuki
14 J Haydon, GB, Ducati
15 A Meklau, Aut, Ducati

Standings – 1 Kocinski 34;
2 Fogarty 33; 3 Crafar 32;
4 Slight 25; 5 Bayliss 22;
6 Edwards 20

Round 2 – San Marino
Misano, 20 April
Race 1
 1 P Chili, Ita, Ducati
 2 J Kocinski, USA, Honda
 3 C Fogarty, GB, Ducati
 4 A Slight, NZ, Honda
 5 S Crafar, NZ, Kawasaki
 6 C Edwards, USA, Yamaha
 7 N Hodgson, GB, Ducati
 8 P Bontempi, Ita, Kawasaki
 9 P Riba Cabana, Spa, Honda
10 C Lavieille, Fra, Honda
11 G Cantalupo, Ita, Ducati
12 R Assirelli, Ita, Yamaha
13 I Jerman, Slo, Kawasaki
14 J Mrkyvka, CZ, Honda
15 B Scatola, Ita, Kawasaki

Race 2
 1 J Kocinski, USA, Honda
 2 A Slight, NZ, Honda
 3 C Fogarty, GB, Ducati
 4 N Hodgson, GB, Ducati
 5 A Yanagawa, Jap, Kawasaki
 6 S Russell, USA, Yamaha
 7 S Crafar, NZ, Kawasaki
 8 C Edwards, USA, Yamaha
 9 P Riba Cabana, Spa, Honda
10 C Lavieille, Fra, Honda
11 J Haydon, GB, Ducati
12 M Hale, USA, Suzuki
13 G Cantalupo, Ita, Ducati
14 B Scatola, Ita, Kawasaki
15 J Mrkyvka, CZ, Honda

Standings – 1 Kocinski 79;
2 Fogarty 65; 3 Slight 58; 4 Crafar 52;
5 Edwards 38; 6 Russell 29

Round 3 – Great Britain
Donington Park, 4 May
Race 1
1 A Slight, NZ, Honda
2 C Fogarty, GB, Ducati
3 S Crafar, NZ, Kawasaki
4 N Hodgson, GB, Ducati
5 C Edwards, USA, Yamaha
6 S Russell, USA, Yamaha
7 N Mackenzie, GB, Yamaha
8 J Whitham, GB, Suzuki
9 J Reynolds, GB, Ducati
10 J Kocinski, USA, Honda
11 P Bontempi, Ita, Kawasaki
12 C Lindholm, Swe, Yamaha
13 G Lavilla, Spa, Ducati
14 S Emmett, GB, Ducati
15 M Hale, USA, Suzuki

Race 2
1 C Fogarty, GB, Ducati
2 P Chili, Ita, Ducati
3 A Slight, NZ, Honda
4 S Crafar, NZ, Kawasaki
5 J Kocinski, USA, Honda
6 C Edwards, USA, Yamaha
7 S Russell, USA, Yamaha
8 N Mackenzie, GB, Yamaha
9 N Hodgson, GB, Ducati
10 J Whitham, GB, Suzuki
11 J Reynolds, GB, Ducati
12 S Emmett, GB, Ducati
13 G Lavilla, Spa, Ducati
14 J Haydon, GB, Ducati
15 A Meklau, Aut, Ducati

Standings – 1 Fogarty 110;
2 Slight 99; 3 Kocinski 96;
4 Crafar 81; 5 Edwards 59;
6 Russell 48

Round 4 – Germany
Hockenheim, 8 June
Race 1
1 A Slight, NZ, Honda
2 J Kocinski, USA, Honda
3 S Russell, USA, Yamaha
4 C Fogarty, GB, Ducati
5 P Chili, Ita, Ducati
6 N Hodgson, GB, Ducati
7 C Edwards, USA, Yamaha
8 A Yanagawa, Jap, Kawasaki
9 M Hale, USA, Suzuki
10 A Meklau, Aut, Ducati
11 P Bontempi, Ita, Kawasaki
12 C Lindholm, Swe, Yamaha
13 J Schmid, Ger, Kawasaki
14 J Whitham, GB, Suzuki
15 U Mark, Ger, Suzuki

Race 2
1 C Fogarty, GB, Ducati
2 A Yanagawa, Jap, Kawasaki
3 J Whitham, GB, Suzuki
4 S Russell, USA, Yamaha
5 C Edwards, USA, Yamaha
6 S Crafar, NZ, Kawasaki
7 P Chili, Ita, Ducati
8 N Hodgson, GB, Ducati
9 J Schmid, Ger, Kawasaki
10 A Meklau, Aut, Ducati
11 P Bontempi, Ita, Kawasaki
12 C Lindholm, Swe, Yamaha
13 G Lavilla, Spa, Ducati
14 J Kocinski, USA, Honda
15 U Mark, Ger, Suzuki

Standings – 1 Fogarty 148;
2 Slight 124; 3 Kocinski 118;
4 Crafar 91; 5 Edwards 79;
6 Russell 77

Round 5 – Italy
Monza, 22 June
Race 1
1 J Kocinski, USA, Honda
2 A Slight, NZ, Honda
3 C Fogarty, GB, Ducati
4 S Crafar, NZ, Kawasaki
5 S Russell, USA, Yamaha
6 J Whitham, GB, Suzuki
7 P Chili, Ita, Ducati
8 A Yanagawa, Jap, Kawasaki
9 P Bontempi, Ita, Kawasaki
10 M Hale, USA, Suzuki
11 A Meklau, Aut, Ducati
12 J Haydon, GB, Ducati
13 J Schmid, Ger, Kawasaki
14 J-P Ruggia, Fra, Yamaha
15 I Jerman, Slo, Kawasaki

Race 2
1 P Chili, Ita, Ducati
2 J Kocinski, USA, Honda
3 J Whitham, GB, Suzuki
4 C Fogarty, GB, Ducati
5 A Slight, NZ, Honda
6 P Bontempi, Ita, Kawasaki
7 S Crafar, NZ, Kawasaki
8 S Russell, USA, Yamaha
9 M Hale, USA, Suzuki
10 J Schmid, Ger, Kawasaki
11 P Riba Cabana, Spa, Honda
12 U Mark, Ger, Suzuki
13 J Haydon, GB, Ducati
14 J-M Deletang, Fra, Yamaha
15 G Cantalupo, Ita, Ducati

Standings – 1 Fogarty 177;
2 Kocinski 163; 3 Slight 155;
4 Crafar 113; 5 Chili 99; 6 Russell 96

Round 6 – USA
Laguna Seca, 13 July
Race 1
1 J Kocinski, USA, Honda
2 C Fogarty, GB, Ducati
3 M DuHamel, Can, Honda
4 S Crafar, NZ, Kawasaki
5 D Chandler, USA, Kawasaki
6 S Russell, USA, Yamaha
7 A Slight, NZ, Honda
8 J Whitham, GB, Suzuki
9 P Bontempi, Ita, Kawasaki
10 A Yanagawa, Jap, Kawasaki
11 S Crevier, Can, Honda
12 T Kipp, USA, Yamaha
13 P Picotte, Can, Suzuki
14 M Hale, USA, Suzuki
15 I Jerman, Slo, Kawasaki

Race 2
1 J Kocinski, USA, Honda
2 C Fogarty, GB, Ducati
3 M DuHamel, Can, Honda
4 S Russell, USA, Yamaha
5 A Yanagawa, Jap, Kawasaki
6 P Chili, Ita, Ducati
7 P Bontempi, Ita, Kawasaki
8 T Kipp, USA, Yamaha
9 N Hodgson, GB, Ducati
10 A Slight, NZ, Honda
11 A Yates, USA, Suzuki
12 S Crevier, Can, Honda
13 I Jerman, Slo, Kawasaki
14 M Krynock, USA, Suzuki

Standings – 1 Fogarty 217;
2 Kocinski 213; 3 Slight 170;
4 Crafar 126; 5 Russell 119;
6 Chili 109

Round 7 – Europe
Brands Hatch, 3 August
Race 1
1 P Chili, Ita, Ducati
2 S Russell, USA, Yamaha
3 J Kocinski, USA, Honda
4 N Hodgson, GB, Ducati
5 A Yanagawa, Jap, Kawasaki
6 A Slight, NZ, Honda
7 J Whitham, GB, Suzuki
8 P Bontempi, Ita, Kawasaki
9 M Hale, USA, Suzuki
10 C Walker, GB, Yamaha
11 M Rutter, GB, Honda
12 R Stringer, GB, Kawasaki
13 P Riba Cabana, Spa, Honda
14 B Sampson, GB, Kawasaki
15 P Giles, GB, Kawasaki

Race 2
1 C Fogarty, GB, Ducati
2 J Kocinski, USA, Honda
3 M Rutter, GB, Honda
4 A Yanagawa, Jap, Kawasaki
5 S Russell, USA, Yamaha
6 N Hodgson, GB, Ducati
7 S Crafar, NZ, Kawasaki
8 A Slight, NZ, Honda
9 J Whitham, GB, Suzuki
10 C Walker, GB, Yamaha
11 M Hale, USA, Suzuki
12 P Bontempi, Ita, Kawasaki
13 P Riba Cabana, Spa, Honda
14 P Giles, GB, Kawasaki
15 I Jerman, Slo, Kawasaki

Standings – 1 Kocinski 249;
2 Fogarty 242; 3 Slight 188;
4 Russell 150; 5 Crafar 135;
6 Chili 134

Round 8 – Austria
A1-Ring, 17 August
Race 1
1 C Fogarty, GB, Ducati
2 A Yanagawa, Jap, Kawasaki
3 A Slight, NZ, Honda
4 P Chili, Ita, Ducati
5 J Kocinski, USA, Honda
6 S Crafar, NZ, Kawasaki
7 S Russell, USA, Yamaha
8 N Hodgson, GB, Ducati
9 P Bontempi, Ita, Kawasaki
10 J Whitham, GB, Suzuki
11 M Hale, USA, Suzuki
12 C Walker, GB, Yamaha
13 U Mark, Ger, Suzuki
14 J Schmid, Ger, Kawasaki
15 A Meklau, Aut, Ducati

Race 2
1 A Yanagawa, Jap, Kawasaki
2 A Slight, NZ, Honda
3 J Kocinski, USA, Honda
4 S Russell, USA, Yamaha
5 P Bontempi, Ita, Kawasaki
6 J Whitham, GB, Suzuki
7 M Hale, USA, Suzuki
8 A Meklau, Aut, Ducati
9 U Mark, Ger, Suzuki
10 C Walker, GB, Yamaha
11 J Schmid, Ger, Kawasaki
12 P Riba Cabana, Spa, Honda
13 I Jerman, Slo, Kawasaki
14 A Gruschka, Ger, Yamaha
15 G Scudeler, Bra, Ducati

Standings – 1 Kocinski 276;
2 Fogarty 267; 3 Slight 224;
4 Russell 172; 5 Chili 147;
6 Yanagawa 146

Round 9 – Holland
Assen, 31 August
Race 1
1 J Kocinski, USA, Honda
2 C Fogarty, GB, Ducati
3 P Chili, Ita, Ducati
4 A Slight, NZ, Honda
5 N Hodgson, GB, Ducati
6 S Russell, USA, Yamaha
7 J Whitham, GB, Suzuki
8 A Yanagawa, Jap, Kawasaki
9 S Crafar, NZ, Kawasaki
10 C Walker, GB, Yamaha
11 M Hale, USA, Suzuki
12 P Riba Cabana, Spa, Honda
13 J Schmid, Ger, Kawasaki
14 U Mark, Ger, Suzuki
15 E Korpiaho, Fin, Kawasaki

Race 2
1 C Fogarty, GB, Ducati
2 P Chili, Ita, Ducati
3 J Kocinski, USA, Honda
4 A Slight, NZ, Honda
5 N Hodgson, GB, Ducati
6 S Crafar, NZ, Kawasaki
7 A Yanagawa, Jap, Kawasaki
8 S Russell, USA, Yamaha
9 C Walker, GB, Yamaha
10 P Bontempi, Ita, Kawasaki
11 J Whitham, GB, Suzuki
12 J Schmid, Ger, Kawasaki
13 U Mark, Ger, Suzuki
14 I Jerman, Slo, Kawasaki
15 P Riba Cabana, Spa, Honda

Standings – 1 Kocinski 317;
2 Fogarty 312; 3 Slight 250;
4 Russell 190; 5 Chili 183;
6 Yanagawa 163

Round 10 – Spain
Albacete, 21 September
Race 1
1 J Kocinski, USA, Honda
2 A Slight, NZ, Honda
3 S Crafar, NZ, Kawasaki
4 A Yanagawa, Jap, Kawasaki
5 P Chili, Ita, Ducati
6 P Bontempi, Ita, Kawasaki
7 G Lavilla, Spa, Ducati
8 M Hale, USA, Suzuki
9 J Schmid, Ger, Kawasaki
10 C Walker, GB, Yamaha
11 P Riba Cabana, Spa, Honda
12 U Mark, Ger, Suzuki
13 I Jerman, Slo, Kawasaki
14 G Cantalupo, Ita, Ducati
15 J Mrkyvka, Cz, Honda

Race 2
1 J Kocinski, USA, Honda
2 S Crafar, NZ, Kawasaki
3 A Slight, NZ, Honda
4 A Yanagawa, Jap, Kawasaki
5 S Russell, USA, Yamaha
6 P Bontempi, Ita, Kawasaki
7 P Chili, Ita, Ducati
8 N Hodgson, GB, Ducati
9 M Hale, USA, Suzuki
10 J Whitham, GB, Suzuki
11 C Walker, GB, Yamaha
12 J Schmid, Ger, Kawasaki
13 P Riba Cabana, Spa, Honda
14 U Mark, Ger, Suzuki
15 J Haydon, GB, Ducati

Standings – 1 Kocinski 367;
2 Fogarty 312; 3 Slight 286;
4 Chili 203; 5 Russell 201;
6 Crafar 198

Round 11 – Japan
Sugo, 5 October
Race 1
1 A Yanagawa, Jap, Kawasaki
2 N Haga, Jap, Yamaha
3 S Crafar, NZ, Kawasaki
4 K Kitagawa, Jap, Suzuki
5 W Yoshikawa, Jap, Yamaha
6 A Slight, NZ, Honda
7 S Takeishi, Jap, Kawasaki
8 K Fujiwara, Jap, Suzuki
9 J Kocinski, USA, Honda
10 T Serizawa, Jap, Suzuki
11 S Itoh, Jap, Honda
12 P Chili, Ita, Ducati
13 C Fogarty, GB, Ducati
14 S Russell, USA, Yamaha
15 N Fujiwara, Jap, Yamaha

Race 2
1 N Haga, Jap, Yamaha
2 S Crafar, NZ, Kawasaki
3 J Kocinski, USA, Honda
4 A Slight, NZ, Honda
5 K Fujiwara, Jap, Suzuki
6 T Serizawa, Jap, Suzuki
7 Y Takeda, Jap, Honda
8 A Ryo, Jap, Kawasaki
9 S Emmett, GB, Ducati
10 M Hale, USA, Suzuki
11 M Suzuki, Jap, Ducati
12 I Asai, Jap, Ducati
13 M Kamada, Jap, Honda
14 I Jerman, Slo, Kawasaki
15 P Riba Cabana, Spa, Honda

Standings – 1 Kocinski 391;
2 Fogarty 317; 3 Slight 310;
4 Crafar 234; 5 Yanagawa 214;
6 Chili 209

Round 12 – Indonesia
Sentul, 12 October
Race 1
1 J Kocinski, USA, Honda
2 A Slight, NZ, Honda
3 C Fogarty, GB, Ducati
4 A Yanagawa, Jap, Kawasaki
5 N Haga, Jap, Yamaha
6 S Russell, USA, Yamaha
7 J Reynolds, GB, Ducati
8 M Hale, USA, Suzuki
9 J Whitham, GB, Suzuki
10 I Jerman, Slo, Kawasaki
11 P Riba Cabana, Spa, Honda
12 M Suzuki, Jap, Ducati
13 Y Kusuma, Ind, Kawasaki

Race 2
1 C Fogarty, GB, Ducati
2 A Yanagawa, Jap, Kawasaki
3 N Haga, Jap, Yamaha
4 A Slight, NZ, Honda
5 S Russell, USA, Yamaha
6 J Whitham, GB, Suzuki
7 N Hodgson, GB, Ducati
8 S Emmett, GB, Ducati
9 I Jerman, Slo, Kawasaki
10 M Suzuki, Jap, Ducati
11 P Riba Cabana, Spa, Honda
12 C Lavieille, Fra, Honda
13 Y Kusuma, Ind, Kawasaki

Final Standings – 1 Kocinski 416;
2 Fogarty 358; 3 Slight 343;
4 Yanagawa 247; 5 Crafar 234;
6 Russell 226

1998 SEASON
Round 1 – Australia
Phillip Island, 22 March
Race 1
1 C Fogarty, GB, Ducati
2 T Corser, Aus, Ducati
3 N Haga, Jpn, Yamaha
4 P Chili, Ita, Ducati
5 A Yanagawa, Jpn, Kawasaki
6 M Willis, Aus, Suzuki
7 C Edwards, USA, Honda
8 N Hodgson, GB, Kawasaki
9 A Slight, NZ, Honda
10 S Russell, USA, Yamaha
11 G Lavilla, Spa, Ducati
12 P Bontempi, Ita, Kawasaki
13 L Pedercini, Ita, Ducati
14 M Campbell, Aus, Ducati
15 I Jerman, Slo, Kawasaki

Race 2
1 N Haga, Jpn, Yamaha
2 A Slight, NZ, Honda
3 C Fogarty, GB, Ducati
4 P Goddard, Aus, Suzuki
5 A Yanagawa, Jpn, Kawasaki
6 T Corser, Aus, Ducati
7 C Edwards, USA, Honda
8 S Russell, USA, Yamaha
9 M Willis, Aus, Suzuki
10 S Martin, Aus, Ducati
11 G Lavilla, Spa, Ducati
12 J Whitham, GB, Suzuki
13 S Giles, Aus, Honda
14 C Connell, Aus, Ducati
15 A Gramigni, Ita, Ducati

Standings – 1 Haga & Fogarty 41;
3 Corser 30; 4 Slight 27;
5 Yanagawa 22; 6 Edwards 18

Round 2 – Great Britain
Donington Park, 13 April
Race 1
1 N Haga, Jpn, Yamaha
2 T Corser, Aus, Ducati
3 P Chili, Ita, Ducati
4 A Slight, NZ, Honda
5 A Yanagawa, Jpn, Kawasaki
6 C Edwards, USA, Honda

7 C Fogarty, GB, Ducati
8 J Whitham, GB, Suzuki
9 P Goddard, Aus, Suzuki
10 S Hislop, GB, Yamaha
11 C Walker, GB, Kawasaki
12 N Hodgson, GB, Kawasaki
13 S Russell, USA, Yamaha
14 P Bontempi, Ita, Kawasaki
15 J Haydon, GB, Suzuki

Race 2
1 N Haga, Jpn, Yamaha
2 T Corser, Aus, Ducati
3 C Fogarty, GB, Ducati
4 A Slight, NZ, Honda
5 P Chili, Ita, Ducati
6 N Mackenzie, GB, Yamaha
7 C Edwards, USA, Honda
8 J Whitham, GB, Suzuki
9 S Hislop, GB, Yamaha
10 P Goddard, Aus, Suzuki
11 S Russell, USA, Yamaha
12 C Walker, GB, Kawasaki
13 P Bontempi, Ita, Kawasaki
14 J Haydon, GB, Suzuki
15 T Rymer, GB, Suzuki

Standings – 1 Haga 91; 2 Corser 70;
3 Fogarty 66; 4 Slight 53; 5 Chili 40;
6 Edwards 37

Round 3 – Italy
Monza, 10 May
Race 1
1 C Edwards, USA, Honda
2 A Slight, NZ, Honda
3 T Corser, Aus, Ducati
4 N Hodgson, GB, Kawasaki
5 P Chili, Ita, Ducati
6 C Fogarty, GB, Ducati
7 P Goddard, Aus, Suzuki
8 J Whitham, GB, Suzuki
9 N Haga, Jpn, Yamaha
10 G Lavilla, Spn, Ducati
11 A Meklau, Aut, Ducati
12 A Gramigni, Ita, Ducati
13 I Jerman, Slo, Kawasaki
14 L Pedercini, Ita, Ducati
15 E Korpiaho, Fin, Kawasaki

Race 2
1 C Edwards, USA, Honda
2 C Fogarty, GB, Ducati
3 P Chili, Ita, Ducati
4 T Corser, Aus, Ducati
5 J Whitham, GB, Suzuki
6 A Yanagawa, Jpn, Kawasaki
7 N Hodgson, GB, Kawasaki
8 P Goddard, Aus, Suzuki
9 A Meklau, Aut, Ducati
10 N Haga, Jpn, Yamaha
11 P Bontempi, Ita, Kawasaki
12 I Jerman, Slo, Kawasaki
13 A Gramigni, Ita, Ducati
14 L Pedercini, Ita, Ducati
15 E Korpiaho, Fin, Kawasaki

Standings – 1 Haga 104; 2 Corser 99;
3 Fogarty 96; 4 Edwards 87;
5 Slight 73; 6 Chili 67

Round 4 – Spain
Albacete, 24 May
Race 1
1 P Chili, Ita, Ducati
2 T Corser, Aus, Ducati
3 G Lavilla, Spa, Ducati
4 A Slight, NZ, Honda
5 C Edwards, USA, Honda
6 S Russell, USA, Yamaha
7 N Hodgson, GB, Kawasaki

8 A Gramigni, Ita, Ducati
9 C Fogarty, GB, Ducati
10 N Haga, Jpn, Yamaha
11 J Whitham, GB, Suzuki
12 P Bontempi, Ita, Kawasaki
13 A Yanagawa, Jpn, Kawasaki
14 P Goddard, Aus, Suzuki
15 E Korpiaho, Fin, Kawasaki

Race 2
1 C Fogarty, GB, Ducati
2 A Slight, NZ, Honda
3 T Corser, Aus, Ducati
4 N Haga, Jpn, Yamaha
5 P Chili, Ita, Ducati
6 P Bontempi, Ita, Kawasaki
7 A Yanagawa, Jpn, Kawasaki
8 P Goddard, Aus, Suzuki
9 S Russell, USA, Yamaha
10 J Whitham, GB, Suzuki
11 J-M Deletang, Fra, Yamaha
12 I Jerman, Slo, Kawasaki
13 F Protat, Fra, Ducati
14 N Hodgson, GB, Kawasaki
15 J Mrkyvka, CZ, Honda

Standings – 1 Corser 135;
2 Fogarty 128; 3 Haga 123;
4 Slight 106; 5 Chili 103;
6 Edwards 98

Round 5 – Germany
Nürburgring, 7 June
Race 1
1 A Slight, NZ, Honda
2 C Edwards, USA, Honda
3 P Chili, Ita, Ducati
4 A Yanagawa, Jpn, Kawasaki
5 N Haga, Jpn, Yamaha
6 P Goddard, Aus, Suzuki
7 T Corser, Aus, Ducati
8 P Bontempi, Ita, Kawasaki
9 J Whitham, GB, Suzuki
10 A Gramigni, Ita, Ducati
11 S Russell, USA, Yamaha
12 L Pedercini, Ita, Ducati
13 C Fogarty, GB, Ducati
14 I Jerman, Slo, Kawasaki
15 R Xaus, Spa, Suzuki

Race 2
1 P Chili, Ita, Ducati
2 C Edwards, USA, Honda
3 T Corser, Aus, Ducati
4 A Slight, NZ, Honda
5 A Yanagawa, Jpn, Kawasaki
6 G Lavilla, Spa, Ducati
7 N Haga, Jpn, Yamaha
8 P Goddard, Aus, Suzuki
9 P Bontempi, Ita, Kawasaki
10 J Whitham, GB, Suzuki
11 N Hodgson, GB, Kawasaki
12 U Mark, Ger, Suzuki
13 C Fogarty, GB, Ducati
14 L Pedercini, Ita, Ducati
15 I Jerman, Slo, Kawasaki

Standings – 1 Corser 160;
2 Chili & Slight 144; 4 Haga 143;
5 Edwards 138; 6 Fogarty 134

Round 6 – San Marino
Misano, 21 June
Race 1
1 A Slight, NZ, Honda
2 T Corser, Aus, Ducati
3 C Edwards, USA, Honda
4 C Fogarty, GB,Ducati
5 A Yanagawa, Jpn, Kawasaki
6 J Whitham, GB, Suzuki
7 N Hodgson, GB, Kawasaki

8 S Russell, USA, Yamaha
9 A Meklau, Aut, Ducati
10 U Mark, Ger, Suzuki
11 A Gramigni, Ita, Ducati
12 L Pedercini, Ita, Ducati
13 P Blora, Ita, Ducati
14 A Stroud, NZ, Kawasaki
15 I Jerman, Slo, Kawasaki

Race 2
1 A Slight, NZ, Honda
2 T Corser, Aus, Ducati
3 C Fogarty, GB, Ducati
4 C Edwards, USA, Honda
5 A Yanagawa, Jpn, Kawasaki
6 S Russell, USA, Yamaha
7 G Lavilla, Spa, Ducati
8 N Hodgson, GB, Kawasaki
9 A Meklau, Aut, Ducati
10 I Jerman, Slo, Kawasaki
11 P Bontempi, Ita, Kawasaki
12 A Gramigni, Ita, Ducati
13 U Mark, Ger, Suzuki
14 L Pedercini, Ita, Ducati
15 A Stroud, NZ, Kawasaki

Standings – 1 Corser 200;
2 Slight 194; 3 Edwards 167;
4 Fogarty 163; 5 Chili 144;
6 Haga 143

Round 7 – South Africa
Kyalami, 5 July
Race 1
1 P Chili, Ita, Ducati
2 C Fogarty, GB, Ducati
3 G Lavilla, Spa, Ducati
4 J Whitham, GB, Suzuki
5 P Goddard, Aus, Suzuki
6 A Yanagawa, Jpn, Kawasaki
7 N Haga, Jpn, Yamaha
8 A Slight, NZ, Honda
9 C Edwards, USA, Honda
10 S Russell, USA, Yamaha
11 A Gramigni, Ita, Ducati
12 P Bontempi, Ita, Kawasaki
13 I Jerman, Slo, Kawasaki
14 A Stroud, NZ, Kawasaki
15 F Protat, Fra, Ducatii

Race 2
1 P Chili, Ita, Ducati
2 C Fogarty, GB, Ducati
3 N Haga, Jpn, Yamaha
4 C Edwards, USA, Honda
5 A Yanagawa, Jpn, Kawasaki
6 P Goddard, Aus, Suzuki
7 T Corser, Aus, Ducati
8 A Slight, NZ, Honda
9 S Russell, USA, Yamaha
10 P Bontempi, Ita, Kawasaki
11 I Jerman, Slo, Kawasaki
12 A Stroud, NZ, Kawasaki
13 L Pedercini, Ita, Ducati
14 A Gramigni, Ita, Ducati
15 F Protat, Fra, Ducati

Standings – 1 Slight 210;
2 Corser 209; 3 Fogarty 203;
4 Chili 194; 5 Edwards 187;
6 Haga 168

Round 8 – USA
Laguna Seca, 12 July
Race 1
1 T Corser, Aus, Ducati
2 A Yanagawa, Jpn, Kawasaki
3 D Chandler, USA, Kawasaki
4 B Bostrom, USA, Honda
5 C Fogarty, GB, Ducati
6 J Whitham, GB, Suzuki

7 P Chili, Ita, Ducati
8 A Slight, NZ, Honda
9 N Hodgson, GB, Kawasaki
10 J Hacking, USA, Yamaha
11 C Edwards, USA, Honda
12 A Yates, USA, Suzuki
13 G Lavilla, Spa, Ducati
14 P Goddard, Aus, Suzuki
15 S Russell, USA, Yamaha

Race 2
1 N Haga, Jpn, Yamaha
2 T Corser, Aus, Ducati
3 B Bostrom, USA, Honda
4 P Chili, Ita, Ducati
5 J Whitham, GB, Suzuki
6 N Hodgson, GB, Kawasaki
7 J Hacking, USA, Yamaha
8 P Goddard, Aus, Suzuki
9 A Gramigni, Ita, Ducati
10 C Edwards, USA, Honda
11 I Jerman, Slo, Kawasaki
12 L Pedercini, Ita, Ducati
13 R Orlando, USA, Kawasaki

Standings – 1 Corser 241.5;
2 Slight 214; 3 Chili 111.5;
4 Fogarty 208.5; 5 Edwards 195.5;
6 Haga 193

Round 9 – Europe
Brands Hatch, 2 August
Race 1
1 C Edwards, USA, Honda
2 A Slight, NZ, Honda
3 S Russell, USA, Yamaha
4 C Fogarty, GB, Ducati
5 J Whitham, GB, Suzuki
6 N Mackenzie, GB, Yamaha
7 T Corser, Aus, Ducati
8 S Hislop, GB, Yamaha

9 P Chili, Ita, Ducati
10 P Goddard, Aus, Suzuki
11 S Emmett, GB, Ducati
12 N Haga, Jpn, Yamaha
13 T Bayliss, Aus Ducati
14 M Llewllyn, GB, Ducati
15 A Gramigni, Ita, Ducatii

Race 2
1 T Corser, Aus, Ducati
2 C Fogarty, GB, Ducati
3 J Whitham, GB, Suzuki
4 C Edwards, USA, Honda
5 A Slight, NZ, Honda
6 P Chili, Ita, Ducati
7 N Haga, Jpn, Yamaha
8 S Russell, USA, Yamaha
9 N Hodgson, GB, Kawasaki
10 N Mackenzie, GB, Yamaha
11 S Hislop, GB, Yamaha
12 J Haydon, GB, Suzuki
13 P Goddard, Aus, Suzuki
14 J Reynolds, GB, Ducati
15 T Bayliss, Aus, Ducati

Standings – 1 Corser 275.5;
2 Slight 245; 3 Fogarty 241.5;
4 Edwards 233.5; 5 Chili 228.5
6 Haga 206

Round 10 – Austria
A1-Ring, 30 August
Race 1
1 A Slight, NZ Honda
2 P Chili, Ita, Ducati
3 C Fogarty, GB, Ducati
4 A Yanagawa, Jpn, Kawasaki
5 J Whitham, GB, Suzuki
6 T Corser, Aus,Ducati
7 C Edwards, USA, Honda
8 N Hodgson, GB, Kawasaki

9 N Haga, Jpn, Yamaha
10 P Goddard, Aus, Yamaha
11 G Lavilla, Spn, Ducati
12 S Russell, USA, Yamaha
13 A Gramigni, Ita, Ducati
14 A Meklau, Aut, Ducati
15 I Jerman, Slo, Kawasaki

Race 2
1 A Slight, NZ, Honda
2 C Fogarty, GB, Ducati
3 P Chili, Ita, Ducati
4 A Yanagawa, Jpn, Kawasaki
5 T Corser, Aus, Ducati
6 J Whitham, GB, Suzuki
7 G Lavilla, Spa, Ducati
8 P Goddard, Aus, Suzuki
9 C Edwards, USA, Honda
10 N Hodgson, GB, Kawasaki
11 S Russell, USA, Yamaha
12 N Haga, Jpn, Yamaha
13 A Meklau, Aut Ducati
14 A Gramigni, Ita, Ducati
15 I Jerman, Slo, Kawasaki

Standings – 1 Corser 296.5;
2 Slight 295; 3 Fogarty 277.5;
4 Chili 264.5; 5 Edwards 249.5;
6 Haga 217

Round 11 – Holland
Assen, 6 September
Race 1
1 P Chili, Ita, Ducati
2 C Fogarty, GB, Ducati
3 T Corser, Aus, Ducati
4 A Slight, NZ, Honda
5 C Edwards, USA, Honda
6 P Goddard, Aus, Suzuki
7 A Yanagawa, Jpn, Kawasaki
8 N Haga, Jpn, Yamaha
9 S Russell, USA, Yamaha
10 N Hodgson, GB, Kawasaki
11 A Gramigni, Ita, Ducati
12 I Jerman, Slo, Kawasaki
13 M Innamorati, Ita, Kawasaki
14 E Korpiaho, Fin, Kawasaki
15 S Stroud, NZ, Kawasaki

Race 2
1 C Fogarty, GB, Ducati
2 A Slight, NZ, Honda
3 T Corser, Aus, Ducati
4 C Edwards, USA, Honda
5 J Whitham, GB, Suzuki
6 A Yanagawa, Jpn, Kawasaki
7 P Goddard, Aus, Suzuki
8 N Haga, Jpn, Yamaha
9 N Hodgson, GB, Kawasaki
10 I Jerman, Slo, Kawasaki
11 M Innamorati, Ita, Kawasaki
12 E Korpiaho, Fin, Kawasaki
13 A Stroud, NZ, Kawasaki
14 H Platacis, Ger, Kawasaki

Standings – 1 Corser 328.5;
2 Slight 328; 3 Fogarty 322.5;
4 Chili 289.5; 5 Edwards 273.5;
6 Haga 233

Round 12 – Japan
Sugo, 4 October
Race 1
1 K Kitagawa, Jpn, Suzuki
2 A Ryo, Jpn, Suzuki
3 C Fogarty, GB, Ducati
4 A Yanagawa, Jpn, Kawasaki
5 S Russell, USA, Yamaha
6 N Hodgson, GB, Kawasaki
7 A Slight, NZ, Honda
8 S Itoh, Jpn, Honda

9 W Yoshikawa, Jpn, Yamaha
10 P Goddard, Aus, Yamaha
11 J Whitham, GB, Suzuki
12 P Chili, Ita, Ducati
13 C Edwards, USA, Honda
14 S Takeishi, Jpn, Kawasaki
15 Y Takeda, Jpn, Honda

Race 2
1 N Haga, Jpn, Yamaha
2 A Yanagawa, Jpn, Kawasaki
3 A Ryo, Jpn, Suzuki
4 C Fogarty, GB, Ducati
5 K Kitagawa, Jpn, Suzuki
6 A Slight, NZ, Honda
7 W Yoshikawa, Jpn, Yamaha
8 K Haga, Jpn, Yamaha
9 J Whitham, GB, Suzuki
10 P Goddard, Aus, Suzuki
11 S Takeishi, Jpn, Kawasaki
12 S Russell, USA, Yamaha
13 C Edwards, USA, Honda
14 Y Takeda, Jpn, Honda
15 G Lavilla, Spn, Ducati

Final Standings – 1 Fogarty 351.5;
2 Slight 347; 3 Corser 328.5;
4 Chili 293.5; 5 Edwards 279.5;
6 Haga 258

1999 SEASON
Round 1 – South Africa
Kyalami, 28 March
Race 1
1 C Fogarty, GB, Ducati
2 T Corser, Aus, Ducati
3 A Slight, NZ, Honda
4 N Haga, Jpn, Yamaha
5 C Edwards, USA, Honda
6 A Yanagawa, Jpn, Kawasaki
7 P Chili, Ita, Suzuki
8 G Lavilla, Spn, Kawasaki
9 D Romboni, Ita, Ducati
10 R Ulm, Aut, Kawasaki
11 K Fujiwara, Jpn, Suzuki
12 V Guareschi, Ita, Yamaha
13 A Meklau, Aut, Ducati
14 L Isaacs, RSA, Ducati
15 A Gramigni, Ita, Yamaha

Race 2
1 C Fogarty, GB, Ducati
2 A Slight, NZ, Honda
3 T Corser, Aus, Ducati
4 C Edwards, USA, Honda
5 A Yanagawa, Jpn, Kawasaki
6 G Lavilla, Spn, Kawasaki
7 P Goddard, Aus, Aprilia
8 P Chili, Ita, Suzuki
9 D Romboni, Ita, Ducati
10 K Fujiwara, Jpn, Suzuki
11 R Ulm, Aut, Kawasaki
12 L Pedercini, Ita, Ducati
13 V Guareschi, Ita, Yamaha
14 L Isaacs, RSA, Ducati
15 I Jerman, Slo, Kawasaki

Standings – 1 Fogarty 50;
2 Slight & Corser 36; 4 Edwards 24;
5 Yanagawa 21; 6 Lavilla 18

Round 2 – Australia
Phillip Island, 18 April
Race 1
1 T Corser, Aus, Ducati
2 C Fogarty, GB, Ducati
3 C Edwards, USA, Honda
4 A Slight, NZ, Honda
5 A Yanagawa, Jpn, Kawasaki
6 N Haga, Jpn, Yamaha
7 D Romboni, Ita, Ducati

8 C Connell, Aus, Ducati
9 K Fujiwara, Jpn, Suzuki
10 A Meklau, Aut, Ducati
11 S Giles, Aus, Suzuki
12 I Jerman, Slo, Kawasaki
13 V Guareschi, Ita, Yamaha
14 R Ulm, Aut, Kawasaki
15 J Mrkyvka, CZ, Ducati

Race 2
1 T Corser, Aus, Ducati
2 C Fogarty, GB, Ducati
3 C Edwards, USA, Honda
4 A Slight, NZ, Honda
5 N Haga, Jpn, Yamaha
6 A Yanagawa, Jpn, Kawasaki
7 S Martin, Aus, Ducati
8 D Romboni, Ita, Ducati
9 C Connell, Aus, Ducati
10 K Fujiwara, Jpn, Suzuki
11 A Meklau, Aut, Ducati
12 S Giles, Aus, Suzuki
13 P Chili, Ita, Suzuki
14 L Pedercini, Ita, Ducati
15 V Guareschi, Ita, Yamaha

Standings – 1 Fogarty 90;
2 Corser 86; 3 Slight 62;
4 Edwards 56; 5 Yanagawa 42;
6 Haga 34

Round 3 – Great Britain
Donington Park, 2 May
Race 1
1 C Fogarty, GB, Ducati
2 A Slight, NZ, Honda
3 C Edwards, USA, Honda
4 C Walker, GB, Kawasaki
5 A Yanagawa, Jpn, Kawasaki
6 T Corser, Aus, Ducati
7 J Reynolds, GB, Ducati
8 S Hislop, GB, Kawasaki
9 S Emmett, GB, Ducati
10 N Haga, Jpn, Yamaha
11 D Romboni, Ita, Ducati
12 N Mackenzie, GB, Yamaha
13 K Fujiwara, Jpn, Suzuki
14 I Jerman, Slo, Kawasaki
15 F Protat, Fra, Ducati

Race 2
1 C Edwards, USA, Honda
2 C Fogarty, GB, Ducati
3 T Corser, Aus, Ducati
4 A Yanagawa, Jpn, Kawasaki
5 P Chili, Ita, Suzuki
6 N Haga, Jpn, Yamaha
7 J Reynolds, GB, Ducati
8 D Romboni, Ita, Ducati
9 S Hislop, GB, Kawasaki
10 N Mackenzie, GB, Yamaha
11 K Fujiwara, Jpn, Suzuki
12 R Ulm, Aut, Kawasaki
14 A Gramigni, Ita, Yamaha
15 F Protat, Fra, Ducati

Standings – 1 Fogarty 135;
2 Corser 112; 3 Edwards 97;
4 Slight 82; 5 Yanagawa 66;
6 Haga 50

Round 4 – Spain
Albacete, 16 May
Race 1
1 N Haga, Jpn, Yamaha
2 A Yanagawa, Jpn, Kawasaki
3 C Fogarty, GB, Ducati
4 A Slight, NZ, Honda
5 P Chili, Ita, Suzuki
6 G Lavilla, Spa, Kawasaki
7 T Corser, Aus, Ducati

8 K Fujiwara, Jpn, Suzuki
9 V Guareschi, Ita, Yamaha
10 P Goddard, Aus, Aprilia
11 I Jerman, Slo, Kawasaki
12 A Meklau, Aut, Ducati
13 R Ulm, Aut, Kawasaki
14 A Gramigni, Ita, Yamaha
15 L Pedercini, Ita, Ducati

Race 2
1 C Edwards, USA, Honda
2 A Yanagawa, Jpn, Kawasaki
3 C Fogarty, GB, Ducati
4 G Lavilla, Spa, Kawasaki
5 P Chili, Ita, Suzuki
6 T Corser, Aus, Ducati
7 A Slight, NZ, Honda
8 K Fujiwara, Jpn, Suzuki
9 V Guareschi, Ita, Yamaha
10 P Goddard, Aus, Aprilia
11 A Meklau, Aut, Ducati
12 I Jerman, Slo, Kawasaki
13 R Ulm, Aut, Kawasaki
14 A Gramigni, Ita, Yamaha
15 L Pedercini, Ita, Ducati

Standings – 1 Fogarty 167;
2 Corser 131; 3 Edwards 122;
4 Yanagawa 106; 5 Slight 104;
6 Haga 75

Round 5 – Italy
Monza, 30 May
Race 1
1 C Fogarty, GB, Ducati
2 C Edwards, USA, Honda
3 P Chili, Ita, Suzuki
4 T Corser, Aus, Ducati
5 A Slight, NZ, Honda
6 N Haga, Jpn, Yamaha
7 A Yanagawa, Jpn, Kawasaki
8 G Lavilla, Spn, Kawasaki
9 P Goddard, Aus, Aprilia
10 A Meklau, Aut, Ducati
11 V Guareschi, Ita, Yamaha
12 I Jerman, Slo, Kawasaki
13 L Pedercini, Ita, Ducati
14 R Ulm, Aut, Kawasaki
15 L Isaacs, RSA, Ducati

Race 2
1 C Fogarty, GB, Ducati
2 C Edwards, USA, Honda
3 P Chili, Ita, Suzuki
4 T Corser, Aus, Ducati
5 A Yanagawa, Jpn, Kawasaki
6 N Haga, Jpn, Yamaha
7 G Lavilla, Spn, Kawasaki
8 A Meklau, Aut, Ducati
9 K Fujiwara, Jpn, Suzuki
10 V Guareschi, Ita, Yamaha
11 P Goddard, Aus, Aprilia
12 A Gramigni, Ita, Yamaha
13 A Antonello, Ita, Aprilia
14 L Isaacs, RSA, Ducati
15 M Lucchiari, Ita, Yamaha

Standings – 1 Fogarty 217;
2 Edwards 162; 3 Corser 157;
4 Yanagawa 126; 5 Slight 115;
6 Haga 95

Round 6 – Germany
Nürburgring, 13 June
Race 1
1 C Fogarty, GB, Ducati
2 A Slight, NZ, Honda
3 T Corser, Aus, Ducati
4 G Lavilla, Spa, Kawasaki
5 P Goddard, Aus, Aprilia
6 K Fujiwara, Jpn, Suzuki

7 V Guareschi, Ita, Yamaha
8 A Meklau, Aut, Ducati
9 C Lindholm, Swe, Yamaha
10 J Schmid, Ger, Kawasaki
11 L Pedercini, Ita, Ducati
12 A Gramigni, Ita, Yamaha
13 G Bussei, Ita, Suzuki
14 J Ekerold, RSA, Kawasaki
15 F Protat, Fra, Ducati

Race 2
1 T Corser, Aus, Ducati
2 A Slight, NZ, Honda
3 A Yanagawa, Jpn, Kawasaki
4 C Edwards, USA, Honda
5 P Chili, Ita, Suzuki
6 N Haga, Jpn, Yamaha
7 K Fujiwara, Jpn, Suzuki
8 P Goddard, Aus, Aprilia
9 V Guareschi, Ita, Yamaha
10 A Meklau, Aut, Ducati
11 R Ulm, Aut, Kawasaki
12 I Jerman, Slo, Kawasaki
13 L Pedercini, Ita, Ducati
14 C Lindholm, Swe, Yamaha
15 F Fogarty, GB, Ducati

Standings – 1 Fogarty 243;
2 Corser 198; 3 Edwards 175;
4 Slight 155; 5 Yanagawa 142;
6 Haga 105

Round 7 – San Marino
Misano, 27 June
Race 1
1 C Fogarty, GB, Ducati
2 T Corser, Aus, Ducati
3 A Yanagawa, Jpn, Kawasaki
4 P Chili, Ita, Suzuki
5 A Slight, NZ, Honda
6 C Edwards, USA, Honda
7 G Lavilla, Spa, Kawasaki
8 N Haga, Jpn, Yamaha
9 V Guareschi, Ita, Yamaha
10 P Goddard, Aus, Aprilia
11 L Pedercini, Ita, Ducati
12 L Isaacs, RSA, Ducati
13 M Lucchiari, Ita, Yamaha
14 K Fujiwara, Jpn, Suzuki
15 I Jerman, Slo, Kawasaki

Race 2
1 C Fogarty, GB, Ducati
2 T Corser, Aus, Ducati
3 A Yanagawa, Jpn, Kawasaki
4 A Slight, NZ, Honda
5 G Lavilla, Spa, Kawasaki
6 P Chili, Ita, Suzuki
7 C Edwards, USA, Honda
8 V Guareschi, Ita, Yamaha
9 K Fujiwara, Jpn, Suzuki
10 R Ulm, Aut, Kawasaki
11 M Lucchiari, Ita, Yamaha
12 I Jerman, Slo, Kawasaki
13 A Gramigni, Ita, Yamaha
14 L Pedercini, Ita, Ducati
15 L Isaacs, RSA, Ducati

Standings – 1 Fogarty 293;
2 Corser 238; 3 Edwards 194;
4 Slight 179; 5 Yanagawa 174;
6 Chili 119

Round 8 – USA
Laguna Seca, 11 July
Race 1
1 A Gobert, Aus, Ducati
2 B Bostrom, USA, Ducati
3 A Yanagawa, Jpn, Kawasaki
4 C Edwards, USA, Honda
5 C Fogarty, GB, Ducati

6 T Corser, Aus, Ducati
7 P Chili, Ita, Suzuki
8 J Hacking, USA, Yamaha
9 A Slight, NZ, Honda
10 E Bostrom, USA, Honda
11 K Fujiwara, Jpn, Suzuki
12 G Lavilla, Spa, Kawasaki
13 I Jerman, Slo, Kawasaki
14 L Isaacs, RSA, Ducati
15 A Gramigni, Ita, Yamaha

Race 2
1 B Bostrom, USA, Ducati
2 T Corser, Aus, Ducati
3 P Chili, Ita, Suzuki
4 C Fogarty, GB, Ducati
5 C Edwards, USA, Honda
6 A Slight, NZ, Hondai
7 E Bostrom, USA, Honda
8 G Lavilla, Spa, Kawasaki
9 P Goddard, Aus, Aprilia
10 N Haga, Jpn, Yamaha
11 K Fujiwara, Jpn, Suzuki
12 A Yanagawa, Jpn, Kawasaki
13 J Hacking, USA, Yamaha
14 F Protat, Fra, Ducati
15 A Gramigni, Ita, Yamaha

Standings – 1 Fogarty 317;
2 Corser 268; 3 Edwards 218;
4 Slight 196; 5 Yanagawa 194;
6 Chili 144

Round 9 – Europe
Brands Hatch, 1 August
Race 1
1 C Edwards, USA, Honda
2 A Slight, NZ, Honda
3 P Chili, Ita, Suzuki
4 J Reynolds, GB, Ducati
5 T Corser, Aus, Ducati
6 A Yanagawa, Jpn, Kawasaki
7 N Haga, Jpn, Yamaha
8 N Mackenzie, GB, Yamaha
9 J Haydon, GB, Suzuki
10 C Walker, GB, Kawasaki
11 A Meklau, Aut, Ducati
12 P Goddard, Aus, Aprilia
13 I Jerman, Slo, Kawasaki
14 K Fujiwara, Jpn, Suzuki
15 V Guareschi, Ita, Yamaha

Race 2
1 C Edwards, USA, Honda
2 A Slight, NZ, Honda
3 N Haga, Jpn, Yamaha
4 C Fogarty, GB, Ducati
5 A Yanagawa, Jpn, Kawasaki
6 S Emmett, GB, Ducati
7 N Mackenzie, GB, Yamaha
8 J Reynolds, GB, Ducati
9 P Goddard, Aus, Aprilia
10 G Lavilla, Spa, Kawasaki
11 J Haydon, GB, Suzuki
12 A Meklau, Aut, Ducati
13 T Corser, Aus, Ducati
14 V Guareschi, Ita, Yamaha
15 K Fujiwara, Jpn, Suzuki

Standings – 1 Fogarty 330;
2 Corser 282; 3 Edwards 268;
4 Slight 236; 5 Yanagawa 215;
6 Chili 160

Round 10 – Austria
A1-Ring, 29 August
Race 1
1 C Edwards, USA, Honda
2 C Fogarty, GB, Ducati
3 V Guareschi, Ita, Yamaha
4 R Ulm, Aut, Kawasaki

5 G Lavilla, Spa, Kawasaki
6 B Morrison, GB, Yamaha
7 M Lucchiari, Ita, Yamaha
8 A Gramigni, Ita, Yamaha
9 F Protat, Fra, Ducati
10 L Pedercini, Ita, Ducati
11 J Mrkyvka, CZ, Ducati
12 A Rechberger, Aut, Suzuki
13 C Macias, Col, Ducati

Race 2
1 P Chili, Ita, Suzuki
2 T Corser, Aus, Ducati
3 A Slight, NZ, Honda
4 C Fogarty, GB, Ducati
5 R Kellenberger, Ch, Honda
6 G Bussei, Ita, Suzuki
7 A Meklau, Aut, Ducati
8 C Edwards, USA, Honda
9 M Lucchiari, Ita, Yamaha
10 B Morrison, GB, Yamaha
11 R Ulm, Aut, Kawasaki
12 I Jerman, Svk, Kawasaki
13 F Protat, Fra, Ducati
14 V Karban, Svk, Suzuki
15 L Isaacs, RSA, Ducati

Standings – 1 Fogarty 363;
2 Corser 302; 3 Edwards 301;
4 Slight 252; 5 Yanagawa 215;
6 Chili 185

Round 11 – Holland
Assen, 5 September
Race 1
1 C Fogarty, GB, Ducati
2 T Corser, Aus, Ducati
3 A Slight, NZ, Honda
4 P Chili, Ita, Suzuki
5 C Edwards, USA, Honda
6 A Yanagawa, Jpn, Kawasaki
7 N Haga, Jpn, Yamaha
8 A Meklau, Aut, Ducati
9 G Lavilla, Spa, Kawasaki
10 C Walker, GB, Kawasaki
11 I Jerman, Slo, Kawasaki
12 K Fujiwara, Jpn, Suzuki
13 V Guareschi, Ita, Yamaha
14 R Ulm, Aut, Kawasaki
15 A Gramigni, Ita, Yamaha

Race 2
1 C Fogarty, GB, Ducati
2 T Corser, Aus, Ducati
3 A Slight, NZ, Honda
4 A Yanagawa, Jpn, Kawasaki

5 C Edwards, USA, Honda
6 P Chili, Ita, Suzuki
7 G Lavilla, Spa, Kawasaki
8 N Haga, Jpn, Yamaha
9 A Meklau, Aut, Ducati
10 C Walker, GB, Kawasaki
11 I Jerman, Slo, Kawasaki
12 K Fujiwara, Jpn, Suzuki
13 M Malatesta, Ita, Ducati
14 A Gramigni, Ita, Yamaha
15 L Pedercini, Ita, Ducati

Standings – 1 Fogarty 413;
2 Corser 342; 3 Edwards 323;
4 Slight 284; 5 Yanagawa 238;
6 Chili 208

Round 12 – Germany
Hockenheim, 12 September
Race 1
1 C Fogarty, GB, Ducati
2 A Slight, NZ, Honda
3 A Yanagawa, Jpn, Kawasaki
4 C Edwards, USA, Honda
5 N Haga, Jpn, Yamaha
6 G Lavilla, Spa, Kawasaki
7 K Fujiwara, Jpn, Suzuki
8 P Goddard, Aus, Aprilia
9 I Jerman, Slo, Kawasaki
10 V Guareschi, Ita, Yamaha
11 M Malatesta, Ita, Ducati
12 A Gramigni, Ita, Yamaha
13 R Ulm, Aut, Kawasaki
14 L Pedercini, Ita, Ducati
15 F Protat, Fra, Ducati

Race 2
1 P Chili, Ita, Suzuki
2 C Fogarty, GB, Ducati
3 A Slight, NZ, Honda
4 A Yanagawa, Jpn, Kawasaki
5 C Edwards, USA, Honda
6 A Meklau, Aut, Ducati
7 T Corser, Aus, Ducati
8 G Lavilla, Spa, Kawasaki
9 N Haga, Jpn, Yamaha
10 K Fujiwara, Jpn, Suzuki
11 M Malatesta, Ita, Ducati
12 V Guareschi, Ita, Yamaha
13 J Schmid, Ger, Kawasaki
14 A Gramigni, Ita, Yamaha
15 L Isaacs, RSA, Ducati

Standings – 1 Fogarty 458; 2 Corser 351;
3 Edwards 347; 4 Slight 320;
5 Yanagawa 267; 6 Chili 233

Round 13 – Japan
Sugo, 10 October
Race 1
1 A Ryo, Jpn, Suzuki
2 C Fogarty, GB, Ducati
3 A Yanagawa, Jpn, Kawasaki
4 K Kitagawa, Jpn, Suzuki
5 W Yoshikawa, Jpn, Yamaha
6 T Serizawa, Jpn, Kawasaki
7 P Chili, Ita, Suzuki
8 T Corser, Aus, Ducati
9 C Edwards, USA, Honda
10 M Tamada, Jpn, Honda
11 S Itoh, Jpn, Honda
12 N Haga, Jpn, Yamaha
13 T Tsujimura, Jpn, Yamaha
14 G Lavilla, Spa, Kawasaki
15 Y Takeda, Jpn, Honda

Race 2
1 A Yanagawa, Jpn, Kawasaki
2 A Ryo, Jpn, Suzuki
3 K Kitagawa, Jpn, Suzuki
4 N Haga, Jpn, Yamaha
5 C Fogarty, GB, Ducati
6 W Yoshikawa, Jpn, Yamaha
7 P Chili, Ita, Suzuki
8 T Serizawa, Jpn, Kawasaki
9 C Edwards, USA, Honda
10 M Tamada, Jpn, Honda
11 S Takeishi, Jpn, Kawasaki
12 T Tsujimura, Jpn, Yamaha
13 A Slight, NZ, Honda
14 T Corser, Aus, Ducati
15 H Izutsu, Jpn, Kawasaki

Final Standings – 1 Fogarty 489;
2 Edwards 361; 3 Corser 361;
4 Slight 323; 5 Yanagawa 308;
6 Chili 251

2000 SEASON
Round 1 – South Africa
Kyalami, 2 April
Race 1
1 C Edwards, USA, Honda
2 N Haga, Jap, Yamaha
3 C Fogarty, GB, Ducati
4 T Corser, Aus, Aprilia
5 P Chili, Ita, Suzuki
6 G Lavilla, Spn, Kawasaki
7 H Aoki, Jpn, Ducati
8 K Fujiwara, Jpn, Suzuki
9 B Bostrom, USA, Ducati
10 J Borja, Spn, Ducati
11 A Meklau, Aut, Ducati
12 G Bussei, Ita, Kawasaki
13 L Isaacs, RSA, Ducati
14 S Crafar, NZ, Honda
15 V Guareschi, Ita, Yamaha

Race 2
1 C Edwards, USA, Honda
2 P Chili, Ita, Suzuki
3 T Corser, Aus, Aprilia
4 H Aoki, Jpn, Ducati
5 G Lavilla, Spa, Kawasaki
6 J Borja, Spn, Ducati
7 B Bostrom, USA, Ducati
8 K Fujiwara, Jpn, Suzuki
9 A Antonello, Ita, Aprilia
10 G Bussei, Ita, Kawasaki
11 A Gobert, Aus, Bimota
12 A Meklau, Aut, Ducati
13 S Crafar, NZ, Honda
14 A Gramigni, Ita, Yamaha
15 M Sanchini, Ita, Ducati

Standings – 1 Edwards 50; 2 Chili 31;
3 Corser 29; 4 Aoki 22; 5 Lavilla 21;
6 Haga 20

Round 2 – Australia
Phillip Island, 23 April
Race 1
1 A Gobert, Aus, Bimota
2 C Fogarty, GB, Ducati
3 V Guareschi, Ita, Yamaha
4 L Pedercini, Ita, Ducati
5 C Edwards, USA, Honda
6 R Ulm, Aut, Ducati
7 G Lavilla, Spa, Kawasaki
8 G Bussei, Ita, Kawasaki
9 A Yanagawa, Jpn, Kawasaki
10 N Haga, Jpn, Yamaha
11 A Maxwell, Aus, Kawasaki
12 M Sanchini, Ita, Ducati
13 K Fujiwara, Jpn, Suzuki
14 L Isaacs, RSA, Ducati
15 B Bostrom, USA, Ducati

Race 2
1 T Corser, Aus, Aprilia
2 N Haga, Jpn, Yamaha
3 P Chili, Ita, Suzuki
4 G Lavilla, Spn, Kawasaki
5 C Edwards, USA, Honda
6 A Yanagawa, Jpn, Kawasaki
7 K Fujiwara, Jpn, Suzuki
8 S Crafar, NZ, Honda
9 A Gobert, Aus, Bimota
10 H Aoki, Jpn, Ducati
11 R Ulm, Aut, Ducati
12 M Sanchini, Ita, Ducati
13 L Pedercini, Ita, Ducati
14 B Bostrom, USA, Ducati
15 I Antonello, Ita, Aprilia

Standings – 1 Edwards 72;
2 Corser 54; 3 Chili 47; 4 Haga 46;
5 Lavilla 43; 6 Gobert 37

Round 3 – Japan
Sugo, 30 April
Race 1
1 H Izutsu, Jpn, Kawasaki
2 N Haga, Jpn, Yamaha
3 P Chili, Ita, Suzuki
4 A Ryo, Jpn, Suzuki
5 C Edwards, USA, Honda
6 K Kitagawa, Jpn, Suzuki
7 M Tamada, Jpn, Honda
8 W Yoshikawa, Jpn, Yamaha
9 T Corser, Aus, Aprilia
10 G Lavilla, Spa, Kawasaki
11 A Meklau, Aut, Ducati
12 R Ulm, Aut, Aut, Ducati
13 Y Takeda, Jpn, Honda
14 J Borja, Spa, Ducati
15 G Bussei, Ita, Kawasaki

Race 2
1 H Izutsu, Jpn, Kawasaki
2 W Yoshikawa, Jpn, Yamaha
3 C Edwards, USA, Honda
4 N Haga, Jpn, Yamaha
5 T Corser, Ita, Aprilia
6 A Yanagawa, Jpn, Kawasaki
7 T Serizawa, Jpn, Kawasaki
8 K Kitagawa, Jpn, Suzuki
9 A Ryo, Jpn, Suzuki
10 G Lavilla, Jpn, Kawasaki
11 J Borja, Spa, Ducati
12 A Meklau, Aut, Ducati
13 B Bostrom, USA, Ducati
14 R Ulm, Aut, Ducati
15 M Kamada, Jpn, Honda

Standings – 1 Edwards 99; 2 Haga 79;
3 Corser 72; 4 Chili 63; 5 Lavilla 55;
6 Izutsu 50

Round 4 – Great Britain
Donington Park, 14 May
Race 1
1 C Edwards, USA, Honda
2 P Chili, Ita, Suzuki
3 N Hodgson, GB, Ducati
4 N Haga, Jpn, Yamaha
5 C Walker, GB, Suzuki
6 J Haydon, GB, Ducati
7 A Yanagawa, Jpn, Kawasaki
8 T Corser, Aus, Aprilia
9 A Slight, NZ, Honda
10 J Reynolds, GB, Ducati
11 G Lavilla, Spn, Kawasaki
12 S Hislop, GB, Yamaha
13 R Ulm, Aut, Ducati
14 A Meklau, Aut, Ducati
15 B Bostom, USA, Ducati

Race 2
1 N Hodgson, GB, Ducati
2 C Walker, GB, Suzuki
3 P Chili, Ita, Suzuki
4 N Haga, Jpn, Yamaha
5 A Yanagawa, Jpn, Kawasaki
6 J Haydon, GB, Ducati
7 A Slight, NZ, Honda
8 B Bostrom, USA, Ducati
9 A Meklau, Aut, Ducati
10 H Aoki, Jpn, Ducati
11 A Antonello, Ita, Aprilia
12 J Crawford, GB, Suzuki
13 K Fujiwara, Jpn, Suzuki
14 V Guareschi, Ita, Yamaha
15 A Gramigni, Ita, Yamaha

Standings – 1 Edwards 124;
2 Haga 105; 3 Chili 99;
4 Corser 80; 5 Lavilla 60;
6 Izutsu 50

Round 5 – Italy
Monza, 21 May
Race 1
1 P Chili, Ita, Suzuki
2 C Edwards, USA, Honda
3 A Yanagawa, Jpn, Kawasaki
4 T Bayliss, Aus, Ducati
5 A Slight, NZ, Honda
6 G Lavilla, Spn, Kawasaki
7 B Bostrom, USA, Ducati
8 T Corser, Aus, Aprilia
9 A Antonello, Ita, Aprilia
10 R Ulm, Aut, Ducati
11 K Fujiwara, Jpn, Suzuki
12 V Guareschi, Ita, Yamaha
13 M Sanchini, Ita, Ducati
14 G Bussei, Ita, Kawasaki
15 M Barth, Ger, Yamaha

Race 2
1 C Edwards, USA, Honda
2 P Chili, Ita, Suzuki
3 A Yanagawa, Jpn, Kawasaki
4 T Bayliss, Aus, Ducati
5 N Haga, Jpn, Yamaha
6 T Corser, Aus, Aprilia
7 A Slight, NZ, Honda
8 A Meklau, Aut, Ducati
9 K Fujiwara, Jpn, Suzuki
10 B Bostrom, USA, Ducati
11 A Antonello, Ita, Aprilia
12 M Barth, Ger, Yamaha
13 J Oelschlaeger, Ger, Yamaha
14 L Isaacs, RSA, Ducati
15 P Blora, Ita, Ducati

Standings – 1 Edwards 169;
2 Chili 144; 3 Haga 116;
4 Corser 98; 4 Yanagawa 79;
6 Lavilla 70

Round 6 – Germany
Hockenheim, 4 June
Race 1
1 T Bayliss, Aus, Ducati
2 A Yanagawa, Jpn, Kawasaki
3 N Haga, Jpn, Yamaha
4 C Edwards, USA, Honda
5 A Slight, NZ, Honda
6 A Meklau, Aut, Ducati
7 T Corser, Aus, Aprilia
8 R Ulm, Aut, Ducati
9 A Antonello, Ita, Aprilia
10 B Bostrom, USA, Ducati
11 S Crafar, NZ, Kawasaki
12 J Haydon, GB, Ducati
13 J Borja, Spn, Ducati
14 S Plater, GB, Kawasaki
15 M Barth, Ger, Yamaha

Race 2
1 N Haga, Jpn, Yamaha
2 C Edwards, USA, Honda
3 P Chili, Ita, Suzuki
4 T Bayliss, Aus, Ducati
5 A Slight, NZ, Honda
6 T Corser, Aus, Aprilia
7 A Antonello, Ita, Aprilia
8 A Meklau, Aut, Ducati
9 R Ulm, Aut, Ducati
10 K Fujiwara, Jpn, Suzuki
11 B Bostrom, USA, Ducati
12 J Borja, Spn, Ducati
13 V Guareschi, Ita, Yamaha
14 S Crafar, NZ, Kawasaki
15 M Barth, Ger, Yamaha

Standings – 1 Edwards 202;
2 Chili 160; 3 Haga 157;
4 Corser 117; 5 Yanagawa 99;
6 Lavilla 70

Round 7 – San Marino
Misano, 18 June
Race 1
1 T Corser, Aus, Aprilia
2 T Bayliss, Aus, Ducati
3 K Fujiwara, Jpn, Suzuki
4 J Borja, Spn, Ducati
5 A Yanagawa, Jpn, Kawasaki
6 B Bostrom, USA, Ducati
7 N Haga, Jpn, Yamaha
8 P Goddard, Aus, Kawasaki
9 H Aoki, Jpn, Ducati
10 A Antonello, Ita, Aprilia
11 A Meklau, Aut, Ducati
12 A Gramigni, Ita, Yamaha
13 L Pedercini, Ita, Ducati
14 F Protat, Fra, Ducati
15 L Isaacs, RSA, Ducati

Race 2
1 T Corser, Aus, Aprilia
2 T Bayliss, Aus, Ducati
3 B Bostom, USA, Ducati
4 K Fujiwara, Jpn, Suzuki
5 J Borja, Spa, Ducati
6 A Yanagawa, Jpn, Kawasaki
7 A Antonello, Ita, Aprilia
8 P Goddard, Aus, Kawasaki
9 A Slight, NZ, Honda
10 C Edwards, USA, Honda
11 H Aoki, Jpn, Ducati
12 G Bussei, Ita, Kawasaki
13 A Meklau, Aut, Ducati
14 L Pedercini, Ita, Ducati
15 A Gramigni, Ita, Yamaha

Standings – 1 Edwards 208;
2 Corser 167; 3 Haga 166;
4 Chili 160; 5 Yanagawa 120;
6 Bayliss 104

Round 8 – Spain
Valencia, 25 June
Race 1
1 T Corser, Aus, Aprilia
2 B Bostrom, USA, Ducati
3 N Haga, Jpn, Yamaha
4 T Bayliss, Aus, Ducati
5 C Edwards, USA, Honda
6 P Goddard, Aus, Kawasaki
7 A Slight, NZ, Honda
8 K Fujiwara, Jpn, Suzuki
9 A Antonello, Ita, Aprilia
10 A Yanagawa, Jpn, Kawasaki
11 A Meklau, Aut, Ducati
12 V Guareschi, Ita, Yamaha
13 M Sanchini, Ita, Ducati
14 P Blora, Ita, Ducati
15 M Barth, Ger, Yamaha

Race 2
1 N Haga, Jpn, Yamaha
2 B Bostrom, USA, Ducati
3 T Bayliss, Aus, Ducati
4 C Edwards, USA, Honda
5 T Corser, Aus, Aprilia
6 P Goddard, Aus, Kawasaki
7 A Slight, NZ, Honda
8 J Borja, Spa, Ducati
9 P Chili, Ita, Suzuki
10 K Fujiwara, Jpn, Suzuki
11 H Aoki, Jpn, Ducati
12 A Yanagawa, Jpn, Kawasaki
13 V Guareschi, Ita, Yamaha
14 A Gramigni, Ita, Yamaha
15 M Sanchini, Ita, Ducati

Standings – 1 Edwards 232;
2 Haga 207; 3 Corser 203;
4 Chili 167; 5 Bayliss 133;
6 Yanagawa 130

Round 9 – USA
Laguna Seca, 9 July
Race 1
1 N Haga, Jpn, Yamaha
2 C Edwards, USA, Honda
3 T Corser, Aus, Aprilia
4 B Bostrom, USA, Ducati
5 P Chili, Ita, Suzuki
6 A Yanagawa, Jpn, Kawasaki
7 K Fujiwara, Jpn, Suzuki
8 A Slight, NZ, Honda
9 J Borja, Spa, Ducati
10 G Bussei, Ita, Kawasaki
11 H Aoki, Jpn, Ducati
12 A Meklau, Aut, Ducati
13 L Pedercini, Ita, Ducati
14 M Sanchini, Ita, Ducati
15 I Jerman, Slo, Kawasaki

Race 2
1 T Corser, Aus, Aprilia
2 N Haga, Jpn, Yamaha
3 B Bostrom, USA, Ducati
4 C Edwards, USA, Honda
5 A Yanagawa, Jpn, Kawasaki
6 P Chili, Ita, Suzuki
7 T Bayliss, Aus, Ducati
8 K Fujiwara, Jpn, Suzuki
9 A Slight, NZ, Honda
10 P Goddard, Aus, Kawasaki
11 G Bussei, Ita, Kawasaki
12 L Isaacs, RSA, Ducati
13 L Pegram, USA, Ducati
14 R Ulm, Aut, Ducati
15 L Pedercini, Ita, Ducati

Standings – 1 Edwards 265;
2 Haga 252; 3 Corser 244;
4 Chili 188; 5 Bostrom 152;
6 Yanagawa 151

Round 10 – Europe
Brands Hatch, 6 August
Race 1
1 T Bayliss, Aus, Ducati
2 N Hodgson, GB, Ducati
3 C Walker, GB, Suzuki
4 J Reynolds, GB, Ducati
5 N Haga, Jpn, Yamaha
6 T Corser, Aus, Aprilia
7 A Slight, NZ, Honda
8 P Chili, Ita, Suzuki
9 A Yanagawa, Jpn, Kawasaki
10 C Edwards, USA, Honda
11 J Borja, Spa, Ducati
12 G Lavilla, Spa, Kawasaki
13 A Meklau, Aut, Ducati
14 A Antonello, Ita, Aprilia
15 B Bostrom, USA, Ducati

Race 2
1 N Hodgson, GB, Ducati
2 T Bayliss, Aus, Ducati
3 P Chili, Ita, Suzuki
4 N Haga, Jpn, Yamaha
5 A Yanagawa, Jpn, Kawasaki
6 C Edwards, USA, Honda
7 C Walker, GB, Suzuki
8 G Lavilla, Spn, Kawasaki
9 A Meklau, Aut, Ducati
10 K Fujiwara, Jpn, Suzuki
11 A Gramigni, Ita, Yamaha
12 V Guareschi, Ita, Yamaha
13 M Barth, Ger, Yamaha
14 M Borciani, Ita, Ducati
15 L Isaacs, RSA, Ducati

Standings – 1 Edwards 281;
2 Haga 276; 3 Corser 254;
4 Chili 212; 5 Bayliss 187;
6 Yanagawa 169

Round 11 – Holland
Assen, 3 September
Race 1
1 C Edwards, USA, Honda
2 J Borja, Spn, Ducati
3 N Haga, Jpn, Yamaha
4 T Corser, Aus, Aprilia
5 A Slight, NZ, Honda
6 A Yanagawa, Jpn, Kawasaki
7 D Romboni, Ita, Ducati
8 G Bussei, Ita, Kawasaki
9 J Oelschlaeger, Ger, Yamaha
10 K Fujiwara, Jpn, Suzuki
11 L Pedercini, Ita, Ducati
12 R Ulm, Aut, Ducati
13 I Jerman, Slo, Kawasaki
14 A Gramigni, Ita, Yamaha
15 V Guareschi, Ita, Yamaha

Race 2
1 N Haga, Jpn, Yamaha
2 A Yanagawa, Jpn, Kawasaki
3 J Borja, Spn, Ducati
4 A Slight, NZ, Honda
5 C Edwards, USA, Honda
6 A Gramigni, Ita, Yamaha
7 T Corser, Aus, Aprilia
8 K Fukiwara, Jpn, Suzuki
9 A Meklau, Aut, Ducati
10 R Ulm, Aut, Ducati
11 D Romboni, Ita, Ducati
12 J Oelschlaeger, Ger, Yamaha
13 L Perdecini, Ita, Ducati
14 L Isaacs, RSA, Ducati
15 G Muteau, Fra, Honda

Standings – 1 Edwards & Haga 317;
3 Corser 276; 4 Chili 212;
5 Yanagawa 199;
6 Bayliss 187

Round 12 – Germany
Oschersleben, 10 September
Race 1
1 C Edwards, USA, Honda
2 G Lavilla, Spn, Kawasaki
3 T Bayliss, Aus, Ducati
4 A Yanagawa, Jpn, Kawasaki
5 A Slight, NZ, Honda
6 P Chili, Ita, Suzuki
7 T Corser, Aus, Aprilia
8 A Antonello, Ita, Aprilia
9 N Haga, Jpn, Yamaha
10 B Bostrom, USA, Ducati
11 A Gramigni, Ita, Yamaha
12 W Yoshikawa, Jpn, Yamaha
13 R Ulm, Aut, Ducati
14 K Fujiwara, Jpn, Suzuki
15 M Barth, Ger, Yamaha

Race 2
1 C Edwards, USA, Honda
2 T Bayliss, Aus, Ducati
3 A Yanagawa, Jpn, Kawasaki
4 G Lavilla, Spn, Kawasaki
5 N Haga, Jpn, Yamaha
6 P Chili, Ita, Suzuki
7 B Bostrom, USA, Ducati
8 K Fujiwara, Jpn, Suzuki
9 W Yoshikawa, Jpn, Yamaha
10 R Ulm, Aut, Ducati
11 A Gramigni, Ita, Yamaha
12 A Meklau, Aut, Ducati
13 M Barth, Ger, Yamaha
14 L Isaacs, RSA, Ducati
15 M Borciani, Ita, Ducati

Standings – 1 Edwards 367;
2 Haga 335; 3 Corser 285;
4 Chili 232; 5 Yanagawa 228;
6 Bayliss 223

Round 13 –
Brands Hatch, 15 October
Race 1
1 J Reynolds, GB, Ducati
2 T Bayliss, Aus, Ducati
3 C Walker, GB, Suzuki
4 N Hodgson, GB, Ducati
5 J Borja, Spa, Ducati
6 A Yanagawa, Jpn, Kawasaki
7 T Corser, Aus, Aprilia
8 C Edwards, USA, Honda
9 G Lavilla, Spn, Kawasaki
10 P Chili, Ita, Suzuki
11 K Fujiwara, Jpn, Suzuki
12 V Guareschi, Ita, Yamaha
13 A Slight, NZ, Honda
14 S Plater, GB, Kawasaki
15 M Barth, Ger, Yamaha

Race 2
1 C Edwards, USA, Honda
2 P Chili, Ita, Suzuki
3 T Corser, Aus, Aprilia
4 J Reynolds, GB, Ducati
5 G Lavilla, Spn, Kawasaki
6 C Walker, GB, Suzuki
7 A Yanagawa, Jpn, Kawasaki
8 A Slight, NZ, Honda
9 K Fujiwara, Jpn, Suzuki
10 B Bostrom, USA, Ducati
11 A Gramigni, Ita, Yamaha
12 V Guareschi, Ita, Yamaha
13 S Plater, GB, Kawasaki
14 J Borja, Spa, Ducati
15 R Ulm, Aut, Ducati

Final Standings – 1 Edwards 400;
2 Haga 335; 3 Corser 310;
4 Chili 258; 5 Yanagawa 247;
6 Bayliss 243

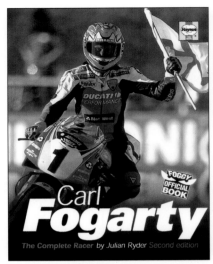
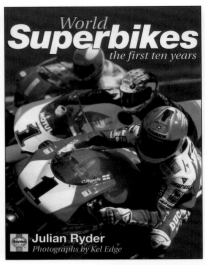
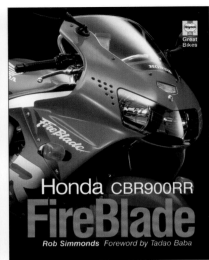

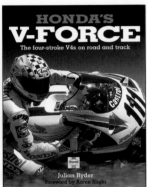

Other titles *of interest*

Carl Fogarty *(2nd Edition)*
Julian Ryder ISBN 1 85960 641 5

World Superbikes: *The first ten years*
Julian Ryder ISBN 1 85960 404 8

Honda CBR900RR FireBlade
Haynes Great Bikes
Rob Simmonds ISBN 1 85960 640 7

The Ogri Collection No.2
Paul Sample ISBN 1 85960 693 8

Mick Doohan *(2nd Edition)*
Mat Oxley ISBN 1 85960 698 9

Honda's V-Force
Julian Ryder ISBN 1 85960 421 8

The Ducati Story *(3rd Edition)*
Ian Falloon ISBN 1 85960 668 7